CREATIVE CONFORMITY

Selected Titles from
the Moral Traditions Series
James F. Keenan, SJ, Series Editor

Aquinas, Feminism, and the Common Good
Susanne M. DeCrane

Aquinas on the Emotions: A Religious Ethical Inquiry
Diana-Fritz Cates

The Banality of Good and Evil: Moral Lessons from the Shoah and Jewish Tradition
David R. Blumenthal

Catholic Moral Theology in the United States: A History
Charles E. Curran

The Church and Secularity: Two Stories of Liberal Society
Robert Gascoigne

The Context of Casuistry
James F. Keenan, SJ, and Thomas A. Shannon, Editors

The Critical Calling: Reflections on Moral Dilemmas since Vatican II
Richard A. McCormick

Defending Probabilism: The Moral Theology of Juan Caramuel
Julia Fleming

Family Ethics: Practices for Christians
Julie Hanlon Rubio

The Global Face of Public Faith: Politics, Human Rights, and Christian Ethics
David Hollenbach, SJ

Heroes, Saints, and Ordinary Morality
Andrew Michael Flescher

Introduction to Jewish and Catholic Bioethics: A Comparative Analysis
Aaron L. Mackler

John Cuthbert Ford, SJ: Moral Theologian at the End of the Manualist Era
Eric Marcelo O. Genilo, SJ

Loyal Dissent: Memoir of a Catholic Theologian
Charles E. Curran

The Moral Theology of Pope John Paul II
Charles E. Curran

Overcoming Our Evil: Human Nature and Spiritual Exercises in Xunzi and Augustine
Aaron Stalnaker

Prophetic and Public: The Social Witness of U.S. Catholicism
Kristin E. Heyer

The Sexual Person: Toward a Renewed Catholic Anthology
Todd A. Salzman and Michael G. Lawler

Theological Bioethics: Participation, Justice, and Change
Lisa Sowle Cahill

United States Welfare Policy: A Catholic Response
Thomas J. Massaro, SJ

CREATIVE CONFORMITY

The Feminist Politics of U.S. Catholic and Iranian Shi'i Women

Elizabeth M. Bucar

Georgetown University Press/Washington, D.C.

Library of Congress Cataloging-in-Publication Data

Bucar, Elizabeth M.
Creative conformity : the feminist politics of U.S. Catholic and Iranian Shi'i women / Elizabeth M. Bucar.
p. cm. — (Moral traditions series)
Includes bibliographical references and index.
ISBN 978-1-58901-739-9 (pbk. : alk. paper)
1. Feminism—Political aspects—United States. 2. Feminism—Political aspects—Iran. 3. Women—Political activity—United States. 4. Women—Political activity—Iran. 5. Catholic women—United States. 6. Muslim women—Iran. 7. Shiites—Political activity—Iran. I. Title.
HQ1206.B795 2011
305.48'68273—dc22

2010036032

∞ This book is printed on acid-free paper meeting the requirements of the American National Standard for Permanence in Paper for Printed Library Materials.

15 14 13 12 11 9 8 7 6 5 4 3 2
First printing

Printed in the United States of America

Contents

Acknowledgments vii

Note on Transcriptions ix

Preface xi

Introduction: *Creative Conformity, Clerical Guidance, and a Rhetorical Turn* 1

Chapter One
What's a Good Woman to Do? Recasting the Symbolics of Moral Exemplars 33

Chapter Two
Surprises from the Laps of Mothers: Leveraging the Gaps in Procreative Virtues 58

Chapter Three
Scripture, Sacred Law, and Hermeneutics: Exploring Gendered Meanings in Textual Records 80

Chapter Four
Performance beyond the Pulpit: Presenting Disorderly Bodies in Public Spaces 109

Chapter Five
Republication of Moral Discourse: Compromise and Censorship as Political Freedom 134

Conclusion 160

Epilogue: Revisiting Shahla Habibi 180

Glossary 185

Bibliography 187

Index 197

Acknowledgments

Substantial portions of this book were written with the support of a postdoctoral fellowship from the Berkley Center for Religion, Peace, and World Affairs at Georgetown University. I thank Tom Banchoff, the center's director, for the gift of time to think and write, and the faculty at Georgetown, who welcomed me warmly into their community during my fellowship year. Writing was also supported by faculty excellence grants from the University of North Carolina at Greensboro and by my colleagues in the department of religious studies who have become invaluable mentors and close friends during the last three years.

The research I conducted in Iran would not have been possible without the generous support provided by the Human Rights Program of the University of Chicago, which funded my travel to Iran in the summer of 2004, and the Institute of Women's Studies and Research in Tehran, which graciously hosted me during my stay and was invaluable in facilitating meetings with key leaders of the Iranian women's movement. To the women who agreed to meet with me in Iran, despite political pressure not to, I owe a debt I can never repay. I also want to thank Roja Fazaeli and Ezzat Goushegir, who helped me with the task of cultural and linguistic translation during the early stages of my research and without whom my fieldwork would not have been nearly as productive.

Portions of the preface, introduction, and epilogue appeared in "Dianomy: Understanding Religious Women's Moral Agency as Creative Conformity," *Journal of the American Academy of Religion* 78, no. 3, (2010): 662–86. Oxford University Press has granted permission to publish them here. The method used in this book and discussed in the introduction draws on two of my earlier publications: "Speaking of Motherhood: The Epideictic Rhetoric of John Paul II and Ayatollah Khomeini," *Journal of the Society of Christian Ethics* 26, no. 2 (2006): 93–123, and "Methodological Invention as a Constructive Project: Exploring the Production of Ethical Knowledge through the Interaction of Discursive Logics," *Journal of Religious Ethics* 36, no. 3 (2008): 355–73. Georgetown University Press and John Wiley and Sons, respectively, have granted permission for portions of these essays to be reproduced here.

This book has benefited from numerous conversations with colleagues. Particular thanks goes to William Schweiker, Aaron Stalnaker, Jonathan

Schofer, Tulasi Srinivas, Abdulaziz Sachedina, and Jean Bethke Elshatin, all of whom read large portions of this manuscript at various stages and pushed me to deepen my analysis. My primary debt is to my partner Alexis Zubrow, who helped me to keep balance throughout this process and to remember that scholarship can be fun.

Note on Transcriptions

This book includes Arabic and Persian terms, written in non-Latin alphabets, that are transliterated according to a modified version of the IJMES style. Words found in Merriam–Webster's dictionary are spelled as they appear there and not treated as technical terms (e.g., hijab). Exceptions include terms on the IJMES word list (e.g., shari'a). All remaining technical terms are italicized and fully transliterated with diacritical marks (macrons and dots). The IJMES style is that diacritics should not be added to personal names, place names, names of political parties and organizations, or titles of books and articles. This convention is followed with the exception of titles of book and articles for which I include diacritics unless a well-known transliteration exists (e.g., *Shahnameh*). Names of living individuals are spelled according to their preferred English spelling.

Preface

It is August in Tehran. I've been walking up and down the same two blocks in the center of the city for an hour. I've asked the attendant at the door of the neighborhood mosque and the man who sells phone cards at the corner, but neither has ever heard of the Iranian Network of Women's NGOs or its director, Shahla Habibi. I try a couple of doorbells on the unmarked buildings, but there is no response. Finally, after the time of my appointment with Habibi has come and gone, I decide to call from a pay phone. Habibi repeats the address I already have, but this time sends her assistant down to open a creaking metal door. I am ushered up three flights of steps. I arrive flustered and sweaty.

The heat, my tardiness, and the difficulty in locating this office have only contributed to a general level of nervousness with which I started the day. Habibi is a prominent post-Revolution figure in national politics. In 1995 President Rafsanjani appointed her as Iran's first presidential advisor on women's affairs, a position that would later become part of the official cabinet.[1] She led the Iranian delegation to the Fourth World Conference on Women in Beijing in 1995 and now (2010) runs a nongovernmental organization in Tehran. These impressive credentials were in the back of my head when I dressed earlier in the morning. I decided, in an attempt to increase my status in her eyes, to wear my most conservative Islamic dress: a knee-length baggy black overcoat or manteau; long, loose pants; black socks with my sandals; and a black head scarf, tied under my chin. This was in strong contrast to more fitted manteaus and brightly colored headscarfs I usually wore to fulfill a woman's legal duty to veil in public. I feel dowdy but respectful.

I am glad for the extra hijabi effort when Habibi greets me at her door in full chador, the traditional form of Iranian dress that became a symbol of Islamic Revolution and is often perceived as the most conservative form of Islamic dress in Iran. She continues to wear the chador within the private space of her office, which is unusual given the heat and the fact that only women—myself, Habibi, and her female assistant—are present. She invites me to remove my headscarf. In response, I tie it even more tightly, feeling that this is some sort of test and hoping to make it clear that I respect the Islamic traditions of my host country.

I am mindful that Habibi has agreed to this interview only because of my affiliation with the well-respected and well-funded Institute of Women's

Studies and Research in Tehran. I begin carefully, treading lightly as I try to determine the limits of what Habibi is comfortable discussing with an American researcher. My questions start out vague and open-ended: What do you think are the most important women's rights issues in Iran today? What are the challenges for women in the Islamic Republic? What do you hope for the future of women? I take my lead from her responses, which steer us toward a discussion about Ruhollah Khomeini's legacy to women's political participation in the Islamic Republic. Habibi is a large woman with a booming voice, and quickly becomes animated in our discussion of Khomeini, whom she calls my Imam, a title that means leader but also invokes the concept of the Imamate whom Shi'a understand to be the rightful leaders of the Muslim community. She shifts forward and back in her chair, explaining the many ways Khomeini changed her life. She confesses that she is also writing a book on Khomeini's rhetoric: a collection of his writings and speeches to be published in Persian, Arabic, and English so that all women can have the benefit of his counsel. She has obviously been touched personally and professionally by Khomeini's words and is pleased that I also recognize how important he is to women's lives and women's morality in Iran.

Into her mini-lectures about Khomeini's life and teaching, Habibi not only weaves her own beliefs about women's primary duties as mothers and wives, but also snipes about how Western women can be too professionally ambitious and neglectful of their families. She asks whether I am married, and on learning that I am not seems reassured that I have not abandoned my duties at home to conduct research in Iran.

We shift to discussing her participation in the United Nations (UN) Beijing conference in 1995. At one point she argues for support of the Convention on the Elimination of All Forms of Discrimination Against Women (CEDAW) in shari'a law and the possibility of a female president being elected in Iran before one is in the United States. When I admit that this is possible, she is pleased and breaks into a quiet, deep chuckle. At this point in our conversation I am completely at ease. Habibi and I can joke about the state of feminist politics in the world today. Feminist politics in Iran is not so different from what it is at home.

In my next question I refer to Habibi as an Islamic feminist. In response, she slams her hands down on her desk, cuts me off mid-sentence, and says, "I am not a feminist. Do not call me a feminist. I do not believe in your feminism."[2] I stammer and apologize, knowing that despite my familiarity with Khomeini's writings and my effort to wear "good hijab," I have at best distanced myself from Habibi and at worst offended her. Our interview stalls. For the next half hour she returns to the feminist label again and again, defining herself against it, bringing up Western women such as Simone de

Beauvoir and Madeline Albright, who, in Habibi's opinion, misunderstand women's proper roles and the significance of religious women's actions.

Later I cannot get Habibi's assertion that she does not believe in my feminism out of my head. I am extremely embarrassed that I offended her on a personal level. But I am also uncomfortable because her rejecting my label was questioning my right to interpret her argument and actions. In her words I heard echoed my own doubts about my scholarship, especially my ability to work cross-culturally.

Accusing me of wrongly attributing "my feminism" to her, Habibi signaled that she was aware, even if I was not yet, that I had in mind a specific conception of what freedom was for women, and was hearing only that type of freedom in her arguments. She was quite right to realize that I was more interested in her arguments about shari'a support for CEDAW, which is essentially a UN treaty that couches women's freedom in legal equality, than I was in those about a woman's duty to her family. The more I thought about our interaction, the more I realized that my assumptions about what women are or what they want limited my ability to see what they actually do. This meant that, in essence, I was learning from Habibi only what I already knew. I had slid into a sort of academic ventriloquism, "throwing my voice" to the women I studied, becoming the subject of my own scholarship.

But I was not the only one engaged in a form of interpretation based on prior conceptions of women. Habibi was hearing me through an interpretative framework as well. For example, her rant about feminism was not just about separating herself from Western feminist assumptions about women. Her critique of what she called my feminist ideology was based on her understanding of what she considered women's natural roles to be. She too was neglecting the cross-cultural diversity of what women want and thus what their political actions might actually do. We were engaged in a mutual act of ventriloquism, mishearing, misreading, and ultimately misunderstanding each other.

What I said to Habibi, her reaction to it, and my subsequent reaction to her reaction led to the central question of this book: How can a scholar understand religious women's political arguments without her own feminist commitments interfering? This question is based on two challenges Habibi indirectly raises for my project. The first is the need to question categories I am given by my own secular, liberal framework. Secularism is by no means neutral in its approach toward religion. Even in forms tolerant of religiosity in the political sphere, it assumes that certain actions are more legitimate than others, such as those that promote equality and empowerment.[3]

For example, this project began as a cross-cultural study of gender equality or women's empowerment. Using this approach, I had planned to focus on feminist resources in the teachings of Pope John Paul II and Ayatollah Khomeini. This is the sort of project most colleagues still assume I am doing given my case study: a boxing match, if you like, between two villains of women's empowerment, a match to be scored and judged by the tenets of liberal feminism. But as my conversation with Habibi suggests, women do not necessarily agree on what counts as equality or as empowerment.[4] This means that a conceptual ignorance, perhaps even arrogance, characterized my initial approach. After my encounter with Habibi, however, my feminist faux pas became a litmus test for my engagement with women and their writings. I often stop to ask myself whether I am throwing my voice again or being careful to question my own categories.

The second challenge is how to understand the diversity among women's arguments. This diversity exists among traditions, within a single community, and even at times within the feminist politics of individual women, which can vary contextually and biographically. Differences between traditions are expected, given variations in theology, local political conditions, and historical women's movements. But can something be learned from these differences? Does such a thing as cross-cultural feminist politics exist? If it does, how can it be studied in comparison without privileging one community's action over another's?

A further difficulty is how to make sense of diversity among women in the same local context. For example, when some of the other women I interviewed in Iran learned that I was interviewing Habibi, they were surprised: "She is very conservative, do you know that?" "She does not agreed with us on many issues." "She will be very suspicious of you." "You will get only regime propaganda from Mrs. Habibi." This raises the question of who gets to represent "proper feminist politics" within one community and for the scholar complicates her selection criteria for subjects of study. Certainly Habibi herself would be critical of women's political actions in Iran that did not share her understanding of women's essential qualities.

Finally, given that several discourses of gender exist within the same culture, and several discourses about the moral life circulate within a religious community, any given individual woman is exposed to multiple visions of womanhood. Even when she intends to subscribe to a particular discourse, as some of the women studied in the volume do, this discourse is often not the only influence on her.[5] This understanding of overlapping, complex systems of ethical knowledge may be helpful for a thick description of moral agency, but it greatly complicates how to isolate specific contributions of women to a community's ethical understanding.

These challenges are not unrelated. Both derive from a concern with discursive contexts, whether my own (secular liberal feminism) or the discursive context of the women I study. I address both challenges in this book by attempting to engage feminist politics at the ground level, which involves defining what counts as feminist politics in this study as well as selecting a case study that can isolate aspects of women's political engagement in order to analyze how it has productive power within a religious tradition.

ENGAGING FEMINIST POLITICS

If Shahla Habibi frames the conceptual approach in my research, Frances Kissling, who is discussed in chapter 5, is the first creative conformer I was exposed to and the original inspiration for this project. I worked for Kissling from 1998 to 1999, when she was president of Catholics for a Free Choice. To take this job I left my work with more secular liberal human rights organizations (Human Rights Watch, Lawyers Committee for Human Rights, International Women's Judges Foundation) and entered the world of faith-based activism. The discursive shift to Kissling's world was jarring. I observed her at meetings with congressional representatives, leaders of women's rights organizations, and diplomats at UN events. It quickly became clear that her message was moral and feminist in ways different than those to which I was accustomed. Her arguments about safe motherhood were based on different assumptions, sources, and logic than those of Kate Michelman of NARAL or Patricia Ireland of NOW. It is not only women's autonomy or choice that are at stake for Kissling, but women's physical, mental, and spiritual health. Kissling bristles at environmentalists' arguments that spin contraception and abortion in terms of population control. Her discourse is ethical and theological.

Kissling made me appreciate the diversity of feminist politics, particularly those within religious communities. At the same time, I found that her politics pushed me to reexamine my own, and her discourse seemed to have had a similar effect on some international women's human rights activists. This led me to wonder what else might be learned from arguments by religious women about womanhood. Were there other ways religious discourse could fill out or deepen gender-based politics? If taken seriously, would it change what counted as political and as women? These questions inspired, or at least gave rise to, this project.

It is important to acknowledge that labeling any project focused on religious communities feminist is problematic for at least two reasons. There are historical-political reasons to be concerned with a feminist approach to understanding religious women. It is a well-known narrative in gender and postcolonial studies that feminism was co-opted by those in the West who used the excuse of "protecting brown women from their brown men" to implement a wide range of agendas that had little to do with improving women's lives.[6] But while those of us in the progressive left are quick to critique the deployment of feminism against "the Other," we often neglect how feminism has mistreated religious minorities in Western settings. Rosemary Radford Ruether, for example, has pointed out the vilification of the Catholic working class by feminists in the United States around the issue of temperance.[7] One doesn't have to look far in current media coverage to find assertions that link Islam to women's oppression.

The anecdote that begins this preface makes very clear that feminism is also a problematic term for some of the women I study, and yet in this project I have decided to continue to use the term *feminist politics* to describe the types of discursive practices studied. In part this is because to reject the term *feminist* outright is to privilege the more problematic definitions of feminism that neglect cultural and economic differences between women and the scholarly work done on its behalf. Judith Butler's work is immensely helpful on this point. She writes, "one might continue at the same time to interrogate and to use the terms of universality."[8] With regards specifically to feminism she argues, "to question a term, a term like feminism, is to ask how it plays, what investments it bears, what aims it achieves, what alterations it undergoes." However, and most important, acknowledging "the changeable life of that term does not preclude its use."[9]

On another level, retaining feminist is an acknowledgment that the women I interview base their form of political action on a conception of woman, no matter how diverse or problematic they understand this concept to be. Even if scholars are trained to deconstruct and problematize such conceptual frameworks, feminisms have motivating power in the real world. In other words, the concept of woman remains relevant to the production of ethical knowledge within religious communities not only because of the gendered anthropologies of male clerics, but also because of the moral praxis of religious women.

What do I mean by feminist if not the imperialistic feminism of which Habibi was so suspicious? I understand feminism to include any system of thought that challenges stereotypes that misrepresent women's experiences.[10] But this definition intentionally leaves undefined stereotypes because misrepresentation depends on one's perspective. I retain the feminist label for this project but keep in mind that alternative definitions of feminism do exist and that feminism is as much an historically varied and philosophically contested tradition as Roman Catholicism in the United States or Shi'i Islam in Iran. There are liberal feminists, naturalist feminists, care feminists, social-constructionist feminists, radical feminists, and so on.

This diversity is part of my motivation for exploring religious women's brands of "feminism" as a possible way to expand, rather than narrow, our understanding of productive feminist actions. I hope the way I claim feminism leaves me and the reader open to learn from women within settings different from our own.

A further distinction between feminist description, feminist analysis, and feminist politics is possible, and will help clarify what I mean by feminist politics.[11] Feminist description seeks to provide details of the experience of living female-gendered lives. This can be pursued through social scientific studies or ethnography that consciously attempts to convey women's experiences in their own words.[12] The question feminist description addresses is this: what is going on in particular women's lives?

Feminist analysis goes a step further, attempting to explain why women are like they are. More than just description, analysis searches for reasons between the actions and beliefs of women, as well as for external factors that create and influence these actions.[13] This second line of inquiry is important because it counters a tendency in ethnographic work to accept at face value the self-understanding of women.[14] For example, feminist analysis can look at the conscious reasons articulated for an action, but it can also uncover an agent's contradictory logics or consider sociological motivations for a specific action, thereby explaining "a craftiness that does not know itself."[15] This type of feminist analysis does not, however, necessarily imply that individuals are incapable of self-reflection (false consciousness theory) but rather assumes that certain dimensions of politics cannot be explained by an agent's intentions alone.[16]

Feminist politics is the most proscriptive or normative of the group. I define feminist politics as a form of action that attempts to reshape the conditions of women's individual or collective existence.[17] It often begins with assumptions about women's constrained freedom under particular conditions and a desire to eradicate these conditions.[18] In other words, feminist politics begins with some normative claim (e.g., women are equal to men) and a normative agenda of insurgency (e.g., women must be treated as equal to men). In contrast, although both feminist description and feminist analysis begin with the assumption that by looking at women we can learn something that is neglected in gender-neutral analysis (or that women and men are different, if not ontologically, at least in how they are treated or understood in a variety of arenas), they do not necessarily imply any normative agenda.

A problem in cross-cultural work on women is a tendency to slide from description (is) to prescription (ought), without attention to explanation (why). In the case of Habibi, I moved from description (she supports CEDAW) to prescription (she ought to be engaged in subversive political action based on a secular liberal model) too quickly. Following Pierre Bourdieu's assertion that "it is because subjects do not, strictly speaking, know what they are doing that what they do has more meaning than they know,"[19] this book is an explicit attempt to begin with and make central feminist analysis in order to explain the "more meaning" that women themselves might not know.

Feminist politics still occupies a central role in this project, but the feminist politics I try to highlight are of the women I study, not my own. In other words, what counts as a political claim and political agenda is determined by the practices of the women I investigate. This is not to say that I am disinterested. My role as a scholar is still feminist insofar as I have chosen to describe and explain the feminist politics in two communities. I study these women because I am personally committed to women's freedom, even if I am aware that what constitutes freedom may be different among different women. If this book has a political agenda, it is that this diversity is productive for feminist thinking and action. But I also study Catholic and Shi'i women because I believe that they are doing something innovative within their communities that is important to even a secular understanding of women's flourishing. For this project then, feminist politics is the way I characterize the actions of Catholic and Shi'i women: I attempt to isolate their engagement with tradition on the specific issue of women's proper action, and how their engagements contribute to the tradition's gendered moral vision.

Finally, continuing to label my project as feminist to some extent foregrounds the tensions within feminism—between divergent philosophical articulations of feminism and political, analytical, and descriptive feminisms. I cannot get beyond the contributions and challenges that feminism's legacy brings to this project. But if I keep this tension at the surface, it might prove productive. In some cases, disclosing my understanding of and commitment to a type of feminism provides an opportunity for a deeper conversation. In the case of Habibi, once it became clear that I was a feminist and she was not (according to her definition of a feminist), we were able to move past these labels to her argument of the coherence of equitable rights and distinct duties for men and women under shari'a.

SELECTION OF THE CASE STUDY

This book uses a transnational (United States and Iran), intertradition (Catholic and Shi'i) comparison between the feminist politics of different religious women. Using texts and some ethnography, the arguments of eleven women are analyzed against the pronouncements of Ayatollah Khomeini and Pope John Paul II, who each provide a local religious context. The goal is to isolate what sorts of traditional logics of womanhood the women draw on and which others they reform. The focus is not on specific issues of feminist politics (reproductive rights, leadership roles, status in the family) but rather on the rhetorical tactics. This means that selection of examples discussed in each chapter is based primarily on similarity at the tactical level and only secondarily on similarity at the thematic level. In the end, this book is not only about how women engage with various structures of authority in a process that creates wisdom and allows them to live moral lives, but also about how women contribute to the logics of the religious tradition beyond specific women's issues.

To orient the reader, it is helpful to provide initial justification for a number of dimensions of this case study, which although treated separately here, evolved together: mainly the selection of the two traditions, two clerics and eleven women, and the rationale for a comparative case study in the first place.

Catholicism and Shi'i Islam

Catholicism and Shi'i Islam are two traditions that have antiliberal, and anti-women reputations. This is especially so at the level of clerical pronouncements, where papal encyclicals and ayatollah fatwas are assumed to limit the freedom of Catholic and Shi'i women, respectively. My case study is selected in part to demonstrate how these liberal secular assumptions about these traditions are only partly correct and importantly misleading. I find that the practices of Catholic and Shi'i women are not only determined by but also contribute to the ethical and political landscape in their respective religious communities. This means that I am challenging the orthodoxies of liberal feminist politics (a sort of fundamentalist feminism, if you will) in order to ultimately strengthen feminism as a scholarly endeavor. If these two religious communities have something constructive to add to feminist politics, which I believe they do, further study of religion, rhetoric, and authority in gender studies can contribute to feminist thought in general.

A Clerical Context

Returning to my anecdote, my interaction with Habibi made it clear that to determine the ethical impact of what she was saying, I had to juxtapose it against a specific context. At times she engaged UN treaties, at other times *tafsīr,* at still others nationalist ideology. And her words could be understood to be productive in different ways from these different implied discursive contexts. During that initial interview, I was particularly keyed to her argument about CEDAW because I was considering her arguments from an international women's human rights framework. Choosing this framework, however, contributed to my neglect of some of her ethical arguments because although it is fundamental to liberal feminist politics, it is not the only framework that Habibi works within. I realized that to understand how women's arguments engage their local religious traditions, I had to find a discursive context that would allow me to see women's political actions as religious discursive practices. I had to find a new place to stand in order to see more than myself in the mirror.

It was during an initial set of interviews with prominent lay leaders in both communities that I found that many shared a common context: clerical rhetoric. That is, when pressed, they each acknowledge they respond to the ethical teachings of a particular religious leader: John Paul II or Ayatollah Khomeini. There is a wide range of opinions among the women studied about whether clerical rhetoric is good or bad, but general agreement that, given its authority in the community, this rhetoric warrants engagement. By focusing on this engagement, either direct or indirect, I work to understand how women place themselves within a religious tradition and at what point they work to reaffirm, critique, or innovate the teachings of their respective religious leaders. The place I stand is within the logic of clerical teaching on women, to better understand what women's discursive practices do with this logic.

This book challenges the facile assumptions that the authoritarian structures of the papacy and the Iranian theocracy are uniformly and necessarily bad for women. I am interested in a different sort of inquiry: If these clerical leaders are in fact patriarchal, how exactly do they construct their visions of women? What are their gendered moral anthropologies? How do they attempt to convince women that their vision of women's proper roles is the correct one? In other words, my focus on rhetoric is meant to provide a more nuanced way to understand these leaders' authority.

A causal relationship between the clerical discourse and feminist politics of women is not posited. Rather the clerical discourse represents one source of authority within the community and this study uncovers the almost shocking fact that even when attempting to control women within religious structures, clerical authority provides the tools for a wide variety of feminist politics. Nor do I intend to overstate the influence of clerical authority in these communities. In fact, the ultimate focus of this book is on how women are producers of moral knowledge. Nevertheless, the Roman Catholic Church and Shi'i Islam in Iran are two contexts in which the authority of clerics plays a crucial role in gender politics, so this book uses clerical rhetoric to provide a context for analysis.

Some readers will object to the coupling of Pope John Paul II and Ayatollah Khomeini in this study. This concern is addressed in the introduction through an argument about their shared forms of charismatic authority, but a few words about the reasons for the selection of these specific thinkers are appropriate here. As mentioned previously, interviews of American Catholic and Iranian Shi'i women made it clear that John Paul II and Khomeini were each an important source of local understandings about morality for women. Both thinkers were religious leaders who became immensely influential in their respective community's understanding of proper practice, particularly on the issue of women's proper roles. There is also some parity in their background and thought. Both studied and lectured on philosophy and mysticism early in their careers, wrote passionately about the importance of ethical living, and were concerned with the challenges raised by the social, political, and economic context of the twentieth century. Finally, both were centrally concerned with the political actions of women. More than any other cleric within their respective communities in the last quarter of the twentieth century, John Paul and Khomeini wrote about and spoke to women.[20] Through their arguments about women's moral and political lives, they made womanhood a legitimate topic of religious discourse and increased women's opportunities to contribute to an ongoing conversation about the ideal conditions of women's collective existence.

The Creative Conformers

The primary data for this book is the moral discourse of eleven women. I spent the summer and fall of 2004 meeting with a number of potential "creative conformers" in the United States and Iran. Even though I could not include all the women I spoke with, these conversations determined the ultimate selection my creative conformers and the themes of conformity I focus on (the subjects of the five chapters). It was challenging to limit myself, particularly given the wide range of political activities of Catholic women in the United States and Shi'i women in Iran, and subsequent arguments that support these activities. To make the selection, I came up with three criteria based on my ethnographic work.

First, all the creative conformers are recognizable public intellectuals in their local communities. Anyone who has studied Catholic feminism in the United States will already be familiar with the women discussed in this book: Lisa Cahill, Diana Hayes, Helen Hitchcock, Ada María Isasi-Díaz, and Frances Kissling. The same can be said of my selection of Shi'i women in Iran: Mahboubeh Abbas-Gholizadeh, Leila Arshad, Monir Gurji, Elaheh Koulaei, Masoumeh Ebtekar, and Shahla Sherkat. Public intellectuals were studied on one hand because their discursive practices have particular productive power given their visibility. But a more important reason exists: Given the present pressures faced by those politically active in Iran, I did not want to argue that a particular woman's discourse was meant to be public and political unless her position already made this dimension of her argumentation clear. The eleven women have held a variety of positions, including nun, member of parliament, missionary, candidate for president, academic, theologian, Qur'anic interpreter, leader of a church group, journalist, and director of a civil society organization. They write for scholarly journals, mainstream religious publications, and publish their own journals and newletters. They are by no means representative of all Catholic women in the United States or Shi'i women in Iran because they all would be considered elite. But they each have been enormously influential on contemporary Catholic and Shi'i feminist politics.

Second, I selected women who I believe engage John Paul's and Khomeini's moral guidance through a wide range of tactics rather than only thematically. My initial attempts to line up the women on core issues of religious leadership, reproductive rights, and public dress was problematic; Iranian Shi'i and American Catholic women are simply not concerned with the same set of issues, and to force a comparison on the issue of abortion, for instance, was to misrepresent the range of feminist tactics in Iran. In addition, tactical similarities emerged through comparison of radically different conceptual debates. A Catholic argument over women's ordination involved logics and tactics similar to a Shi'i debate over religious dress; discourse about natural family planning in the United States becomes an interesting counterpoint to debates about a woman's right to custody of her children after divorce in Iran. In addition to ideological diversity among the women studied, and more important, there is both tactical variety and overlap.

Third, it was not my intent to identify the strongest articulations of dissent, but rather responses that construct new and intriguing rhetorical spaces through their architectonics, content, and logic. In each section I mention relevant direct refutations, but my focus is on arguments that work indirectly. For example, although Frances Kissling is best known for her articulation of a pro-choice Catholic position, I have selected a lesser-known speech in which she considers the value of fetal life. An indirect response may be more difficult to identify in a woman's rhetorical performance, perhaps even impossible to see, without the groundwork of deconstructing the clerical rhetoric. Ultimately, however, I argue indirect responses do more to redefining religious feminist politics than a direct rebuttal based on secular-liberal assumptions.

Fourth, I determined that I needed a text to work from.[21] This decision was due in part to the limits of my fieldwork: Given the diplomatic relations between Iran and the United States, or lack of them, I was not able to conduct a second stint of fieldwork in Iran. This meant that I had to rely more heavily on textual sources collected in the field than I initially anticipated. But a conceptual need for a text also emerged during my interviews of the Iranian women: it became clear I was sometimes being told what the women thought I wanted to hear. This is the flipside of the academic ventriloquism. I was not the only one throwing my voice. During interviews the women themselves sometimes fell into a pattern of channeling my voice. In an interview I had no way of knowing when an argument was being constructed for my benefit, as a Western feminist scholar. A similar problem emerged when I interviewed Catholic women: Some of them made assumptions about my project, given my institutional training or the juxtaposition of John Paul and Khomeini in the same book, and were suspicious, defensive, or overly enthusiastic. Referring to a text, I can more easily isolate arguments directed explicitly to the community of believers. For example, Iranian women, not American researchers, are the primary audience for a text written in Persian and published in Iran. The types of texts I select—editorials, interviews, published speeches, and academic essays—also attempt to isolate discursive arguments aimed at a particular local audience of adherents.

WHY COMPARE?

This book puts comparison at the center of its analysis. Each chapter works among and between two traditions, clerics and laity, and different women's visions of the moral life. Comparison places the features of each religious tradition's gender teachings in relief and thus de-centers the unconscious and unspoken norms of prominent feminist models. Working within the religious understanding of gender in two traditions prevents us from passing moral judgment over one or the other. The ability to remain open to multiple perspectives is especially important given recent geopolitical events when the United States seems poised for war with Iran. Considering the Shi'i perspective alongside one that is more prominent in U.S. politics will help counter impressions of Iran as backward, irrational, or evil.

In many ways, working comparatively (among traditions and nations) makes both my and the reader's job more difficult. This book asks you to keep in mind two traditions, two clerics, and a number of diverse feminist politics. Technical definitions from each tradition are explained, historical contexts for rhetorical events provided, all of which might mean losing the goal of describing feminist politics in the details. However, we are simply unable to describe or explain feminist tactics in the way that allows for cross-cultural diversity without this complexity. For this particular project, comparison opens up the possibility for Western readers to both understand Islamic women and rethink Western feminism more than a study focused solely on Iran would. As Michel de Certeau writes, "Other laws restore to us what our own culture has seen fit to exclude from its own discourse."[22]

NOTES

1. This post was later held by Zahra Shojaei under President Khatami, and by Nasrin Soltankhah during President Mahmoud Ahmadinejad's administration.

2. "Man fimīnīst nīstam. Man rā bih 'unvān-i fimīnīst ḥisāb nakunīd. I'tiqād bih fimīnīzm nadāram." Shahla Habibi, innterview by the author, Tehran, August 12, 2004.

3. Saba Mahmood provides an excellent discussion of the how secularism lends itself to a specific form of hermeneutics, important particularly in U.S. foreign policy, which is no less literal or inflexible than traditional religious forms of hermeneutics. "Secularism, Hermeneutics, and Empire," 323–47.

4. Talal Asad has helpfully pointed out that empowerment was originally a legal term (meaning giving power to someone, or having the power to act), which has come to be understood by some liberal theorists as "a metaphysical quality defining human subjectivity, its objective as well as precondition." "Agency and Pain," 35.

5. For a discussion of how these overlapping discourses of gender function in the Iranian context, see Torab, "Piety as Gendered Agency," 236–39. See also her most recent monograph, *Performing Islam*, 242–49.

6. Spivak, "Can the Subaltern Speak?" 271–316.

7. "When feminism became linked with temperance at the turn of the century, the anti-Catholic bias sometimes became explicit, vilifying the growing Catholic working-class political leadership cities, such as Boston and Chicago, as the epitome of 'rum, Romanism, and rebellion.'" Ruether, "The War on Women," 3.

8. Butler, *Undoing Gender*, 180.

9. Ibid., 178–79.

10. This definition is informed by Marilyn Strathern's discussion of feminist anthropology in "An Awkward Relationship," 287.

11. For other discussions of the analytical and political dimensions of feminist scholarship see Mahmood, *Politics of Piety*; Mahmood, "Feminist Theory, Embodiment and the Docile Agent;" Butler, *Gender Trouble*; Mohanty, "Under Western Eyes"; Strathern, "An Awkward Relationship."

12. For an example of feminist descriptive work in the American Catholic context, see Isasi-Díaz, *En la Lucha*, 86–140. For an example of feminist description of Iranian women, see Esfandiari, *Reconstructed Lives*.

13. For an excellent discussion of description versus analysis, see Hollywood, "Gender, Agency and the Divine," 514–28.

14. My thanks to Aaron Stalnaker for pushing me to clarify this point.

15. De Certeau, "On the Oppositional Practices of Everyday Life," 18.

16. Azam Torab has written eloquently on this subject and proposes a theory of multiple selves that are constituted through the web of multiple discourses that individuals find themselves within. *Performing Islam,* 242–49.

17. My definition depends largely on Charles Hirschkind's recent reworking of Hannah Arendt's definition of politics in *The Ethical Soundscape*, 8.

18. For an expanded discussion on feminist analysis versus politics, see Mahmood, *Politics of Piety*, 10; Hirschkind and Mahmood, "Feminism, the Taliban, and Politics of Counter-Insurgency," 339–54.

19. Bourdieu, *Outline of a Theory of Practice*, 79.

20. A possible exception is Ayatollah Murtaza Mutahhari, from whom Khomeini draws many of his understandings of the moral life. But, unlike Khomeini, Mutahhari did not speak directly to large groups of women in Iran.

21. The one exception to focus on a text is Arshad's rhetoric on custody discussed in chapter two. In this case I draw from our interview. The argument Arshad gave me verbally is similar to the one I heard from a number of women active in that reform campaign, including Shirin Ebadi and Elaheh Koulaei. However, I was unable to locate an article from my source publications, *Farzānah* and *Zanān,* devoted to the justification for the custody reform.

22. De Certeau, "On the Oppositional Practices of Everyday Life," 14.

INTRODUCTION

Creative Conformity, Clerical Guidance, and a Rhetorical Turn

This book uses a comparative study of women's moral discourse to describe and explain one way in which women produce ethical knowledge. I work within and between women, clerics, and traditions to describe both the citation and innovation of women's moral discourse, as well as the dynamic interactions between clerics and laity. The goal of the study is to challenge views of women as merely victims of male authority by showing how women negotiate with powerful clerical moral guidance. Themes include how clerical rhetoric works as moral guidance, how authority creates diversity of response, how the logical parameters of discursive contexts shift, and how religious women contribute to their community's moral anthropology.

This introduction lays out the background for the chapters, which focus on textual analysis informed by ethnography. First, I offer an overview of the theory of moral agency this study assumes. I propose the neologism *dianomy*, meaning dual sources of the moral law, to account for moral agency that relies neither exclusively on the self nor exclusively on religious traditions as a source of moral authority. With dianomy, tactical moves, actions that are not intentionally chosen, and even happy accidents can be studied as productive of ethical knowledge within religious communities. I call these types of actions—which confound the theories of autonomy, heteronomy, and theonomy—*creative conformity*.

Second, because I work among two traditions, I briefly introduce ethics within Catholicism and Shi'i Islam through the theme of moral guidance. Given my selection of clerical rhetoric to provide a context for women's arguments, I discuss the nature of Pope John Paul II's and Ayatollah Ruhollah Khomeini's charismatic leadership, particularly as it relates to their ethical teachings for female believers. The roots of their moral guidance are considered through their training in emotional connection to audiences and their unique positions in their respective religious communities.

Third, I describe the technical method of rhetorical analysis used in this study. Invention of this method proved necessary to break clerical rhetoric down into discrete pieces to better serve as a background for the women's indirect responses. Specific categories of informal argument are key to this method and are informed by Aristotle's classical definition of the mode of epideictic rhetoric and by the recent work on argumentation by Chaïm Perelman and Stephen Toulmin.

These three overviews, related to moral agency, the authority of clerics, and discrete components of argumentation, make up the framework that will allow the reader to better understand the analysis in this book. Although discussed separately, these conceptual issues are closely interrelated. A thick description of moral agency is needed to account for a wide range of women's arguments as the proper subject for a study on feminist politics. Understanding traditional forms of ethical knowledge, particularly as conveyed through clerical rhetoric, is needed to isolate moments when women are offering something distinct. To identify the tactics used in women's arguments and their rhetorical impact, a technical method of rhetorical analysis has to be developed. These are also the three conceptual areas where my assumptions and methodology were rethought and reinvented in the process of this study. So, although they appear at the beginning of this book, they are also some of the most important payoffs of this comparative analysis.

MORAL AGENCY AS CREATIVE CONFORMITY

The lessons I learned from my interaction with Habibi, described in the preface, were important first steps toward trying to rethink how to theorize women's agency in a cross-cultural and interreligious study. But I was still left with the challenge of how to describe and explain the full range of women's moral discourse. Specifically, I wondered how both to acknowledge that the clerical rhetoric (among other external forces) influences women's discourse and that women's discourse has its distinct logic and therefore power in religious communities. To resolve this dilemma, I needed to specify what sorts of actions are considered as feminist politics in this book and to articulate a theory of moral agency grounding these actions that can account for multiple sources of the moral law. In the first case, Michel de Certeau's distinction between strategy and tactic proved helpful; in the second, a survey of existing scholarship on moral agency led me to the invention of the neologism *dianomy* to account for a theory of moral law that incorporates both the insights of autonomy and heteronomy.

Tactical Actions within the Game

In his general introduction to *The Practice of Everyday Life*, de Certeau writes that his goal is "to bring to light the clandestine forms taken by the dispersed, tactical, and make-shift creativity of groups or individuals already caught in the nets of 'discipline.'"[1] In a similar way, this book seeks to understand how religious women, my example of individuals caught in the nets of discipline, are nevertheless creative.

The way de Certeau draws a distinction between tactics and strategies is helpful for specifying what sorts of women's actions I consider as part of feminist politics. He defines strategy as "the calculus (or the manipulation) of relations of force which becomes possible whenever a subject of will and power . . . can be isolated."[2] Strategies intend to critique, reform, threaten, or rebel. If we use a game as a metaphor for the moral life, strategies are attempts to referee from the sidelines, introduce different rulebooks, or even break up the game entirely.[3] But exclusive focus on strategies comes with a price. First, we risk reading as resistance even those actions that do not mean to resist, thereby assigning intentions to women's actions that are not their own.[4] Second, we risk judging any action that looks like obedience as not "truly free."

This book tries to avoid some of these analytical traps by focusing on what de Certeau calls tactics instead of strategies. He writes,

> A *tactic* is a calculated action determined by the absence of a proper locus. No delimitation of an exteriority, then, provides it with the condition necessary for autonomy. The space of a tactic is the space of the other. Thus it must play on and with a terrain imposed on it and organized by the law of a foreign power. . . . It takes advantage of "opportunities" and depends on them, being without any base where it could stockpile its winnings, build up its own position and plan raids. What it wins it cannot keep. . . . It must vigilantly make use of the cracks that particular conjunctions open in the surveillance of the proprietary powers. It poaches in them. It creates surprises in them. It can be where it is least expected. It is a guileful ruse.[5]

Considering feminist politics to include tactics helps avoid some of the shortcomings of an exclusive focus on strategies, and provides a complex enough conceptual understanding of action to allow for dimensions of creativity and conformity within the same act. When applied to the subject of this book, the "terrain imposed" on the subject is the religious tradition as interpreted and conveyed by the clerics. Women within the religious communities "take advantage of opportunities" on this terrain. The conformity of the feminist politics is how women stay within the game by using clerical logics; the creativity is the logical surprises and ruptures of the women's discourse that are unanticipated, and yet made possible, by the clerical rulebook.

For the most part, de Certeau's tactics are the sorts of actions envisioned in feminist politics as creative conformity. I do, however, disagree with de Certeau on three issues. First, he understands the production of representation "taught by preachers, educators, and popularizers" to be the original production of the representation (in my study, ethical knowledge is the representation at stake).[6] For him, users or the audience for such production (in my study, religious women) are engaged in the secondary process of utilization. In contrast, I understand even the original representation to invoke women, at least insofar as clerics must attune to their audience's assumptions to be persuasive. More important, use itself affects the representation: women's moral praxis shifts the local meaning of women's proper roles. Second, de Certeau calls tactics the tools of the weak.[7] I have difficulty affirming his duality between strong and weak, which misrepresents the nature of power by privileging some forms of authority and action over others. Finally, it is also important that I do not investigate the intentionality behind the women's rhetoric. De Certeau's use of the adjective "calculated" to describe not only strategies but also tactics might merely be an assertion of the free will of agents. But it could also imply that an agent's intent is the litmus test for the success or impact of a tactical action. In the preface I argue for the importance of feminist scholarship in being able to describe not only the intent of the agent, but also its unintended impact. Specifically, I am interested in how women construct visions of their moral lives using traditional religious components of informal argumentation, even when they see themselves as dissenting from this logic, and shift others, even when they see themselves to be reiterating clerical visions of women's proper roles. In fact, the issue of intended orthodoxy or reform is finally irrelevant in this analysis because in creative conformity, obedience can be innovative as unanticipated, and dissent can be submissive as citational.

Dianomy: Getting beyond the Good and Bad Girls

Given a decision to focus on tactics, the next question becomes how to conceptualize the model of agency framing tactical actions. At issue is how to maintain both a sense of free will necessary for moral action and an acknowledgment that the terrain of tactics is to some extent externally imposed. In ethical scholarship, this is sometimes expressed as a tension between the autonomous and heteronomous sources of the moral law.

Autonomy emphasizes the importance of the individual in the moral life and sees her as the source of her freedom and innovation. However, a study of religious women that assumes autonomy tends to focus only on women's dissent from religious traditions (the bad girls of religion), rejecting that actions that look like obedience might be done freely or be creative. Heteronomy, in contrast, places women within a system of external forces and emphasizes the role of habituation for the moral life. This focuses scholarly inquiry on how women enact religious traditions (the good girls of religion). However, heteronomy tends to obscure free subjects, or reject their existence outright, and neglects how enactment itself can be ambiguous or innovative.[8]

To correct how each of these theories neglect dimensions of moral agency, I propose dianomy. Dianomy is dual insofar as both the autonomous and heteronomous laws are acknowledged as sources of the moral life. They are held together in an unresolved tension, the emphasis being on the process by which they interact. In addition to signifying two sources of the moral law, the *dia* is meant to invoke exchange akin to dialectic between two individuals, such as a lay-woman and a cleric, who share a group of premises. The model of agency implied in dianomy is also double: a woman is formed within a specific discursive and performative environment, but she is also able to interrogate that environment. I developed this model through the study of religious women, but it can be applied to any agent.

Dianomy has a number of advantages over assuming strict autonomy or heteronomy in interpreting women's actions. The most general lesson it incorporates from heteronomy is that the possibilities of actions are to some extent local. In this way dianomy is not meant to be a universal theory of agency, other than an assertion that to understand women's actions we need to understand some aspect of their context. In my current project, clerical rhetoric is used to provide such a context: inquiry into arguments about women are used to understand what women say. However, in contrast to some theories of heteronomy, dianomy retains an understanding of free will. It does so without resorting to an autonomous understanding of freedom that depends on escaping external power structures, but instead by considering how free will itself can be a habituated norm within a tradition. Dianomy thus provides a way to consider the ability to critique as part of the model of habituation: even as local discursive contours create the possibilities of and restraints on action, freedom can exist as a situated norm within the discursive space.

In contrast to autonomy, which focuses on individual reason as a source of the moral law, dianomy focuses on the interaction between reasons and habits, multiple sources of external norms, and clerical and lay *nomos*. This dual nature of dianomy embraces the ambiguity, partiality, and imperfection in the moral life. Because agents have direct access only to autonomous moral law, their ethical actions and arguments in some way depend on a creative process of perceiving and negotiating multiple sources of heteronomous law. The movement from law to practice is also ambiguous because it relies on the unpredictable processes of hearing, understanding, and interpreting discourse. In dianomy, the importance of the individual (auto) is not primarily as a source of moral law, but rather as the site for interpretation, negotiation, and application.

Dianomy is not purely my invention, even if the neologism is. Many scholars work with theories akin to dianomy, and a group of feminist scholars have been particularly instructive.[9] For instance, a motivation behind developing dianomy is to account for a process of critique that does not assume an agent is able to stand outside the tradition she critiques. My understanding of how such critique can occur, even unintentionally, is informed by Judith Butler's analysis of the role of citation in hate speech.

Butler writes, "Indeed, racist speech could not act as racist speech if it were not *a citation of itself*; only because we already know its force from its prior instances do we know it to be so offensive now, and we brace ourselves against its future invocations."[10] Butler's situating of speech's meaning within a specific context acknowledges that traditions (whether racism or Catholicism or Islam) strongly determine what sorts of things a subject can believe, say, or do. However, Butler is also interested in a critical moment of rhetorical response, in the possibility of breaking from this process of citation.[11] This response is critical "in the sense that it will not comply with a given category, but rather constitute an interrogatory relation to the field of categorization itself, referring at least implicitly to the limits of the epistemological horizon within which practices are formed."[12] This is how critique can be understood as not distinct from a habituated skill, but instead as a cross-cultural virtue (perhaps the only truly universal virtue) necessary to navigate our habituation within multiple traditions, including many that stress the good of free will.

Butler argues that this critical moment is possible because the intention and meaning of speech are not as closely linked as some scholars have claimed and that discourse is "always in some ways out of our control," free to be fought over, to be defined and redefined by both the original speaker and audience.[13] This means that creativity occurs in part because of the difference between the performed and ideal status of moral claims, virtues, and embodied skills. This same conceptualization can be applied to the speech of a religious leader who may attempt to limit how practitioners believe or act. Even though this argument is deployed from a position of authority, we cannot necessarily predict how women will respond to it.[14]

The work of Azam Torab, a social anthropologist who studies Iranian women, has also been helpful in formulating a dianomous understanding of the moral life. Her work on prayer meetings in Tehran explores women's "simultaneous processes of complicity as well as resistance," which resonates with my notion of creative conformity.[15] Torab argues that this "complicit resistance" is possible because women have multiple selves in that they are formed by several discourses at the same time: "The notion of multiple selves does not mean the disappearance of powerful discourses, but their realignment under contest. It is therefore not simply that there are multiple discourses within cultures, but in addition, individuals themselves are multiply constituted, which allows them the scope to act on the world in which they live."[16]

If we put Torab's insight into the language of moral agency, her suggestion is that moments of creative conformity occur because it is within the individual that multiple heteronomous norms are realigned. This realignment or negotiation is necessary for an individual to act; it is possible in the first place because being constituted in multiple traditions creates a type of skillful flexibility within individuals.

A similar concept of negotiation grounds dianomy, but my work differs from Torab's in two important ways. First, her study is meant to represent how women envision their actions. In other words, she is concerned with the intentions behind actions in a way that I am not. Second, although Torab describes a process of realignment that I find helpful for explaining tactics, her concern is with resistance in a more strategic form, one that assumes a prior teleology of women's empowerment.

R. Marie Griffith's work on charismatic evangelical women also theoretically informs dianomy, in that she attempts to explain the "meaning of women's continued adherence to the doctrine of submission and authority."[17] Her work, published in 1997, was groundbreaking at the time for introducing a different approach to conservative religious women as objects of academic study. Griffith finds that women's devotional narratives uncover a "dialectic of female submission and empowerment"[18] through which "women rework the social roles they inhabit."[19] For example, she discovers "a high degree of innovation, not to mention historical development, in [Aglow Fellowship] women's interpretation of female submission."[20] This is all similar to the types of creative conformity I hope to capture with dianomy.

Griffith's work and mine conceptually diverge, however, in two ways. First, although to a lesser degree than Torab, there is concern in Griffith's work with representing women as they see themselves, which results in privileging their stated intentions.[21] Second, despite her self-disclosed struggle "against the temptation to romanticize resistance," she tends to focus on how the evangelical women "continuously redraw and renegotiate the boundaries of power and authority."[22] This is because one of Griffith's claims is that much historical work on twentieth-century religious women is based on a disdain for women who are perceived as "conservative religious women." In Butler's terms, Griffith is concerned with highlighting conservative women's critique to rehabilitate their agency; in my terms, she is emphasizing the creative part of the creative conformity. However, creativity does more than critique, it can also reconstitute a tradition. I offer dianomy not only to rehabilitate the actions of conservative women as signs of real agency, but also to understand that even the actions of women perceived as "progressive religious women" (such as Muslims who reject the Islamic veil) are no more creative and no less conforming than those of the women Griffith studies. In other words, dianomy is trying to understand the tactical moves of a wide range of women within religious communities to further unsettle the notion that religious women are necessarily more constrained than any other group.

In this way, dianomy confronts one of the potentially glaring weaknesses of ethnographic-based research: the tendency to accept at face value the self-understanding of one's subjects, rather than interpret and even interrogate it as in part ideological. This tendency is seen to some extent in Torab's and even Griffith's work. Scholars should question our sources and informants. We should be able to both respect these women and yet not allow their intent to dictate what can be understood about their actions. In my own work, for example, I do not investigate the intentionality behind the women's rhetoric. I am interested in the process women use to construct their own visions of their moral lives using components of informal argumentation within a religious tradition. Even when they see themselves as dissenting from these logics, they reproduce them; even when they see themselves to be reiterating clerical visions of women's proper roles, they shift them. Dianomy interprets all obedience as potentially innovative and creative, and all dissent as potentially submissive and conforming. In the next section I focus on why some religious norms have been recognized as particularly important for tactical engagement. Specifically I discuss how the guidance of John Paul II and Ayatollah Khomeini has "ethical heft" in these two communities.

JOHN PAUL II, AYATOLLAH KHOMEINI, AND ETHICAL HEFT

While I was conducting research in Iran, my Iranian roommate Ziba wanted to introduce me to her group of young friends.[23] We had decided to meet in Inqilab (Revolution) Square. Earlier that day I had been collecting sources at the premier institute that archives, compiles, and publishes Khomeini's writings. Because of sanctions on Iran, many of these books are not available in the United States and I wanted to have copies to ship home. I was running late, however, and ended up lugging a heavy bag of books as I made my way from the northern suburb of Tajrish to Tehran's center in a series of three shared taxis in stifling heat.

When I finally arrived at the coffee shop, sweating and disheveled, I joked with Ziba in my formal beginner's Persian: "Khumaynī khaylī sangīn ast" (Khomeini is really heavy). As each person joined our group, Ziba and I would complain about Khomeini's weight, offering the bag as evidence. The last to arrive was Saeed, who works for a reformist group.[24] "Give me Khomeini," he said, "I want to see how heavy he is." After testing the bag he handed it back to me and said with a shrug: "You shouldn't complain. You have only carried Khomeini for one hour. We have had to carry him for twenty-five years."

Saeed's comment suggests that it is still very appropriate, if not necessary, to consider the effect of Khomeini's rhetoric on feminist politics in the Islamic Republic of Iran. This was also confirmed by the Iranian women I interviewed, who argued that in terms of women's rights and duties, Khomeini remains heavy. In a similar way, Pope John Paul II emerged through my conversations with Catholic women as an important source for, or obstacle to, women's political activism for the U.S. Catholic community. Even women who find the pronouncements of these two clerics problematic acknowledge that, given their ethical heft, they warrant engagement. In other works, despite debate over whether John Paul's and Khomeini's authority can be justified by theological, ethical, or democratic ideals, they do, in fact, function as moral guides for the Iranian Shi'i and U.S. Catholic communities. Khomeini was heavy. John Paul was heavy. Although they are both now dead, Khomeini since 1989 and John Paul since 2005, their teachings remain touchstones for debate about the moral lives of women.

Despite this ethical heft, my case study is sure to garner at least a few objections from practitioners. For example, a practicing Catholic might bristle at the thought of equating John Paul and Khomeini on any terms given that Khomeini is perceived as a political tyrant, unlike the benevolent head of the Church. And practicing Shi'a might object to the comparison on the grounds that the pope is part of a hierarchical institution and that no comparable governing body exists for Shi'a Islam. These objections might originate from a place of suspicion of the other tradition, but they point to a serious problem: a pope's and an ayatollah's moral discourse is not theologically the same. This complicates use of them in a comparative project.

Scholars of Christianity and Islam might object to clerical comparison on similar grounds, though they would most likely couch objections in theories of authority. For example, from the point of view of Max Weber's influential typology of authority, John Paul and Khomeini differ in traditional and juridical forms.[25] John Paul was elected the 264th head of the Roman Catholic Church. This sort of institutional structure does not exist in Shi'i Islam, where religious leadership is provided by a group of independent scholars. The leaders also do not have the same role in the national politics of the two countries I study. In the United States, given our formal separation of church and state, John Paul was a foreign diplomat. By contrast, Khomeini had a central political role in Iran as leader of the national Islamic Revolution of 1979 and his subsequent position in the Islamic Republic as the supreme leader. His opinions on shari'a became the source for national laws. From the perspective of traditional authority, a papal office is stronger than a mere ayatollah, but from a juridical one, Khomeini's authority seems more established. Viewing either leader's authority in purely institutional-traditional or political-juridical terms could also lead to conclusions about the moral discourse of these clerics. One could assume, for example, that a pope does not need to be persuasive given his authoritarian religious office, or that a supreme leader simply declares what is obligatory rather than tries to persuade about what is good.

However, this analysis relies on only two dimensions of Weber's authority typology. Attention to the third type, charisma, can be a foundation for understanding the parity of these clerics' moral authority. Charisma can also be used to explain the ethical heft of clerics, specifically in terms of how discursive moral authority is conveyed through affectivity. A charismatic leader will kindle enthusiasm for his vision using what Weber calls *Ergriffenheit* (emotional seizure). This quality is not necessarily part of traditional or legal training, and therefore may allow us to understand an often-overlooked dimension of clerical persuasion. Although a pope and ayatollah might differ radically in what Weber would call traditional and juridical authority, exceptional ones might share dimensions of charismatic authority, making comparison possible. Charismatic guidance is therefore a link between two traditions that otherwise differ in form of religious authority.

Attention to the early biography and unusual training of these clerics is helpful for explaining how competency in emotional seizure helped make these clerics heavy in the first place. It will also allow a revisiting of Weber's strict differentiation between pure and routinized charisma, which is complicated by the biographies of these exceptional clerics.

Affective Training on Theatrical and Political Stages

Addressing a crowd in St. Peter's Square in Italian, as the first non-Italian head of the Roman Catholic Church in more than three centuries, John

Paul II demonstrated his ability to connect to his audience: "I have come from a far-away country—far away, but always so close in the communion of faith. I do not know whether I can express myself in your—in our—Italian language. If I make mistakes, you will correct me."[26] John Paul II went on to serve as the 264th bishop of Rome from his election in 1978 until his death in 2005. He was the most widely seen pope, and when his television and radio addresses are considered, he is among the most widely heard people in the second half of the twentieth century.

The life story of John Paul, who was born Karol Wojtyla, has been the subject matter of numerous renditions, including television miniseries, biographies, and even a marvel comic.[27] He was named man of the year by *Time* magazine in 1994.[28] It is difficult at times to separate historical fact from revisionist gloss, but by most accounts Karol as a young boy was interested in the church, athletics, school, and theater. Even if exaggerated, these childhood sufferings and demonstrations of piety are important to contextualize John Paul's rhetoric, as these narratives are told over and over and contribute to how his audience receives his teachings.

Themes often used to describe Karol Wojtyla's life before the papacy include enduring family tragedy, courageously resisting oppression, preserving Polish cultural forms, holding intellectual promise, and having exceptional religious piety, all occurring within the context of a world war, Nazi occupation, and communist rule. But what is not as commonly known or discussed in scholarship as a significant factor in his moral authority is an early theatrical career cut short by World War II.

His brother Edmund, a physician, was the first actor in the family, presenting scenes to his patients to keep them amused. It was Edmund who urged Karol to meet with the local theater director, Mieczyslaw Kotlarczyk (1908–78). Kotlarczyk would eventually take Karol under his wing, training him in Kotlarczyk's particular form of theater, Theater of the Word, which combined the form of simple chanting with the content of Christian beliefs.[29] The focus in Theater of the Word, as with any theatrical performance, was on constructing an "emotional seizure" of the audience. Kotlarczyk understood words to be very powerful in and of themselves: they do not simply communicate, but elicit emotions and understandings of meaning in the audience through the dramatic connection between speaker and listener. He emphasized minimalist production, in which the actors strove to communicate through precise diction the inner consciousness of a given role.

Kotlarczyk provided the earliest systematic training of Karol on any subject. Before Wotjtla's study of Carmelite mysticism, before his study of phenomenology, before his seminary training, Kotlarczyk introduced Karol to a system of religious action that links Christian faith to public performance. It would be fair to say that Karol's theatrical training became important to his later role as pope, particularly given the access he had to the world stage in using radio and television to broadcast his messages to the Catholic faithful. It is also possible that his concern for emotions and affectivity, which runs throughout his early study of mysticism and phenomenology and his later mature Catholic moral theology, also had its roots on the stage. Finally, participation in the Theater of the Word was an early opportunity for John Paul to approach what Weber might call the ultimate center of human values, necessary for any charismatic leader, by modeling certain moral actions.

In contrast, Khomeini's biographical details, as understood in the West, seem to be an obstacle to claiming him as an important moral guide. A quick scan of headlines in the English language press over last twenty-five years hint at the type of events most associated with Khomeini: a revolution that established a modern theocracy; a hostage crisis in the U.S. Embassy in Tehran; imprisonment, torture, and execution of dissidents; compulsatory veiling; and a fatwa against Salman Rushdie's *The Satanic Verses*. He has been labeled in the West (and more quietly in the East) an extremist and a fanatic. He was against the West, unabashedly religious, bearded, cloaked, and turbaned: all traits that make Americans, situated in a climate of hypothetical separation of church and state, uneasy. These impressions of Khomeini are combined with the fact that the position he held as leader of the Islamic Republic has a contested lineage. In fact, it was Khomeini's own arguments for *vilāyat-i faqīh* (guidance of the cleric) that justified his ascension to the role of the supreme leader.[30]

But to a great extent, whether Khomeini was or was not a tyrant or a liberator, a fundamentalist or an innovator, is irrelevant to a discussion of his role as an ethical guide in Iran. His image dominates public political art and graces the walls of many offices—including many of the women I interviewed, for whom Khomeini's teachings are a continuing inspiration for their work. As the founder of the Islamic Republic, established by popular referendum in 1979, his teachings are codified in the constitution and drawn on to justify policies of the Iranian government.[31] His legacy is protected by legislation that makes it illegal to speak against him.[32]

If acting is a key overlooked aspect of John Paul's training, then mystical training is an overlooked aspect of Khomeini's. For example, it might surprise the reader who understands Khomeini primarily as a revolutionary to learn that he began his career as a writer and teacher of *'irfān*, the Shi'i discipline of mystical knowledge.[33] One might even understand an interest in mysticism to be in tension with Khomeini's later political activism: *'irfān* encourages a personal journey toward union with God that focuses both on the other-world and on the individual, independent of political or communal concerns. But Khomeini grew to understand political conditions as an important component of devotional and even mystical matters, even if this was not the opinion held by the majority of Iranian clerics in the twentieth century.[34]

Even if Khomeini's interest in mysticism is unfamiliar to the Western generalist, his prominence in Iran is initially grounded in his expertise in mysticism and ethics. At madrasa (theological college), Khomeini was technically trained to make persuasive arguments that had logical forms. In his study of *'irfān*, the focus shifted to affectivity. It is hard not to speculate, even if it cannot be quantified, that his association with mysticism helped increase his appeal to his followers by both confirming his piety and implying that he had access to special esoteric knowledge. In this very practical way, mysticism contributed to his ability to invoke emotional seizure among Muslims.

Khomeini also evoked emotional seizure by using religious symbols for current political affairs. One of his most reoccurring rhetorical strategies is to connect 'Ashura' and the Battle of Karbala to contemporary politics. During this seventh century battle, Imam Husayn was killed by the Caliph Yazid. According to tradition, Husayn and his companions died slow and painful deaths. This event is commemorated every year by Shi'a on 'Ashura' (the tenth day of Muharram) through the performance of *ta'ziyah* (passion plays) and self-flagellation. In public addresses leading up to the 1979 Islamic Revolution, Khomeini repeatedly equated the Pahlavi Shahs to Yazid and the contemporary Pahlavi tyranny to the tyranny that ended Imam Husayn's life in CE 680.

The role of affectivity in charismatic moral authority encourages us to look at skills necessary for moral leadership in new ways: acting and politicking, not only the study of philosophy and theology, become important for understanding how moral guidance is conveyed within a community. Note that both leaders have an aspect to their training that, though unusual when compared with other clerics in their tradition, increased their ability to invoke emotional responses in believers. John Paul, from his early theatrical career, and Khomeini, by incorporating religious symbols and mysticism into politics, had significant affective skills. This can be seen in part as a shared training in the construction of charisma insofar as charisma depends on the ability to affect, not just effect, believers.

Differences between them are of course also substantial. Although for both leaders an early training in affectivity was important to their charismatic authority, the actual types of training were significantly different. This is because what is capable of invoking an emotional response depends on the set of meta-narratives, cultural values, collective memories, and factual presumptions of a specific audience.

A Third Way: Revisiting Weber's Routinized Charisma

Given the charismatic differences between John Paul II and Khomeini, readers might still object to juxtaposing these clerics in a comparative project. Their charisma is not equivalent. It does not originate, function, or lead in the same way. To equate the two, even provisionally, is to confuse apples and oranges. Weber distinguishes between two significant types of charisma, which help unpack the nature of this objection: pure (genuine) and routinized (transformed) charisma. Pure charisma is the personal ability of an individual to generate excitement. The example Weber most often uses is of a prophet. Over time, Weber argues, for this charismatic authority to survive, it is institutionalized through a process he calls routinization. The institution then derives its authority from its proximity to the original pure charismatic and can take a number of forms. Weber mentions three in particular: kinship charisma (*Gentilcharisma*), bloodline charisma (*Erbscharisma*), and office charisma (*Amtescharisma*). Of these, office charisma seems to hold promise for considering one dimension of a pope's charismatic ethical authority, whereas Shi'i Islam has passed its highest charismatic position (imamate) through the bloodline of the first imam, 'Ali.

However, the biographies of John Paul and Khomeini complicate Weber's strict binary between pure and routinized charisma. A pope (from the Latin *papa*) is the informal title for bishop of Rome and holder of the Petrine office. A pope not only leads the church, he is also a physical embodiment of an exceptional quality that links him to Peter and even, to some extent, to the original charismatic event of the Church: the life and death of Christ. The papal office seems a perfect example of Weber's routinized charismatic authority. However, what is particularly interesting about John Paul is the degree to which he emerges as personally charismatic within the charismatic office. His office does not alone explain his charismatic ethical authority: he embodied pure charisma as well. How else do we explain his immense popularity compared with his successor, Benedict XVI?[35]

Khomeini may not hold an institutionalized office, but he too exists somewhere between pure and routinized charisma. A brief overview of the Shi'i imamate is helpful here. The major break between Sunni and Shi'i sects arose over competing claims about how charisma should be transferred after the Prophet Muhammad's death. Sunnis recognize the caliphs, through the line of Muhammad's companion Abu Bakr, as the legitimate successors of the Prophet Muhammad. Shi'a recognize the imams, following the bloodline of Muhammad's companion and son-in-law 'Ali. These imams are examples of pure charisma: they have a special access to the divine ideal. Using Weber's framework, the imamate itself might be interpreted as a form of routinized charisma. However, for Twelver Shi‘a (Shi‘a who believe in twelve imams, some 89 percent of Iranians), when the last imam "went into hiding" in the ninth century and the Age of Occultation began, the status of the charismatic authority became more complicated: since this time, there has been no recognizable imam, therefore no leader holding an imam-type of charisma.

In the eighteenth century, another form of routinized charisma emerged among Shi‘a as the ulama united behind a few *mujtahidūn*, who were called *marja‘-i taqlīd* (the source of emulation), including Sharhk Murtada al-Ansari (d. 1864), Mirza Hasan Shirazi (d. 1896), and Hossein Borujerdi (d. 1962). These clerics were understood to act as worldly deputies for the absent twelfth Imam. In Iran, a further shift happens in the late twentieth century, supported by Khomeini's theory of *vilāyat-i faqīh* (or guidance of the cleric). With this theory, Khomeini proposes that an exceptional cleric (specifically, an expert in *fiqh*) is the proper figure to assume this authority within the community and to act as the moral leader in the absence of the Imam. This theory becomes the justification for Khomeini's own position as the supreme leader of the Islamic Republic.

Although Khomeini explicitly grounds the need for a clerical ruler in the Qur'an and hadith in his treaty *Islamic Government*,[36] it can also be interpreted as a modernization of the office of *marja‘-i taqlīd*. But Khomeini significantly shifts the parameters of this office through his own theory of the supreme leader. Because he serves as both *marja‘-i taqlīd* and founder of the Islamic Republic, the position of supreme leader has a formal role in governance that *marja‘-i taqlīd* never did. But, from a conceptual point of view, an even larger transformation takes place. The usual path to becoming a *marja‘-i taqlīd* is through recognition as the most learned. This was a highly subjective judgment, but it often rested in part on the cleric's technical expertise. It is a legal-rational, not a charismatic, recognition. By contrast, Khomeini becomes the supreme leader through a more general sense of his overall exceptional quality and in this way, the supreme leader can be understood as a new form of routinized charisma.

Both leaders held a charismatic position within their respective religious communities somewhere between Weber's categories of pure and routinized charisma. For John Paul, the papal magisterium grounds his routinized charismatic authority, but his personal charisma gives him more moral authority than other popes had. Khomeini's personal charisma allowed him to take a leadership role in the Islamic Revolution, but his institutional position as the supreme leader increased his ability to act as a moral guide.

There is a substantial difference between not only the actual charismatic offices the two leaders held, but also in the relation between pure and routinized charisma each leader embodied. On one hand this has to do with a different chronology. John Paul first obtained a charismatic office and then his pure charisma intensified that office's ethical authority. By contrast, Khomeini was able to use his personal charisma to institutionalize a charismatic office, which in turn expanded his ability to function as a moral guide. On the other hand, the shift in the routinized charisma each leader made was substantially different. John Paul took a charismatic office and made its charismatic authority more intense by personally embodying more of the exceptional qualities linked to the original charismatic event of Christianity (for example, emotional and physical suffering). Khomeini in turn shifted a primarily legal office (jurist) into a charismatic one (supreme leader) within a community whose tradition is having a figure, as opposed to an institution, embody charismatic authority. Key here is that neither leader embodies merely a pure or routinized form of charisma, which suggests that a category somewhere between Weber's idealized ones may be more helpful for working comparatively among these two religious leaders.[37]

One final point about charisma: it also provides a way to conceptualize the link between male clerics and religious women. Despite conventional wisdom to the contrary, charisma is not merely the quality of a leader. Rather, charisma is a relation, depending on an exceptional individual and a group that validates that exceptional quality.[38] The core thesis of this book is about this recognition: I argue that a particular process of recognition of the audience (the women's discursive response to clerical rhetoric) contributes to the production of ethical knowledge within a community. This response is theologically grounded in the two religious traditions that are the focus of my research as well as the moral anthropologies of John Paul and Khomeini. In the Catholic tradition, recognition of ethical charisma occurs through the exercise of an individual's conscience, which means all papal moral authority is to some extent charismatic in nature. The question about charismatic recognition comes to a head with the issue of dissent: how or at what point can disagreement with the pope on moral matters happen in a way that still recognizes his ethical charisma? What occurs in practice is that believers accept John Paul as pope, that is, they accept his charismatic office without necessarily agreeing with him on all moral matters. John Paul's understanding of an erroneous conscience in *Veritatis splendor* demonstrates that he himself envisions a situation in which a believer rejects a given papal teaching without rejecting papal authority outright.[39]

In the *Mu'tazila* view of moral agency, which is the epistemological grounding of Shi'i ethics, an individual is responsible for his or her actions. In this way, the counterpoint to the charismatic quality of the supreme leader is the believer's commitment to follow that guidance. Key to this commitment is *taqlīd*, which has two meanings in classical Islamic texts. On the one hand, it has a pejorative sense of unjustified conformity of one person to the teaching of another. This meaning of *taqlīd* was often used to describe the inappropriate substitution of another judgment for one's own, especially in case of two peers (such as two *mujtahidūn*, those who are equally qualified to practice their own *ijtihād*, or individual reasoning) and is more prominent in Sunni discourse.[40] A second meaning of *taqlīd* is more general and refers to the justified conformity of common believers (*muqallidūn*) to specialists (*mujtahidūn*). In this sense, *taqlīd* refers to the necessary process by which those in the community who have specialized in the religious sciences can guide believers who have not.

This second meaning of *taqlīd* is critical to understanding the role of individual free will and recognition in Khomeini's charismatic authority. Although *taqlīd* implies a degree of conformity, the first step of *taqlīd* centers around a free choice: the choice of whose *ijtihād* to follow based on who the believer perceives to have the most reliable interpretation. Once the choice is made, obedience to the cleric's teachings on good action is assumed, but the initial choice is voluntary. Instead of blind or unjustified imitation, *taqlīd* in this sense is best understood as the adherence to the advice of a specialist and is based on a symbiotic charismatic relation between the *mujtahad* and the *muqallid*.

COMPARATIVE RHETORIC: A DISTINCT METHOD

It is no coincidence that I use rhetorical analysis to describe and explain the tactical navigations of feminist politics framed by clerical moral guidance. De Certeau himself suggests that the study of rhetoric offers "models for differentiating among the types of tactics" because, "on the one hand, [rhetoric] describes the 'turns' or tropes of which language can be both the site and the object, and, on the other hand, these manipulations are related to the ways of changing (seducing, persuading, making use of) the will of another (the audience). . . . In the space of a language (as in that of games), a society makes more explicit the formal rules of action and the operations that differentiate them."[41] Because rhetoric is the space where what are known as formal rules of actions are justified, it is also the space where believers rationalize the moral life. This very process of rationalization risks revealing inconsistencies and gaps in traditional moral teachings, which then become the sites of creative conformity. Moreover, rhetorical events are not only the primary data for this study, they define a community of adherents, at least provisionally, because rhetorical performances assume specific audiences. What remains is developing a technique for isolating components of clerical rhetoric in order to see precisely where women contribute distinct logics through their responses. I turn to this task in this section.

One challenge for this project early on was how to analyze discourse that would describe clerical discourse in a way that anticipates the diversity of women's responses to it and explain the logical tactics of women's response. A focus on rhetoric, specifically in its epideictic form, helps to meet both these challenges.[42] According to Aristotle, rhetoric rationally persuades in two ways: logical form and affective logos.[43] To persuade rhetoric would entail some logical structure, though it need not abide by the formal rules of a syllogism. Affective logos is the ability of rhetoric to access the emotional and intuitive commitments of the audience. It is also a way to motivate action by invoking an audience response that is affective as well as cognitive. A technique of rhetorical analysis can work on both levels, attempting to isolate logical form and affective logos. In my own method, I draw categories of analysis from Stephen Toulmin and Chaïm Perelman. Toulmin is helpful for analyzing the logical structure of an argument whose validity cannot be externally judged like a deliberative or judicial one can be, and Perelman helps show what sorts of affective strategies, based on assumed adherence of the audience, each thinker deploys. On one hand is a micro investigation ("getting up close") into what I call the logics of argument to identify an argument's internal rationality in terms of its logical structure. On the other hand, the more macro exploration ("standing back") identifies the general views of communal adherence and provides an opportunity to move from intra- to inter-tradition analysis.

To these two gazes (close up, standing back), I add a third, logics, which bridges intra- and inter-tradition analysis as a meta-category focused on general types of citation. Logics allow us to stand in a middle ground, between the details of logical structure and larger audience assumptions. They entail the intellectual coherence of feminist tactics. Taken together, these strategies of rhetorical analysis illuminate different aspects of persuasion and, ultimately, different opportunities for women to construct and articulate their own conceptions and practices of womanhood.[44]

Breaking Down to Get Up Close: Intra-Tradition Analysis of Logical Form

Toulmin's concern with practical argumentation—how logic functions in real life in our attempts to provide reasons for actions or beliefs—leads him to reject formal logic in the form of a syllogism. Since Aristotle, Toulmin argues, logic has been considered and assessed based on its relation to the deductive syllogistic form: minor premise + major premise = conclusion. But this theory of logic is useful only for understanding a very narrow set of arguments, "namely, the class of unequivocal, analytic, formally valid arguments with a universal statement as 'major premise.'"[45] Arguments in this case are exceptional, argues Toulmin, which "make them a bad example for general study."[46] Assessing all arguments as formal syllogisms is to judge them by a standard to which they may not aim.[47]

Toulmin attempts to build an alternative theory of reasoning by considering actual arguments to assess their "soundness, strength and conclusiveness."[48] He discovers, first, that rather than formal logic's mathematical model, practical arguments are procedural, and best understood in terms of a jurisprudential model.[49] Understanding arguments as a sequence of steps means that, in a clever play on words, Toulmin refocuses inquiry from the form of logic to its formalities.[50] The basic pattern of formalities is connections between different components—or in formal logic's terminology, various types of premises and ways to move between premises. An argument is assessed by how successfully these different components fulfill their assigned tasks. Toulmin's theory also reconceives logic as an empirical and historical study in contrast to an abstract, theoretical, and a priori subject, because its form depends on the specific contexts within which it is found.[51]

This is not to say that informal logic is any less technical or rational. In fact, Toulmin claims that formal logic is actually less binding than informal logic's procedures: in formal logic, the speaker or writer is free to designate their own meanings to symbols, even create their own system of language, independent of its meaningfulness to others or other systems of logic. Formal logic can be judged only by the validity of its syllogistic form as determined by its author. Informal logic will be evaluated based on criteria that the given context requires.

Toulmin's theory of argumentation is highly detailed, he acknowledges that at times it may seem to belabor the obvious, and by using his categories, I run the risk of testing the patience of my reader. Isolating rhetoric's informal components might also flatten the complexity of its function within a community. I take this chance because of the payoff: isolating aspects of arguments is necessary to show how they create opportunities for dynamic response. In addition, my aim in this book is to represent not the full function of moral rhetoric in a community, only how clerical rhetoric allows for certain types of feminist politics.

The specific Toulmin components of an argument I draw on to break down rhetoric as moral praxis are claims, grounds, warrants, backing, modal qualifiers, and possible rebuttals. The claim of an argument is basically the same as the conclusion under the formal model. For Toulmin, it defines both the starting and destination point of the argument and is the conclusion whose merits the speaker is seeking to establish. The question we consider here is simply "What is being claimed?"

The next three categories—grounds, warrants, and backing—signal ways in which premises can have different functions within a practical argument. To consider the grounds of an argument, we look at the evidence explicitly appealed to support the given claim.[52] Here the question is "What do you have to go on?" and the grounds are evaluated based on their sufficiency or relevancy.[53] Warrants, as opposed to the data or facts of grounds, are the rule or law relied on to authorize the step from grounds to the claim. "How do you get there?" or "Do the grounds warrant the claim?" help discover when attention is being drawn to a pattern for significance.[54] Backing is the rationale for why a warrant should be considered reliable, the "generalizations making explicit the body of experience relied on to establish the trustworthiness of the ways of arguing."[55] It can help define this component of an argument in contrast to warrants or grounds. Although grounds have to be produced, backing might remain unstated if the warrant is not challenged. And whereas warrants are "general, hypothetical statements, which can act as bridges,"[56] backing can be expressed as a statement of fact. Backing—which addresses the questions "Is the warrant well founded and reliable?" and "Does it apply to the present case?"—is necessary because warrants are not self-validating.[57] The backing is the place in religious argument, for example, when authority or the community's precedence is often drawn upon.

Modal qualifiers assess the question "How strong is the claim?" in terms of the degree of certainty with which the warrant is being made. Here attention is to what, if any, modals (qualifying phrases) are given—such as *necessary*, *probable*, or *very likely*—which indicate the relative rational strength of the claim being made through the given grounds, warrants, and backing.[58]

Finally, possible rebuttals are the circumstances under which an argument would no longer hold.[59] I shift Toulmin's category slightly from rebuttals to responses to accommodate women's arguments that do not necessarily attempt to refute clerical teachings. This allows me to identify within a rhetorical exchange how a response may not only refute the logic of an argument, but also reiterate it in ways that shift its logical meaning. It also moves my analysis away from the language of rebuttal and refutation, which assumes a more antagonistic relationship between rhetoric and response than in the dianomous model of moral agency. This category will be particularly important to the current project because, even when responses are not stated, considered, or even observed by the speaker, through the act of arguing with a particular set of grounds, warrants, and backing, the possibility of response is always created. My question to help identify this category is "What aspects of the argument create opportunities for counterarguments?"

These categories deconstruct arguments into logical components for two ends. First, this level of analysis can describe the actual practices of justification in moral discourse of a variety of speakers. Moreover, because a speaker aims to persuade a specific audience through this justification, the components of argumentation are also insights into local expectations of the forms of moral discourse. In the case of clerical rhetoric, this level of analysis demonstrates that despite holding positions of traditional or legal authority, clerics are also concerned with providing practical justification for moral teachings. They cannot rely on authoritative status to move believers to right action, but must also justify such action.

Second, this type of breaking down of rhetorics is critical for understanding the interactions of moral discourses. This level of deconstruction allows us to focus discussion on how the informal logical components of rhetoric are discursive building blocks, free to be contested and rearranged for new arguments. Arguments can be compared through the grounds they use, the warrants for those grounds, and the backing for the warrants. This in turn allows us to observe when a woman borrows informal components from a cleric's rhetoric, when she introduces new forms to her community's moral discourse, and thereby the precise production of her creative conformity.

Standing Back to See the Big Picture: Analysis of Audience Assumptions

Analysis of rhetoric can also proceed from the perspective of the audience.[60] One could consider this the standing back process of rhetorical analysis, which works to describe audience assumptions implied in a particular argument.

For Chaïm Perelman, arguments assume "an effective community of minds" and, therefore, for speakers to persuade, they must tap into the web of "opinions, convictions, and commitments."[61] This means the speaker and audience are always mutually dependent. The role of the speaker is to select from this web of agreement the elements that will be given "presence" and set "a value on some aspects of reality rather than others."[62] In other words, for the audience to empathize with a given argument, the rhetoric is often connected to the audience through ideas the audience understands and feels to be significant.

I have used four elements from Perelman's work to isolate the parameters of agreement on which the orator bases his or her argument: facts, presumptions, values, and hierarchies.[63] I draw on these but have shifted them slightly to create more separation between them to make their application to actual rhetoric more precise. Perelman's first category of assumption is facts and truths. I use only facts in my analysis because it became clear that all five categories function as truths in much rhetoric. Facts are agreements held relating to data. If the facts used in an argument are to be accepted, they must conform to the audience's understanding of reality. Given a fact, another fact may be implied. Although reflections of reality, facts can be challenged, either by the introduction of new facts or a change in the audience by the addition of new members who interpret reality differently.

Presumptions are shared opinions and often based on what the audience considers normal or customary. Presumptions can be modified by either new information or a change to what is considered to be normal. An individual within the group might deviate outside the normal and thus modify the normal. Arguments or actions seen as too far outside the normal, however, will usually be ignored or excluded by the group.

Perelman outlines a special relationship between action and values, describing a value as the "admission that an object, a thing, or an ideal" that "must have a specific influence on action and on disposition toward action."[64] Values can take either an abstract or a concrete form, influence action, and are embodied in right action. They therefore provide criteria for judging if a particular practice is morally good. Any value can be disputed, but a community cannot reject all values. In some fields—including religious ethics—values are observed at many levels of the argument.

Hierarchies work to establish "the intensity with which one value is adhered to as compared to another."[65] They can be concrete (humans are higher or more important than animals) or abstract (justice is higher or more important than utility) and work to help order values when simultaneous or equal commitment to two or more values is impossible. For this book, the ways in which gender hierarchies are conceived by clerics and women will be of acute interest.

This level of rhetorical analysis, which focuses on audience assumptions, is important for three reasons. It makes possible investigation not only of the logical structure of rhetoric (which is the focus of the analysis of informal logical form), but also of how affective logos is deployed by references to an audience's assumptions. Without attention to these general assumptions, we neglect one important way that rhetoric persuades. For example, reference to Mary or Fatima may not necessarily make an argument more logical, but may make it more likely to motivate an action by invoking an affective response from the audience.

Second, unlike the analysis of the logical form of a single rhetorical event, in considering audience assumptions we gain insights into a perceived common ethical vision within a community. Just because a speaker uses a particular fact, value, or hierarchy does not mean that he or she believes it to be true. Rather, these categories tell us what the speaker believes the audience assumes is true. This allows for intra-tradition analysis different from the deconstruction of logical components: certain assumptions shared by speakers allow them to be seen as part of a coherent group. For example, at the level of specific claims and informal logical form, the women I study do not agree. Catholic women do not agree on the permissibility of abortion; Shi'i women do not agree on women's right to practice *ijtihād*. But their arguments nevertheless share assumptions about the more general beliefs of their audiences.

Third, this level of rhetorical analysis also allows appropriate comparison among religious traditions. At the level of informal argumentation we would not expect components to line up: what counts as appropriate backing in the Catholic tradition does not in the Shi'i tradition. To assume otherwise would run the risk of assessing the strength or merit of an argument on the logical forms of a different context, or, as Toulmin puts it, "condemning an ape for not being a man or a pig for not being a porcupine."[66] It is not that assumptions will be the same in different religious communities. But all arguments begin with agreements. And if we are able to understand what these agreements are, by analyzing specific arguments, we can consider how they might be the same or different on similar ethical issues. This level of analysis could enable thinking about the possibilities and limitations of developing cross-cultural feminist politics.

Seeing with Bifocals: The Logics of Discourse as Rhetorical Interplay

Logics are general tactics used in an argument that allow it to work within existing logical assumptions, but in innovative ways. As I define them, logics are the intellectual coherence behind transformations of a tradition. The category of logics allows the scholar to stand in a middle ground, between the details of logical structure of the speaker and broader audience assumptions. Logics take various generalizable forms. For example, the logic of concentration chooses one small part of an argument to base another argument, whereas the logic of expansion applies a claim to cases unanticipated by the original speaker. If possible responses are logical deviations anticipated by aspects of the original rhetoric, logics are the method for making these responses without necessarily refuting the original argument.

This level of analysis proved necessary in my research to think more generally about the women's discourse as creatively conforming to clerical teachings. It allows analysis to move from a concern with a speaker's specific construction of an informal argument to understanding the overall logics of arguments in relation to one another.

Taken together, these three modes of rhetorical analysis, which focus on three aspects of rhetoric, illuminate different dimensions of persuasion and, ultimately, different opportunities for women to construct and articulate their conceptions and practices of womanhood. The shift between perspectives allows rhetorical analysis to proceed holistically: not only in terms of the tradition as a whole, but also accounting for the diversity of types of persuasion within.

CHAPTER OVERVIEW

Each chapter is divided into two main sections, Catholic and Shi'i, which are in turn divided into clerical rhetoric subsections and women's response subsections. Holding both traditions together in every thematic chapter encourages comparative analysis, which in turn ensures that focus is not on the specific clerics, traditions, women, or even advocacy issues, but instead on identifying and explaining the tactical logics of women's feminist politics. I selected a variety of themes that are important for creating the parameters of what counts as authentic Catholic and Shi'i teaching on women's roles: moral exemplarity, motherhood, textual interpretation, embodied practices, and public participation. These rhetorical performances deal on a general level with five dimensions of the moral life: moral perfection, family life, the divine human relation, connection of spiritual and material life, and religion and politics.

Within each clerical subsection, I "get up close" to the clerical rhetoric, breaking it down into its procedural components of informal logic. To avoid instances when the two clerics are relying primarily on their institutional or political authority, I consider less formal speeches and writings. This analysis demonstrates that, despite their positions as leaders, John Paul and Khomeini were concerned with proving practical justification for their moral teachings based on local understandings of logical forms.

These clerical architectonics become the context for the women's creative conformity. In separate subsections, women's arguments are analyzed to understand their response to the cleric. I demonstrate the simultaneous citation and transformation of clerical rhetoric in the women's response, and thereby how the women work within traditional discursive parameters as well as shift those parameters. These sections end with an overview of the logics that describe the general ways women rework the clerical rhetoric for their distinct ends.

Chapter 1 explores how women recast clerical rhetoric about moral role models into feminist politics. For the clerics, a role model provides an example of actions and virtues that they try to instill in women. Moral exemplars function quite differently in the women's discursive practices: exemplars become opportunities to discuss unjust conditions imposed on women by others. Fatimah and Hagar are used as examples of how women break out of the mold of what is expected of "good girls" in the tactics of feminist symbolics.

Chapter 2 focuses on how women use clerical logics of motherhood and child rearing in their own moral discourse. For John Paul and Khomeini, being a good mother is made up of a number of actions tied to the physical act of birth. The women understand motherhood in a more expansive way: the tactics of feminist reproduction emphasize the moral meaning of motherhood related to pedagogy, emotionality, and the interdependence of moral knowledge and action.

Chapter 3 describes how women engage and leverage clerical textual interpretations to explore the theological differences between men and women. In the examples analyzed, clerics use two religious texts—the Bible and shari'a as codified in Iran—to define the proper roles of women. Women, in turn, use the clerical forms of textual interpretation to revisit the issue of gender difference. The tactics of feminist hermeneutics work to establish the importance of women's contribution to the local production of ethical knowledge.

Chapter 4 explores how women's proper roles are connected to embodied practices. I consider two issues: women's exclusion from the Catholic priesthood and women's compulsory veiling in Iran. Clerics use these topics to teach about the ethics of women's bodies in the public sphere. The women use these issues to explore embodiment more generally, moving beyond material culture and institutional leadership to disrupt the public order through presenting their bodies as politically disordered.

Chapter 5 concerns the relationship between democracy and theology in the moral discourse of the two communities. I explore competing visions of religious believers' proper roles in global and local politics. The tactic of republication redefines the republic and the role of citizens within it. Women use this approach to transform how religious believers participate in the creation and distribution of political ideology, change the theological significance of citizenry, and propose an expanded role for public theology in the modern nation-state.

The conclusion summarizes the tactics of creative conformity discussed in chapters 1 through 5 with some general observations from my case study about the nature of the productive power of women's practices of creative conformity. In the first section the two communities are considered at the macro-level of shared audience assumptions. This allows something to be said not only about the Catholic and Shi'i women as two groups, but also to see how their rhetoric is tied to local societal assumptions. In the next section the production of ethical knowledge seen through the interaction of clerics and women is summarized through the metaphor of a moral game. Finally, the concept of cross-cultural feminist politics, introduced in the preface, is revisited.

The epilogue revisits Shahla Habibi to reconsider the type of women's agency this study has assumed and ends with some suggestions for future areas of research on creative conformity within religious communities.

NOTES

1. De Certeau, *The Practice of Everyday Life*, xiv–xv.

2. De Certeau, "On the Oppositional Practices of Everyday Life," 35.

3. For a sustained discussion of ethics as a game see Stout, *Democracy and Tradition,* 270–86. Stout uses the game metaphor to demonstrate that ethics in a democracy is both a social practice, aims at objective truth, and involves a symmetrical relation between moral agents. Robert Brandom, who Stout draws on, uses game throughout his *Making It Explicit* to show how the meaning of an expression is determined by how it is used in inferences.

4. Lila Abu-Lughod, an anthropologist who studies women in the Middle East, has discussed this problem in an influential article on the problem of resistance: "The problem has been that those of us who have sensed that there is something admirable about resistance have tended to look to it for hopeful confirmation of the failure—or partial failure—of systems of oppression. Yet it seems to me that we respect everyday resistance not just by arguing for the dignity of heroism of the resistors but by letting their practices teach us about the complex interworkings of historically changing structures of power." "The Romance of Resistance," 53.

5. De Certeau, *The Practice of Everyday Life*, 36–37.

6. Ibid., xiii.

7. De Certeau, "On the Oppositional Practices of Everyday Life," 6.

8. For a more in-depth discussion on these ideal types, drawing on actual scholarship on religious women, see Bucar, "Dianomy," 667–75.

9. It is outside the scope of this chapter to provide a thorough discussion of all the substantial bodies of literatures that are part of the prevailing discourses on agency. However, it is noteworthy to point out that theoretical statements akin to dianomy, insofar as they attempt to balance individual agency with social influence and even control, can be found in many scholarly disciplines, from sociology (e.g., Pierre Bourdieu), to anthropology (e.g., James Clifford, George Marcus, and Henrietta Moore), to philosophy (e.g., Seyla Behabib, Jurgen Habermas, Georg Wilhelm Friedrich Hegel, and Iris Marion Young).

10. Butler, *Excitable Speech*, 80.

11. Ibid., 40.

12. Butler, "What Is Critique?" 217.

13. Butler, *Excitable Speech*, 15.

14. I differ from Butler in that I focus not only not on critical moment of creativity but also on how creativity can reconstitute a tradition. I am indebted to Amy Hollywood for my reading of Butler. See Hollywood, "Performativity, Citationality, Ritualization," 93–115.

15. Torab, "Piety as Gendered Agency," 235.

16. Torab, *Performing Islam*, 248–49.

17. Griffith, *God's Daughters*, 14.

18. Ibid., 199.

19. Ibid., 16.

20. Ibid., 14.

21. Griffith writes, "In attempting to treat my subjects empathically and listen carefully to their stories. . . . I have taken pains to credit their piety as a meaningful source of religious and social power, laden with copious practical strategies for inverting conventional hierarchies and enabling women to influence husbands—perhaps even change or save them—and alter their family lives, as well as to create newly whole and joyful selves." Ibid., 201–2.

22. Ibid., 16.

23. Pseudonym used to preserve confidentiality.

24. Pseudonym used to preserve confidentiality.

25. Weber, *Economy and Society*.

26. The first public words of Karol Wojtyla as Pope John Paul II. McFadden, "Pope John Paul II, Church Shepherd and a Catalyst for World Change," *New York Times*, April 3, 2005, 29.

27. Grant, *The Life of Pope John Paul II*.

28. John Paul shares this honor with Ayatollah Khomeini, who was *Time Magazine*'s Man of the Year in 1979.

29. Karol describes Kotlarczyk "as the pioneer of the original theater, in the most noble sense of the word, and as the voice of the deepest Polish and Christian traditions." Szulc, *Pope John Paul II*, 78. Theater of the Word differed from traditional theater not only in form but also in purpose. Kenneth Schmitz puts this nicely: traditional theater tells a story through actors, Theater of the Word sets forth a human dilemma. For an excellent treatment on the impact of Theater of the Word on John Paul's philosophical anthropology, see Schmitz, "On Stage: New Words for Ancient Truths," 1–29.

30. For a historical and theological tracing of the Shi'i idea of supreme leader see Sachedina, *The Just Ruler in Shi'ite Islam*.

31. *Constitution of the Islamic Republic*, Art. 5, 107, 109.

32. For example, *Islamic Penal Code of Iran,* Book Five *(Ta'azirat)*, Art. 513.

33. The *'irfān* literally means knowing. In the Shi'i tradition it refers to both mysticism and access to spiritual knowledge (sometimes translated as gnosis). It overlaps with Sufism in focus as well as content. While a student at madrasa,

Khomeini studied with a number of *mujtahidūn* who had been trained in mysticism, including Ayatollah Muhammad Ali Shahabadi (1847–1950) under whose tutelage Khomeini became known as scholar of Mulla Sadra (1571–1640).

34. For Khomeini, "spirituality and mysticism have never implied social withdrawal or political quietism, but rather the building up of a fund of energy that finds its natural expression on the socio-political plane." Algar, "Introduction," 14. Khomeini's linking of *'irfān* and politics might have been influenced by the practices of his teacher Shahabadi, who was one of the few ulama who criticized the Pahlavi Dynasty. In a strategy that Khomeini would himself adopt, Shahabadi regularly used the occasion of 'Ashura' commemorations to speak against political decisions of the dynasty. Algar, "The Fusion of the Gnostic and the Political," 1–12.

35. Because Benedict has been pope for only five years, it might be premature to judge his popularity. Nevertheless it seems clear that he does not have the same personal charisma as John Paul, which will most likely affect not only his popularity but also his moral authority. To illustrate, my uncle's mother asked him to purchase a memento of the pope for her when he was in Vatican City in 2008. To specify which pope, she said, "The holy pope," by which she meant John Paul. Indeed, two and a half years after Benedict had taken office there were still more John Paul than Benedict souvenirs offered in the shops that line via della conciliazione in Vatican City.

36. A number of Qur'anic passages are referred to in Khomeini's treaty and Qur'anic suras cited, with page numbers in Algar translation: 16:89 (44); 8:60 (46); 28:4 (48); 4:59 (57); 2:124 (60); 33:6 (65, 103); 57:25, 8:41, 9:103, and 4:59 (77); 4:58–59 (87, 90, 109); 4:60 (92–3); 5:63, 5:78, 9:71 (109); and 9:71 (117). The sura that occurs the most often is known as the authority *aya*: "Believers, obey God and obey the Prophet and those in authority among you" (4:59). Khomeini uses hadith to abrogate an interpretation of this *sura* as a call for political quietism, insisting instead that the Prophet Muhammad and imams made it clear that Islamic jurists are the authorities to be obeyed. In total, fourteen hadiths are used as backing for the argument that Muslim communities need a "trustee" or guide, that jurists are the proper "trustees of the prophets" and therefore obligated to guide the community as the Prophet Muhammad and imams did, and that this trusteeship should take the form of a comprehensive government.

37. For a recent and especially creative treatment of charisma that holds great potential for comparative work, see Tulasi Srinivas, *Winged Faith*. She coins the phrase "nomadic charisma" to explain the mobile charisma of Shri Sathya Sai Baba, leader of the Sathya Sai global religious movement, through extended affiliation strategies.

38. Weber writes, "It is the recognition on the part of those subject to authority which is decisive for the validity of charisma. This recognition is freely given and . . . is a matter of complete personal devotion to the possessor of the quality, arising out of enthusiasm, or of despair and hope." Weber, *Economy and Society*, vol. 1, 242.

39. John Paul II writes, "in the case of the erroneous conscience, it is a question of what man, mistakenly, subjectively considers to be true. . . . It is possible that the evil done as the result of invincible ignorance or a nonculpable error of judgment

may not be imputable to the agent; but even in this case it does not cease to be an evil, a disorder in relation to the truth about the good." *Veritatis splendor*, para. 63.

40. Weiss, "Taqlid," 188.

41. De Certeau, *The Practice of Everyday Life*, xx.

42. In *On Rhetoric*, Aristotle makes what I think is his most important contribution to the study of rhetoric within a religious community. There he argues that there are three and only three types of rhetoric, classified based on their intended audiences: deliberative, judicial, or epideictic (I.3.1–3). Epideictic, or demonstrative, rhetoric is not judged by the audience in the same way as the other two forms because it is built on shared initial understandings. It is important to note that the nonjudged characteristic stems from the existence of a community of adherence, not because the audience has a passive role. A speaker who uses this mode of discourse argues by working to convince the hearer that the specific position being put forward is something she already believed. The most successful rhetorical performances can even appear to the audience as occasions of self-discovery. In this way, epideictic rhetoric is not judged because it does not aim to convince about new abstract truth; it assumes the truth of the community and concerns itself with how to implement this truth. Epideictic rhetoric can be a useful way to theorize arguments within a religious community, particularly those deployed from positions of clerical authority: even this rhetoric must seek to persuade and risks the chance of misfire through the dynamic process of hearing, interpreting, and implementing. For further discussion, see Bucar, "Speaking of Motherhood," 95–96, 98.

43. These two modes of persuasion can be seen in Aristotle's discussion of the rhetorical syllogism: the enthymeme. An enthymeme persuades in part through a logical form conveyed through deductivity, probability, and brevity (*On Rhetoric*, I.1). Rhetorical discourse will have some place for deduction because it aims to persuade an audience and, for Aristotle, we are most likely to be persuaded by arguments we think have been logically proven. At a minimum, enthymemes will have to display a premise-conclusion structure that we have come to expect from deductions. However, because the goal of rhetoric is persuasion and not logical validity per se, it is less important that the enthymeme be a true deduction. In addition to its logical form, enthymeme's use of affectivity allows it not only to convince, but also to motivate. The root of enthymeme, *thymos*, means heart and the verb enthymeme has a range of meanings, including "consider well" or "form a plan." By my reading, two hearts are implicated: the heart of the audience and of the speaker. The heart of the speaker must reflect on the particular circumstances of the audience in order to persuasively respond to that context. The heart of the audience will in turn think deeply about, infer, and conclude. The successful speaker is able to empathize with the audience by not only understanding their factual knowledge base, but also being aware of and sensitive to the value-charged ideas that a community adheres to. Moreover, epideictic rhetoric's goal to persuade is helped when the audience is able to identify themselves with a particular stance of the orator. The heart of the speaker therefore strategically attends to the heart of the audience. For further discussion, see Bucar, "Speaking of Motherhood," 96–97.

44. It is important to note that my order of operation is a reversal of the way in which Toulmin and Perelman themselves conceive of it. Toulmin writes, "The philosopher has a triple task. His responsibilities are, first, to spell out the basic assumptions current in different areas of thought and belief; next, to make explicit the structures of argument from which different kind of belief draw their strength; and finally, to criticize the resulting arguments by universal, public standards." *Knowing and Acting*, 89. Perelman suggests a similar order of operations: "for argumentation to exist, an effective community of minds must be realized at a given moment. There must first of all be agreement. In principle, on the formation of this intellectual community, and, after that, on the fact of debating a specific question." Perelman and Olbrechts-Tyteca, *The New Rhetoric*, 14.

From the orator's point of view, identifying the parameters of shared understandings does precede the actual construction and delivery of a successful rhetorical discourse. By contrast, I understand a reverse order to be more amendable to a scholarly comparative rhetorical analysis. By starting with the structure of informal arguments, we begin with the simplest analysis, the analysis of concrete and definable—therefore manageable—arguments. It seems more difficult and perhaps problematic to begin where Toulmin and Perelman suggest, with a statement of basic assumptions, or sources of authority, and so on. The method I suggest allows the aspects of the discursive traditions to be studied to flow from the actual rhetoric, rather than from a base of assumptions.

45. Toulmin, *The Uses of Argument*, 145.

46. Ibid.

47. Ibid., 256.

48. Ibid., 1.

49. "Instead of dissociating formal arguments from active arguing, for instance, we might alternatively begin by viewing 'arguing' as a function, or performance, which people undertake with certain general purposes in mind. . . . In other words, we might begin, not by asking about firm foundation and strong support, but rather by asking how one can argue for a belief with complete effectiveness, or present a properly convincing case. To do this would of course launch our discussion in a very different direction from before—toward *rhetoric* rather than *formal logic*." Toulmin, *Knowing and Acting*, 86 (emphasis in the original).

50. Toulmin, *The Uses of Argument*, 43.

51. Toulmin, Rieke, and Janik, *An Introduction to Reasoning*, 114.

52. Toulmin uses *facts* instead of *evidence*. By contrast, I reserve the term *fact* to denote the audience's assumptions about reality. See the Perelman level of analysis that follows.

53. Toulmin, Rieke, and Janik, *An Introduction to Reasoning*, 37–39.

54. Ibid., 45–46.

55. Ibid., 61.

56. Toulmin, *The Uses of Argument*, 98.

57. Toulmin, Rieke, and Janik, *An Introduction*, 61–62.

58. Ibid., 85–88.

59. Ibid., 96–97.
60. Perelman, *The New Rhetoric*, 13–14.
61. Ibid., 17.
62. Ibid.
63. Perelman and Olbrechts-Tyteca, *The New Rhetoric*, 67–95.
64. Perelman and Olbrechts-Tyteca, *The New Rhetoric*, 74.
65. Ibid., 81.
66. Toulmin, *The Uses of Argument*, 256.

CHAPTER ONE

What's a Good Woman to Do?

Recasting the Symbolics of Moral Exemplars

✦

Exceptional women tend to become moral exemplars for the rest of us. Sometimes they are born into moral greatness, sometimes selected by divine hand, and sometimes the result of a particularly gracious reaction to fortune or courage in the face of bad luck. Such women become deeply involved in histories of communities, remembered for acting in ways we find admirable: Eleanor Roosevelt in the aftermath of World War II or Rosa Parks in the face of racial segregation. Sometimes they become important on a more intimate level, such as within families: I have been told I share some of the characteristics of my great-grandmother Edna, who was a stanch advocate for women's rights within Protestant circles in New England. What these various women have in common is that their piety is remembered and retold. Their exemplarity is dynamic and evolving in that it is remembered in different ways, in different places, at different times, and by different people. It is thus not only the actions of an exemplar, but also how their actions are referenced discursively that affects our visions of what makes a good woman.

The virtues of exceptional women are important for the moral life of ordinary believers in religious communities as well. Consider how often women in scriptural narratives are referenced in contemporary communities when women's roles are discussed. Ethical heroines are often praised by clerics, and such praise works rhetorically to convey in their image certain types of women. This use, however, is problematic. Christian feminists from the left have complained that Mary's status as virgin and mother is a patriarchal trap, "an unachievable ideal as a way of keeping women in our place."[1] We can never be good women in that way, some complain, and moral exemplarity therefore becomes an opportunity for a direct rebuttal or a strategic response, which questions the entire production and reproduction of role models for women.

My concern here is not with women's dismantling of clerical arguments, but rather with women's use of the clerical logics in innovative ways. I explore how clerical rhetoric about role models becomes recast into feminist politics by creating new functions while maintaining some of the clerical epistemologies related to exemplarity. How are role models transformed when they are engaged by women versus male clerics? What additional resources do women bring to understanding the politics of exemplarity? What happens when different models are chosen or different attributes of models emphasized? What does this tell us about the politics of the production of knowledge?

In this chapter I consider clerical rhetoric on Fatimah and Mary and then the corresponding ways in which Fatimah's exemplarity is shifted by Shi'i Iranian women and U.S. Catholic women's central moral exemplar of a virgin mother with the slave Hagar.

FATIMAH AS MORAL EXEMPLAR

Fatimah was Khomeini's favorite model. She is connected to the beginnings of Islam through her father the Prophet Muhammad and as a participant in the first Muslim community. She is also a foundational figure of Shi'i Islam, particularly through her marriage to 'Ali, whom Shi'a consider the rightful successor to Muhammad. After the death of Muhammad, Abu Bakr and 'Ali both claimed to be the rightful successors to leadership of the community. Abu Bakr was eventually elected by the other companions as the first caliph, but Shi'a recognize an alternative line of succession of imams (leaders) through the bloodline of 'Ali. This makes Fatimah's theological significance even greater because her two sons, Husayn and Hasan, become the second and third imams.

Among Shi'a, Fatimah's status is higher than all others except the Prophet Muhammad and the first imam, her husband 'Ali. In popular devotional practices such as Muharram processions and passion plays, Fatimah is often present as an icon. Her name and its variants, as well as her epithets—Zahra (The Radiant One), Tahira (Virginal), Zakiya (Pure), Razia (Contented), Batul (Virgin), Kaniz (Maiden), Ma'suma (Shielded from Sin)—are popular names for girls in Iran.[2] She is a common theme in public art, often the subject of enormous murals on buildings in major cities like Tehran, represented with her face covered by a veil, holding a martyred soldier in her arms.

Fatimah is also an exemplary figure for men, and Khomeini's discussion of Fatimah can be used to understand his more general views on the moral life.[3] But I focus in this section on the logics behind, and attributes of, Fatimah as a role model for women through two of Khomeini's addresses. The first address was delivered in March 1985, in the midst of the Iran-Iraq War, and war-inspired metaphors are used by Khomeini throughout to illustrate aspects of the moral life.[4] The second is from May 1979, given on the heels of the Islamic Revolution to commemorate Iranian Women's Day, which is celebrated on the anniversary of Fatimah's birth.[5] This speech is used primarily to help clarify the meaning of what Khomeini refers to in his later rhetoric as Fatimah's special spiritual status.

The overall claim of the 1985 address is that women can be good women by imitating Fatimah: "You must imitate her in order to truly accept today [Fatimah's birthday] is Women's Day."[6] The claim is based on the grounds that the angel Gabriel (Jibra'il) appeared to Fatimah after the death of Muhammad while she was in mourning. Reciting in part a hadith from *Uṣūl al-Kāfi*, which is the most explicit backing deployed in the argument, Khomeini states the following:

> "After the death of her father, Fatimah (peace be upon her), lived for seventy-five days. She was in this world, overcome with sadness and grief. Gabriel, the Trusted Spirit, came to visit and console her and tell her of future events." So, according to this tradition, in these seventy-five days that she had contact with Gabriel, he came and went many times. I do not believe that anyone else except the great prophets have had such an experience, in which for seventy-five days Gabriel, the Trusted Spirit, came and went and spoke of things that would take place in the future, that would happen to her ancestors in the future.[7]

That Gabriel appeared to Fatimah alone is not enough of a premise to support the claim the women should imitate her. In other words, the logical movement from grounds (Gabriel's visit) to claim (imitate Fatimah) requires a warrant, and Khomeini gives two: the visit is proof of Fatimah's special spiritual status and demonstrates her excellent moral character.

According to Khomeini, Gabriel's visit is made possible by Fatimah's special spiritual status: "It should not be imagined that Gabriel would appear to just anyone. His appearance requires a parity between the soul of that person to whom Gabriel would appear and that position of Gabriel as the great spirit."[8] Here Gabriel's appearance to Fatimah is evidence of her special spiritual status, but what sort of spiritual status did Khomeini have in mind?

One possibility is that this status is something Fatimah is born with, which is not without precedence in the Shi'i tradition. There is an ontological distinction between the central Shi'i leaders—the prophets and imams—and normal people. Prophets and imams are not made through good deeds, but rather destined to lead the Shi'i community from birth. Their special designation, as vice-regents for God on earth, includes more perfect access to religious knowledge. In the 1979 Women's Day speech, Khomeini invoked a similar idea in discussing Fatimah's special status. He claimed that Fatimah "was not an ordinary woman: she was a spiritual woman, a heavenly woman, a human being in the true sense of the word."[9] Fatimah's cosmic significance is also a common theme in Shi'i hagiographies of her.[10]

Another possible meaning of Fatimah's spiritual status, in the tradition of mysticism that Khomeini studied and taught, is that she had obtained a higher level of spiritual awareness. In the tradition of *'irfān* (Shi'i mysticism), mystics embark on a spiritual journey toward union with God. They aspire to become what Ibn Arabi refers to as *al-insān al-kāmil* (a person who integrated all of God's attributes). This can be achieved by men or women and the result is greater spiritual knowledge. This understanding of Fatimah's status is explicitly referenced in Khomeini's 1979 speech:

> There are various dimensions of woman just as there are of man, and for human beings in general. The observable, natural side is the lowest stage of a human being, be it man or woman. But it is from this low stage that movement towards perfection occurs. A human being is a dynamic entity, moving from the natural stage towards the supernatural stage, towards annihilation in God. In Fatimah Zahra's case, these meanings are manifested. She began from the natural stage and moved forward. She proceeded through the stages of a spiritual movement with the power of Allah, with the invisible hand, and with the teachings of the Messenger of Allah (peace be upon him) until she reached the stage that all others fall short of.[11]

This excerpt is also helpful for understanding some contours of Khomeini's general moral anthropology. The physical embodiment of humans is understood as a necessary but insufficient condition of the moral life. To be successful one must move from a physical to a metaphysical orientation and reality. As it relates to our present inquiry into the backing of Fatimah's status, Khomeini supported the idea that Fatimah attained special spiritual status by moving through different mystical stages, partly because of her own study and effort, and partly because of God's will. Such a journey could, in turn, be part of women's imitation of Fatimah.

Fatimah's special spiritual status is the most prominent warrant suggested as the reason Gabriel appears to her, but another is given later in the 1985 speech: her moral excellence.[12] Khomeini argues that Gabriel's visit to

Fatimah is warranted in part by her virtue and ethical living. The connection between mysticism and ethics in Khomeini's thought strengthens the case that her moral excellence may also be a sign of her mystical achievement.

Fatimah's moral excellence is observed in three interconnected actions—struggle, inspiring men, and suffering—and these are therefore those that women should imitate in the moral life. Take her struggle, for example. Khomeini referenced struggle in the 1985 speech through the concept of jihad.[13] For Khomeini, jihad takes two forms: lesser and supreme. The lesser jihad is the physical struggle against an enemy on the battlefield. The supreme jihad is an ethical struggle. This is a war against one's own improper desires, an ongoing battle necessary to live a moral life. Khomeini makes it clear that the duty to participate in the supreme jihad is directed at both men and women, but is more ambiguous on whether the purpose of struggle is eradication of improper desires (as seems to be the case for Fatimah) or merely the reorientation of these desires to a proper end.[14]

For Khomeini, there is something special for women about this duty to struggle related to inspiring men and suffering. The former comes through in a war metaphor Khomeini uses to describe the role of women in the community's moral life: "If, for example, a group of women enter an area, like a war zone, then in addition to the fighting they do, they also encourage men to double their efforts because men have special feelings toward women. Men are sensitive where women are concerned. . . . If a man sees a hundred other men being killed, he may do nothing, but if he sees one woman who is being disrespected, he will feel offended, even if that woman is a stranger."[15] Here women inspire men to do the right thing on the battlefield. The same logic applies to why women's virtue is important in general: not only are their own moral lives at stake, but also their ability to inspire, or corrupt, men.

Fatimah's moral excellence in the face of suffering is also emphasized by Khomeini's speech. Recall that it was during a time of immense suffering and grief after her father's passing that Gabriel visits her. Fatimah also sees her husband and then her two sons murdered during her lifetime. She is the eternal Shi'i weeper because the important men in her life hold key roles in the Shi'i tradition as prophet and imams.

Khomeini's entire argument for emulating Fatimah is qualified by his understanding that Fatimah is a moral ideal that we can never completely achieve. There is no expectation that Gabriel will visit us, for example, but rather only that we should try to follow Fatimah's example. This qualification anticipates to some extent creative conformity to her moral exemplarity since perfect conformity is not realistic.

Possible responses are also created by the logic of Khomeini's rhetoric. Fatimah could be upheld by the women as a moral exemplar, but for different grounds. In particular, the ambiguity of the origins of Fatimah's special spiritual status creates an opportunity for response. Depending on how he is heard, Khomeini's argument to imitate Fatimah is warranted by either her special ontological status, which makes her closer to spiritual beings like Gabriel and the imams, or her mystical status, obtained from a process of spiritual growth. Khomeini might have seen these as two interrelated grounds, and not at all contradictory: Fatimah is ontologically different and a successful mystic. However, from the audience's point of view and in terms of the internal logic of the rhetoric, it does matter which of these grounds the claim really hinges on. Could she have been as good without special ontological status? If not, how can we imitate her? In addition, a response could shift the practical content of her moral exemplarity away from Khomeini's emphasis on double responsibility for the moral life of the community, struggle, and personal suffering. Khomeini mentioned only in passing Fatimah's political role of confronting "the governments of the time and judging them."[16] These public roles will be central in the women's response we consider in the next section.

RECASTING FATIMAH AS THE MODEL OF POLITICAL PARTICIPATION

Fatimah is a strong icon for many of the women I interviewed in Iran. When I visited Mrs. Qasanvapur, special advisor on women's affairs to the governor of Isfahan, in her office at the governor's mansion, the only artwork that graced her walls was an enormous painting of Fatimah, at whose feet Khomeini stood, head bowed. Mahboubeh Abbas-Gholizadeh, discussed in detail in chapter 3, shared with me a dream in which Fatimah visited her; a dream she credits with her decision to become an advocate for women's rights.[17] It is therefore not suprising that Fatimah is invoked in much women's public rhetoric in Iran. I focus in this section on an essay published in 1997 titled "The Life and Status of Fatimah Zahra: A Woman's Image of Excellence."[18] Its authors, Monir Gurji and Masoumeh Ebtekar, are key figures in the Iranian women's movement. Gurji was among the first group of women elected to the Majles (Iranian parliament) after the Islamic Revolution, as well as the most prominent female Qur'anic interpreter in Iran. Ebtekar was the first female vice president in Iran, serving under former President Muhammad Khatami. She also played an important role in the Islamic Revolution by acting as spokesperson for the student group that took over the American Embassy in 1979.[19] These women are both *khaṭ-i imāmī*, the Persian term, which literally means "the line of the imam," to reference generally a follower of Khomeini's thought or specifically the student protestors of the 1979 revolution who were supporters of Khomeini.

Gurji's and Ebtekar's claim on a general level is identical to Khomeini's. They write, "Fatimah set a consistent example of the rights, roles, and status of the Muslim woman during her turbulent lifetime."[20] They refer to Fatimah as "leader of the world's women," an "ideal person," a "role model," and a "flawless individual" whose "exemplary role has transcended the boundaries of time and place."[21] The way their argument is structured, however, involves a number of more specific claims about how women should follow Fatimah, which transforms Khomeini's logic of moral exemplarity.

The first difference is the grounds offered for Fatimah as a moral exemplar. Khomeini relied on the angel Gabriel's visit to Fatimah, while she mourns the death of the Prophet, as proof of her special status. In this way, her position is externally conferred by (the Prophet Muhammad) and confirmed by (the angel Gabriel) others. Gurji and Ebtekar provide three grounds that focus on Fatimah herself as the source of her special status: Fatimah's unique character traits, her influence on sociopolitics of her time, and her popularity among Muslims.

The use of different grounds, in turn, leads to different characteristics of Fatimah that women should imitate. For example, in contrast to Khomeini's focus on Fatimah's struggle as suffering, Gurji and Ebtekar focus on this struggle as an educational process: "Fatimah received a holistic spiritual and material education and training according to the best standards. She experienced the most difficult circumstances only to become one of the most learned, knowledgeable, and elevated personalities of her era."[22] The authors also describe Fatimah's education as two-fold: social and spiritual. The social component of her education allows her to become a source of knowledge of the community, especially important for "educating other women."[23] Her "spiritual elevation" is the result of a spiritual development and not merely ontological.[24] Note also how in the cited passage Fatimah's suffering is highly productive—a path toward greater social and spiritual knowledge—and not merely suffering for its own sake.

Fatimah's influence on sociopolitical events of her time are Gurji's and Ebtekar's second ground for her role as moral exemplar. Two events are discussed in the essay: Fatimah's defense of her husband's right to succeed Muhammad as leader of the Muslim community and Fatimah's claim to her right of inheritance from her father. These two political actions are commonly attributed to Fatimah in the Shi'i tradition, but the authors' interpretation of the significance of these events is particularly creative.

After the death of the Muhammad, Abu Bakr and 'Ali (Fatimah's husband) both claimed to be the rightful successors to leadership of the community. Abu Bakr was elected by the other companions as leader. Gurji and Ebtekar summarize Fatimah's response in the following passage: "While her husband 'Ali had chosen to refrain from any power struggle and believed that during the course of time the people would realize the truth, Fatimah insisted on promoting a strategy of awareness raising in order to inform the people of her concerns, as the daughter of the font of revelation."[25] In this passage, Gurji and Ebtekar read the historical event as evidence of Fatimah's assertion of her place among the highest level of decision makers of the community, her independence from her husband and even from her father, and her decisive advocacy.[26]

Fatimah's second major political action was her claim to inheritance of her father's orchard (Fadak), which Abu Bakr refused to cede to her. There are accounts in a number of hadiths of a speech Fatimah gave supporting her inheritance in a mosque in Medina.[27] In this essay, Gurji and Ebtekar consider different records of the account and summarize the event as follows: "Fatimah initially provided decisive evidence including witnesses that Fadak belonged to her. When the court refused the evidence, she proved again that she may have gained access to Fadak through inheritance. At this point she began a powerful discussion referring to the various verses of the Holy Qur'an on the right to inheritance and the examples of prophets like Solomon and David."[28] Note how this event is interpreted in terms of moral exemplarity: she fights for her right to inheritance through her own Qur'anic interpretation based on her "vast knowledge and analytical capabilities"[29] and "provides a strong philosophical and logical background on the foundations of Islamic religion and thought."[30] On a general level, Gurji and Ebtekar argue that Fatimah's sermon is an expression of her rights, especially freedom of expression and economic rights.[31] The women shift Fatimah from a passive moral exemplar, who observes and mourns the political life of the men in her life, to an active one who not only participates in political life, but also helps construct the community's understanding of women's rights.

The third ground for Fatimah's role as a moral exemplar in this essay is her popularity among Muslims. The positive reception of Fatimah by Shi'a, both then and now, reflects interplay between religious authority and common believers: Fatimah's ethical guidance is authorized by her followers. In this way, Gurji and Ebtekar invoke a nonhierarchical access to religious knowledge and moral teachings. The people know the truth when they see it.

Particularly because the focus is on Fatimah's social and political actions, Gurji and Ebtekar assume her example can and should be followed by all women. They write, "She sends a piercing message to the women and men of all times, a message of nonconformity to injustice, which remains to be analyzed and understood."[32] If any qualification is provided, it is in terms of how imperfectly Fatimah's role is currently understood.[33]

The backing for the claim is provided on a number of levels. First is the usual use of hadith. The women, however, engage in their own interpretation of the hadith, selecting passages from different collections, piecing them together for a coherent argument. There are also a number of footnotes. It is a common strategy that, in most controversial arguments, women in Iran return to the authority of men, especially male clerics, to shore up their grounds and warrants. It is therefore not surprising that Gurji and Ebtekar use a number of men in this way. However, although they reference, for example, 'Ali Shariati's *Fatimah Is Fatimah*, they neglect to mention passages in which their own argument and Shariati's radically differ.[34] Another backing is an appeal to human rights discourse, which is assumed to further authorize the virtue of Fatimah's actions. Khomeini, by contrast, was acutely suspicious of the human rights regime.[35]

Because Gurji and Ebtekar's claim so closely lines up with Khomeini's, I have been able to identify areas where the women draw on components of Khomeini's rhetoric, especially his claim (Fatimah as moral exemplar) and grounds (Fatimah's suffering and spiritual status). The women's essay also serves as a reconstruction of Khomeini's rhetoric in a number of ways. In terms of the actual structure of the argument, Gurji and Ebtekar provide different grounds for Fatimah's status as moral exemplar. Khomeini, for example, relies primarily on the visit of Gabriel to Fatimah as evidence of her status. In contrast, the women use Fatimah's own actions, character traits, and reception by the community as their grounds. Khomeini focuses on Fatimah's cosmic significance, especially as it derives from her relationship to her special father (the Prophet Muhammad) and husband (Imam 'Ali). Gurji and Ebtekar, however, emphasize Fatimah's ordinary life experiences: arguing for her rights in public forums and opposing unjust political leadership. In the grounds the women use, Fatimah's importance does not derive from her father and husband, but in how she sets herself apart from them. Fatimah, not 'Ali, fights publicly for his right to succession. Fatimah, not her father, ensures her Qur'anic right to inheritance. In neither event is a male figure standing behind her authorizing her actions. In both cases, Gurji and Ebtekar argue, she acts independently.

Fatimah's spiritual status also functions very differently in the two cases of rhetoric. Khomeini and Gurji and Ebtekar agree that Fatimah has this status, but for Khomeini it is bestowed by God. In this way, Khomeini implies that Fatimah is not an average human being, which complicates how average women could imitate her. Gurji and Ebtekar instead emphasize

Fatimah's spiritual status as obtained through her spiritual education, which is easier for the common believer to imitate. The women are thereby using the logic of *'irfān* for different ends by recasting Fatimah as a spiritual leader within the context of political action.

Finally, Khomeini's original speech and the women's response emphasize different aspects of Fatimah's life as worthy of imitation. Khomeini's Fatimah is a model of perfection, a quasi-celestial being, who struggles and suffers for the Muslim community in her supreme jihad against evil. The eternal weeper, she is a model of submission to God, to her father, and to her husband. Gurji and Ebtekar's Fatimah is strikingly different. She participates at the highest level of decision making. She passes judgment on leaders around her, provides her own interpretation of the Qur'an, and is independent and assertive: she is the ultimate political advocate for the Shi'a. She is exemplary not because she did what she was told, but rather because she did what she knew to be just.

MARY AS MORAL EXEMPLAR

Mary's theological significance has evolved in the Roman Catholic church through a number of official dogma: Mary was officially recognized as the mother of God in 431. In 651 she was declared a perpetual virgin, denying that Christ was conceived from human sexual activity or that Mary had other children by Joseph. In 1854, Pope Pius IX proclaimed the dogma of Immaculate Conception, referring not to Christ, but to Mary herself, who was said to have been born without original sin. In 1950 the most recent Marian dogma—the Assumption—was proclaimed by Pope Pius XII. This dogma declared that Mary was taken to heaven after her death, body and soul. There was an unsuccessful attempt in the late 1990s to have yet another Marian dogma declared: Mary, with Christ, co-redemptrix of humanity.[36] In the rhetorical performance I focus on in this section, John Paul is concerned with elaborating the moral import of the earliest Marian dogma: Mary as mother of God.

Mary is a powerful rhetorical exemplar for John Paul; he felt he had a special connection to her through his own physical and emotional sufferings.[37] He produced numerous meditations on her role as the mother of God, including an encyclical in 1987 titled *Redemptoris mater*, and he often concludes his writings and speeches with a short reflection on Mary. For the sake of rhetorical analysis, I consider here one section of John Paul's apostolic letter, *Mulieris dignitatem* (The Dignity of Women).[38] Published in 1988, this document covers many themes relating to the moral life of women, including Eve, Christ's relationships to women, the reconcilability of virginity and motherhood, and the role of love in a mother's moral life.

My focus is on the first section of this letter devoted to "woman-mother of God" (*theotókos*). Two claims are found in this section related to the moral life. First, Mary is the model for all of humanity. The grounds for Mary as this exemplar include her place, "at the center of [the] salvific event. . . which determines the ultimate finality of the existence of every person both on earth and in eternity. From this point of view, the 'woman' is the representative and the archetype of the whole human race: she represents the humanity which belongs to all human beings, both men and women."[39] Here John Paul asserts that Mary's representation of all humankind in the saluific event makes her an exemplar for us all.

John Paul emphasizes how during this event "*Mary* attains *a union with God that exceeds* all the expectations of the human spirit."[40] For John Paul, Mary's union with God is not merely spiritual, but rather has an embodied component. The physical aspect of the union is described metaphorically, however, to warrant his claim that she is a model for all kinds of gendered bodies. Mary's physical conception and pregnancy therefore becomes a symbol of a spiritual union with God: "Mary conceived a man who was the Son of God, of one substance with the Father. Therefore she is truly the Mother of God, because motherhood concerns the whole person, not just the body."[41] The virgin womb becomes a metaphor for readiness to be filled with God's grace.

In addition to a physical and spiritual component of Mary's union with God, John Paul provides a third ground: an intentional and voluntary component of the union as seen through her response to learning that she would become the mother of the son of God with her *fiat* "Let it be done to me."[42] John Paul's use of her *fiat* is slightly strange here. *Fiat* is the Latin subjunctive of the verb "to become." Usually one responds by *fiat* ("let it be done") not by one's *fiat*. The possessive quality of *fiat* in John Paul's letter makes Mary's declaration more personal and implies the conception of Christ is voluntary on her part. She presents herself to God for this task of her own free will. The concept of *fiat* becomes important in the women's response as well as they confirm the exemplarity of free will even as they recast it for different ends.

The move to the claim (Mary as a model for humankind) from these three grounds (Mary at the center of the saluific event, her union with God, and her *fiat*) is warranted by the assumption that Mary can be considered independent of her gender. In this way, the three grounds also give us a glimpse of John Paul's understanding of the goals of the gender-neutral moral life: aimed at salvation, open to God's grace, and an exercise of free will.

At the same time, in this section of the letter John Paul forwards a second claim specific to women: Mary is an especially important model for women, the "essential horizon of reflection on the dignity and vocation of women."[43] On one hand Mary represents the ultimate human dignity that is shared by men and women (claim 1), but on the other hand, "the event at Nazareth highlights a form of union with the living God which can *only belong to the 'woman,'* Mary: *the union between mother and son.*"[44] Here John Paul argues that Mary's message for women is that motherhood is central to their dignity.

Motherhood is a theme particularly favored by John Paul and some scholars suggest that it was the tragic loss of his mother at a young age that lead to his particular affinity for Mary. In chapter 2 I consider an address focused on the vocation of child rearing. In this letter, however, motherhood is defined differently. Take John Paul's use of the Greek *theotókos* in his rhetoric to describe the woman-mother of God. Although John Paul uses the term interchangeably with Mother of God, *theotókos* is the Greek compound of god and childbirth, and a more literal translation would be God-bearer. This is not merely a question of semantics. Whereas in other addresses John Paul emphasizes the role of child rearing, in this letter his focus is the physical act of carrying Jesus in the womb and giving birth.

The move from the ground (Mary as child bearer) to the claim (that reproduction is central to women's moral life) is warranted by the nature of grace and its role in Mary's immaculate conception. Invoking Augustine, John Paul writes,

> Grace never casts nature aside or cancels it out, but rather perfects it and ennobles it. Therefore the *"fullness of grace"* that was granted to the Virgin of Nazareth, with a view to the fact that she would become "*Theotókos*," also signifies the fullness of the perfection of "*what is characteristic of woman*," of "*what is feminine*." Here we find ourselves, in a sense, at the culminating point, the archetype, of the personal dignity of women.[45]

Grace perfected Mary's nature so that she was born without original sin in order for her to become *theotókos*. But even normal women have a nature that reflects an aspect of Mary's special dignity and therefore John Paul implies here that the child bearer is the essence of women's nature.

The reproductive component of women's nature is grounded in a later section of the letter in scientific research. Biology "fully confirms that the very physical constitution of women is naturally disposed to motherhood—conception, pregnancy and giving birth."[46] John Paul also references women's "psycho-physical structure," which makes them "more capable than men of paying attention to another person," and "motherhood develops this predisposition even more."[47]

In addition to the warrant of the role of grace in perfecting Mary's feminine nature, the maternal nature of her *fiat* authorizes the move from grounds to claim in this rhetoric. Whereas in the first claim Mary's *fiat* was not gendered because it functioned as a ground for her gender neutral exemplarity, in this second claim her *fiat* is gendered. For example, John Paul refers to how Mary exercises her free will as an expression "of her personal and feminine 'I' in the event of the Incarnation," implying that Mary's consent to conception, not merely the capacity to conceive, is specifically feminine.[48]

The Bible is the central backing for both claims about Mary as exemplar. As discussed in chapter 3, John Paul used Genesis in his rhetoric about a gendered moral anthropology. Here, however, the focus is on the record of Christ's birth in the New Testament (Galatians 4:4). In addition, the Second Vatican Council, Pius XII, and John XXIII are mentioned by John Paul in his introduction to the Apostolic Letter as having similar concern for the dignity and vocation of women. In terms of John Paul's understanding of Mary as *theotókos*, the Third Ecumenical Council at Ephesus in 431 is cited.

John Paul offers no explicit qualification in his rhetoric, though that Mary is a model for both men and women arguably works as a qualification within the rhetorical performance. In addition, Mary's unobtainable level of moral perfection, signaled in part by her special ontological status and her immaculate conception, limits a normal person's ability to follow her moral example.

The logic of John Paul's discussion of Mary as a model for the moral life leads to several possible responses. For example, we can already imagine upholding Mary as a model, and yet making this claim with different grounds or warrants, thereby shifting the content of her exemplarity. Or a different woman from the history of Christianity could be claimed as a model, perhaps defended as one more specified for women given that Mary serves for all humankind. Finally, John Paul assumes woman is a universal category and that Mary's moral exemplarity for all women is the same. To accommodate an assumption of radical religious, ethnic, or racial differences between women, John Paul's rhetoric would need to be revised, especially in how it references natural law.

REFOCUSING ON HAGAR AS THE HOPE OF BLACK WOMEN

In the late twentieth century, efforts from the right and left have tried to make Mary respectively more and less important in church teaching. Prominent conservative Catholics, including New York's Cardinal John O'Connor, petitioned John Paul to declare Mary, in cooperation with Jesus, co-redemptrix of humanity. Although John Paul has referred to Mary as co-redemptrix, he refused to make this belief dogma. At the same time, some women have stepped up their critiques of Mary as an unobtainable model of moral perfection. What both these actions have in common is a strategic attempt to change the logics of Mary's exemplarity: either elevating her status theologically beyond a moral exemplar or eradicating it. In contrast, my concern here is how women remain within the logics of clerical use of moral exemplars and still recast what this exemplarity means.

An example of an expositor of this tactical middle ground is Diana Hayes, currently a professor of systematic theology at the Jesuit-run Georgetown University, and the first African American woman to receive the Pontifical Doctor of Sacred Theology degree from the Catholic University of Louvain, Belgium. Hayes is well known for her pioneering work as a womanist theologian.[49] According to Hayes, a womanist seeks liberation, "not simply for herself but for all of her people and, beyond that, for all who are also oppressed by reason of race, sex, and/or class."[50] In addition to locating herself within black feminist theology, Hayes is Catholic, and situates herself within the history of the American Catholic Church, giving special attention to the church's historical role in justifying slavery.[51]

In what follows, I consider two claims made by Hayes, which serve as responses to John Paul's vision of Mary as a moral exemplar for woman. The first claim is that a womanist perspective changes the moral exemplarity of Mary. In her 1998 essay, "And When We Speak," Hayes makes the claim, similar to John Paul's, that Mary is a role model.[52] But her grounds are very different. It is not Mary's role as *theotókos*, God bearer, but her status as oppressed, poor, marginalized, and an unwed pregnant woman and the strength of her faith that breaks through the limitations put on her by society that makes her a moral exemplar for women. Instead of John Paul's use of the warrant that God's grace perfects her nature, Hayes' claim is warranted by the fact that aspects of Mary's life resonate with black women's experiences. In Hayes's reading, Mary becomes a vision of hope in the context of struggle and a model for black women as the vessel, quite literally, of the future black church.

When Hayes is asked to give the Saint Mary's College Madeleva Lecture in 1995,[53] it is Hagar, and not Mary, whom Hayes posits as a model for black Catholic women. In this lecture, "Hagar's Daughters: Womanist Ways of Being in the World," Hayes claims, "We are the daughters. . . of Hagar, the rejected and cast-out slave, mother of Ishmael, concubine of Abraham and threat to Sarah, his barren wife."[54] Hagar as exemplar is the second claim I consider.

My understanding of the account of Hagar in Genesis 16 and 21 is greatly informed by Tikva Frymer-Kensky and the biblical translations I use in this section are hers.[55] Hagar, which sounds like the Hebrew *ha-ger* (outsider), is the Egyptian slave-woman of Sarai, wife of Abram, in Genesis 16 and 21. When Sarai has difficulty conceiving a child, she suggests that Abram use Hagar as a surrogate. When Hagar does become pregnant, Sarai feels her position in the household is threatened; Sarai begins to treat Hagar very poorly until Hagar decides to run away. At this point, an angel visits the pregnant Hagar and commands her to return to Sarai and Abram,[56] which she does and gives birth to her son Ishmael. Years later, Sarai also conceives and bears a son, Isaac. She comes to perceive Ishmael as a threat to her son and urges Abram to banish Hagar and Ishmael. Hagar and Ishmael are cast out into the desert without adequate provisions, but saved from death by a direct intervention by God, who proclaims a great future for Ishmael: "Arise, lift up the boy, and hold your hand on him, for I will make him a great nation" (Genesis 21:18). Ishmael goes on to found a community in Mecca.[57]

Hayes anticipates her audience's confusion of Hagar as a role model: "Why Hagar, you ask?"[58] Hayes acknowledges that in the biblical account, Hagar is in many ways passive and that her story is often read as one of surrogacy.[59] Nevertheless, she provides three reasons for Hagar as moral exemplar. First, Hagar is triply oppressed.[60] As a slave, she is oppressed for her race. As a concubine, she is oppressed for her gender. Hayes gives particular attention to Hagar's oppression based on her class at the hands of Sarai, who "lost sight of the reality that she and Hagar had more in common as women in that society than 'that which divided them as Hebrew master and Egyptian slave woman.'"[61] This is especially ironic when we remember that Sarai was herself a slave of the house of Pharaoh.[62] In this way, Hayes reminds us of how white women have exploited black women through our historic "inability to recognize our shared commonalities and rejoice in our differences."[63] Models that do not account for differences among women in the same way can be exploitative. Note that already we see several rhetorical reinterpretations by Hayes that work to increase the affectivity of her words. For example, race in Israelite narratives is not the same thing as race in the modern United States, and yet the connection is rhetorically powerful given Hayes's audience.

A second ground for Hagar as a womanist exemplar is her suffering. Hagar is enslaved, forced to serve as concubine, mistreated by Sarai, and finally abandoned in the desert. For Hayes, this abandonment is shared by Catholic African Americans, who are disregarded by the church, where they are invisible "outsiders-within,"[64] and neglected by white feminists and black Protestants. When Hayes speaks about her background and experience, she makes it clear that she feels this abandonment on a deeply personal level.[65]

The final ground for Hagar as an exemplar is the fact of her survival, and the manner in which she survives. Hayes argues, "God reaches out to Hagar in her abandonment and provides her with 'new vision to see survival resources where she had seen none before'. . . . And as Hagar learned how to survive and acquire an 'appropriate quality of life' for herself and her son, so also did the African slaves."[66]

Not only does Hagar not parish in the desert, through what Hayes calls "direct contact" with God, she gains new hope and is able to realize a full life, in a context when the ability to flourish seemed impossible. This is, according to Hayes, similar to the experience of African Americans: "It is our experience, not as victims, but as survivors, that is the foundation for the renewal of the Black community. Like Hagar, we have been harshly used in this world yet we have found strength in ourselves and in our faith in a God who fights on the side of the oppressed and we have continued to 'move on up a little higher.'"[67]

The move from these three grounds (Hagar as oppressed, abandoned, yet a survivor) to Hagar as a womanist model is warranted on a number of levels. For example, Hayes implies a difference between white and black values, a statement she has made explicitly elsewhere.[68] So though Mary, as a model of moral perfection, might work for some women, African American women need a model that provides hope for survival within difficult, externally imposed, circumstances. Hayes suggests that it is not the heroines but the tragic figures of the Bible who may provide better models. The warrant that moral exemplars must reflect contemporary experience is also operative in Hayes' rhetoric. Hagar is a role model because her story resonates with black women. The concrete, particular experiences of women, and not biblical stories, are the starting point of Hayes's ethics. This signals another warrant operative in Hayes's rhetoric: the Roman Catholic Church has something to learn from the experience of black women. Black women's authenticity as Catholics is "worthy not only of being preserved but also of being shared with the Church as a whole."[69]

In addition to the biblical story of Hagar, Hayes backs her claim with the black literary tradition, especially the work of Alice Walker and Toni Morrison, "as a source for discovering and recovering the spiritual values and voice of Black women."[70] This is very similar to the way literature has been a central source for Protestant womanists, such as Katie Cannon.[71]

Hayes's discursive performance can be considered citational of John Paul. They share the claim that Mary is a significant moral exemplar for women, grounded by her place at the center of the major Christian salvific event. But, in terms of the components of informal argumentation, the similarity ends there. Ignoring John Paul's additional ground of Mary as the bearer of God, Hayes provides two of her own: Mary's status as an oppressed unwed mother, and her ability to do more than society thought she could. In contrast to the facts about Mary that John Paul invokes, which are highly theological, Hayes relies on Mary's concrete actions. The emphasis on Mary's role as mother is also shifted from a literal bearer of God to a mother who struggles to pass on tradition under difficult circumstances. If John Paul is concerned with conceiving and birthing the child, Hayes focuses on Mary's survival, the survival of her child, and the survival of the new Christian community.

Another major shift in Hayes's rhetoric is her trumpeting Hagar as the quintessential female biblical exemplar. Both John Paul and Hayes look to the Bible for a moral exemplar, but the choice of Hagar requires radically different grounds. On a general level, picking a moral exemplar like Hagar, instead of Mary, recasts the goal of the role model, and by extension the moral life, in a different light. Whereas Mary is perfectly pious, Hagar is resourceful under difficult circumstances. The selection of Hagar as a model implies a vision of the moral life that stresses realistic goals under difficult circumstances rather than perfect piety.

The warrants that authorize this shift are where we can most clearly see what is at stake for Hayes in her response to John Paul's rhetoric. Whereas John Paul is concerned with speaking to all women, Hayes insists on differences between women, especially based on race: Hagar is primarily a model for black women. This complicates John Paul's vision of women as a cohesive group defined by natural law. Hayes's emphasis on the difference means not only will the Roman Catholic Church have to work hard to acknowledge and include black women, but also black women's exemplars, so long neglected, who have something to teach the magisterium about womanhood.

SUMMARY OF CREATIVE CONFORMITY

Both male clerics and laywomen use moral exemplars in their rhetoric about the gendered moral life. John Paul and Khomeini do not determine the conception of role models in women's feminist politics, but women work to some extent within the same logical parameters as the clerics on this theme. Gurgi, Ebtekar, and Hayes argue for the same claim (Fatimah and Mary are exemplars for women). The women use some of John Paul's and Khomeini's grounds (Fatimah's spiritual status and Mary's position at the center of the salvific event) and use backings similar to those in the clerical rhetoric (the hadith and the Bible). Hayes's discourse shares with John Paul II an emphasis on the connection between Mary and Hagar and their sons as central to their exemplarity.

Even as women conform to some of the components of the clerical rhetoric, they demonstrate creativity by shifting it on two levels: logical structure (architectonics), and logical tactics (logics). At the level of architectonics (claim, grounds, warrants, backings, and qualifiers), the women rearrange and re-conceptualize components of clerical rhetoric. Hayes affirms John Paul's claim that Mary is a moral exemplar, but also offers Hagar as a better exemplar for African American women. Although Gurji and Ebtekar, like Khomeini, claim Fatimah as a moral exemplar for women, they do so by introducing different grounds and warrants, which radically shift the content of that moral exemplarity.

Women's discussion of models for the moral life also shares several logical tactics with the clerical rhetoric on the same theme. Thus discursive interplay among the clerics and women results in a shift, adding complexity and depth in the communities' discursive references to moral exemplars. Some of these logics are specific to each community; some are shared.

We find the logic of expansion: the application of the original clerical claim to cases he might not have intended. This is in part the justification of Fatimah as a model of political participation. Hayes applies the logic of expansion to biblical mentors in order to include Hagar, a figure John Paul might not see as exemplary. The flipside to expansion is the logic of specification: applying specific requirements to an argument. This is the tactic behind Hayes's shift to the African American context. Whereas John Paul's rhetorical performances assume a more universal Catholic audience, Hayes articulates a narrower vision—the gendered moral life in the United States for black women. This leads her to focus on a number of issues unanticipated by John Paul's rhetoric, including black experiences in the American Catholic Church.

A tactic related to perspective is used, which we can call the logic of relocation: shifting the spatial context of an argument. Clerics typically discuss moral models in terms of their virtue in a private ethical struggle (good girls in the home and family), or of the purity of their hearts. By contrast, women's discursive use of the models considers them in the public arena as exemplars. For Gurgi and Ebtekar, Fatimah becomes a model for political participation through her public insistence on her inheritance rights and the succession of her husband as rightful leader of the Muslim community. For Hayes, Hagar is an exemplar because of her ability to overcome the obstacles and abuse of her community by literally relocating and thereby creating a new public space that is safe for her son and his progeny.

Hayes's use of Hagar is based on a sort of tactical citation we can refer to as the logic of substitution: the replacement of a central symbol in an argument with an alternative symbol. When Hayes focuses her argument about moral exemplarity on Hagar instead of Mary, she in effect creates a new symbol within the clerical logic of exemplarity.

Finally, a complex logic of praxis in the women's arguments reworks theoretical arguments into practical ones. For the clerics, moral exemplars function as ideals of moral perfection. From their example we can attempt to deduce the moral code of right action. This exemplarity, however, remains to some extent always on the theoretical level because it can never be perfectly replicated in ordinary women's moral practice. By contrast, the women's discourse about Fatimah and Hagar focuses on their actions, not attributes, to expound the content of their exemplarity. This means status as moral model derives from everyday practice instead of perfection and that exemplarity is only useful insofar as it instructs for the everyday practice of ordinary women. This is why Hayes emphasizes hope: Hagar is a model because she gives black women hope for their struggles. It is also why Fatimah's popularity among Iranians is important to Gurgi and Ebtekar: it demonstrates that she speaks to their everyday needs.

This is a major logical shift from the clerical use of exemplars as models to form certain virtues in women. For the women, exemplarity is earned or learned through life experience, spiritual journey, or necessity, compared with having exemplarity bestowed on them by God or through their connection to prominent male leaders. In feminist politics, women themselves define and authorize which virtues warrant mimicking. Moreover, considering the exemplars in terms of their praxis shifts further what the role model models: in practice, moral exemplars show us not only what to do, but also what is possible when we are told what we cannot do. They celebrate struggle, courage, and innovation under constrained conditions. Fatimah and Hagar are models because they acknowledge and engage circumstances outside their control.

THE TACTIC OF FEMINIST SYMBOLICS

This chapter has worked through three cases in which women use the clerical logic of moral exemplars to construct distinct moral symbols: two clerical exemplars are considered in new light (Fatimah and Mary) and one alternative exemplar is introduced (Hagar). For the women, their discursive practices are not only or even primarily about the theological significance of Fatimah, Mary, or Hagar: these exceptional women become opportunities to discuss the public needs, desires, challenges, and triumphs of women today. The theological significance is moved into the political realm through recasting: Hayes recasts the star of moral exemplarity—moving from Mary to Hagar—which raises an entirely new set of issues that are appropriate to discuss in reference to the moral life; Gurgi and Ibitkar recast the content of the play, giving the same lead actress (Fatimah) a new script, with new plot lines, and new lessons for the audience.

Although these shifts depend on the clerical logic of moral exemplarity, in the end they also shift what defines an exemplar and what an exemplar's moral import for women is. For the clerics, a moral exemplar is an exceptional man or woman whose theological significance or personal piety makes them worthy of mimetic reflection. Fatimah and Mary are the ethical heroines or success stories to whom we should all aspire. They show us the rewards of being a good girl. Discursively this means models serve as examples of actions and virtues clerics try to instill in women; we can use them to deduce moral codes because they show what happens when women do what they ought. Following exemplars benefits the individual, the community, and the world.

Moral exemplars function quite differently in the women's discursive practices. Fatimah and Hagar are outcasts rather than heroines in their religious communities. Their lives become opportunities to discuss unjust conditions imposed on women by others (whether by a Sarai or Sunni leaders in the community after the Prophet's death) and examples of how women break out of the mold of what is expected of good girls. In fact the women's discourse argues that moral perfection in practice reaps no benefits for Fatimah or Hagar, only more struggle and suffering. This adds a new level of complexity to the role of moral exemplars in the communities' ethical discourse. If on one hand the clerical rhetoric works through exemplars to encourage women to reenact conventional roles for women, the women's responses we considered in this chapter do the opposite: they encourage women to move away from convention, through rejecting an understanding of the moral life as a quest for moral perfection. The exemplars are not models of obedience but of creativity, not evidence of the success of the communities' ability to create good women, but of how women are able to be just despite external attempts to misform them. Exemplars demonstrate how the survival of the community is based on sometimes fighting unjust rules and bending others. In the hands of Hayes, Gurgi, and Ebtekar, Hagar and Fatimah become moral guides because of, not despite, their outsider status.

This tactical use of moral exemplars by women, even if not intentionally, critiques a use of exemplarity that might turn specific moral guides into symbolic idols. Clerics use models as opportunities for proscriptive elaborations; in contrast the women ascribe exemplarity to certain exceptional women whose actions they find helpful. Implied is a critique that models in clerical rhetoric can impede women's happiness. Neither of the cases in this chapter say this in so many words, but both turn the logics of exemplarity on its head so that what becomes primary is what women need a model for, not what the model herself might demonstrate.

Finally, it is helpful to note that the grounds and warrants the women use demonstrate that exemplarity derives as least in part through each woman's ability to learn from a situation not of her own making. This is a helpful metaphor for creative conformity: feminist politics comes from the ability to take given discursive situations and create something meaningful to women.

NOTES

1. Kissling, "Should the Trinity Be a Quartet?" 14.

2. See Calmard, "Fatema: In Myth, Folklore, and Popular Devotion," 403; Schimmel, *My Soul Is a Woman*, 30.

3. An interesting comparison between Mary and Fatimah is made in Susan Sered's "Rachel, Mary, and Fatimah," 131–46.

4. Khomeini, "Bayānāt-i Imām Khumaynī bih munāṣibat-i ," 41–46. Hereafter "Women's Day 1985." An English translation of this and the speeches analyzed in chapters 1, 2, 4, and 5 are available in Khomeini, *The Position of Women*. Although I consulted Shaw's and Arezoo's translation, the more literal translations I provide in this chapter and subsequent chapters are my own.

5. Khomeini, "Payām-i Khumaynī bih munāṣibat-i Rūz-i Zan," 28–31. Hereafter "Women's Day 1979."

6. "Shumā bāyad iqtidā' bih ū bikunīd tā paẕīruftah bāshīd kih īn rūz, Rūz-i Zan ast." Khomeini, "Women's Day 1985," 43.

7. "Fatimah salām Allāh 'alayhā ba'd az pidarash 75 rūz zindah būdand, dar īn dunyā būdand va ḥuzn va shiddat barāyishān ghalabih dāsht va Jibrā'īl-i Amīn mī´āmad khidmat-i īshān va bih īshān ta'ziyat'arż mī´kard va masā'ilī az āyandah naql mī´kard. Ẓāhir-i rivāyat īn ast kih dar īn 75 rūz murāvidah´ī būdah ast ya'nī raft va āmad-i Jibrā'īl zīyād būdah ast va gumān nadāram kih ghayr az ṭabaqah-'i avval az anbīyā'-i uẓẓām darbārah-'i kasī īn ṭawr vārid shudah bāshad kih dar ẓarf-i 75 rūz Jibrā'īl-i Amīn raft va āmad dāshtah ast va masā'il rā dar ātīyah´ī kih vāqi' mī´shudah ast, masā'il rā ẕikr kardah ast va ānchih kih bih zurriyah-i ū mī´rasīdah ast dar ātiyah, zikr kardah ast." Ibid., 42.

8. "Khiyal nashavad kih Jibrā'īl barā-yi har kasī mī´āyad va imkān dārad bīāyad īn yak tanāsub lāzim ast bayn-i rūḥ-i ān kasī kih Jibrā'īl mī´khvāhad bīāyad va maqām-i Jibrā'īl kih rūḥ-i a'ẓam ast." Ibid.

9. "Yak zan-i ma'mūlī nabūdah ast, yak zan-i rūhānī, yak zan-i malakūtī, yak insān bih tamām ma'nā insān." Khomeini, "Women's Day 1979," 28.

10. For a summary of Fatimah in Shi'i hagiography and an extensive bibliography on the subject see Amir-Moezzi, "Fātema: In History and Shi'ite Hagiography," 400–402. See also Karen Ruffle's recent work on the role of Fatimah in Shi'i practice. Ruffle, *Gender, Sainthood, and Everyday Practice in South Asian Shi'ism* and "May Fatimah Gather Our Tears."

11. "Az barā-yi zan ab'ād-i mukhtalifah ast, chunānchih barā-yi mard va barā-yi insān. Īn varaq-i ṣūrī-i ṭabī'ī nāzil'tarīn martabah-i insān ast va nāzil'tarīn martabah-i zan ast va nāzil'tarīn martabah-i mard ast. Lākin az hamīn martabah-i nāzil ḥarakat bih sū-yi kamāl ast. Insān mawjūd-i mutaḥarrik ast, az martabah-i ṭabī'at tā martabah-i ghayb, tā fanā bar ulūhiyat. Barā-yi Sadiqah Tahirah īn masā'il, īn ma'ānī ḥāṣil ast. Az martabah-i tabī'at shurū' kardih ast, harakat kardih ast; harakat-i ma'navī, bā qudrat-i ilāhī, bā dast-i ghaybī, bā tartīb-i Rasūl Allāh marāḥil rā ṭay kardih ast tā rasīdah ast bih martabah'ī kih dast-i hamah az ū kūtāh ast." Khomeini, "Women's Day 1979," 29.

12. "Dar har ṣūrat man īn sharāfat va fażīlat rā az hamah-'i fażāyilī kih barā-yi Ḥażrat-i Zahrā ẕikr kardih'and—bā īn kih ānhā ham fażāyil buzurgī ast—īn fażīlat rā man bālātar az hamah mī'dānam kih barā-yi ghayr-i anbīyā 'alayhim al-salām, ān ham nah hamah-'i anbīyā, barā-yi ṭabaqah-i bālā-yi anbīyā 'alayhim al-salām va ba'ż az awliyāyī kih dar rutbah-'i ānhā hast, barā-yi kasī dīgar ḥāṣil nashudah." ("I consider the fact that Gabriel appeared to her when he had appeared to no one other than the prophets and some of the saints who rank among them, to show her nobility and moral excellence more than any other virtue which has been attributed to Fatimah, even though those other virtues are also great virtues.") Khomeini, "Women's Day 1985," 43.

13. Ibid.

14. Ibid., 44.

15. "Agar chunānchih yak 'iddah az zan vārid bishavand dar farż kunīd yak maḥallī kih maḥall-i jang ast, 'alāvah bar īn kih khvudashān jang mī'kunand, mard'hā rā kih yak iḥsāsi dārand nisbat bih zan'hā, ḥassāsiyyat dārand nisbat bih zan'hā, mard'hā rā quvvah'ashān rā dū chandān mī'kunand. . . . Mard ḥassās ast nisbat bih zan, mard agar, ṣad nafar mard rā bibīnad kih mī'kushand, mumkin ast khaylī chīz nashavad, ammā agar yak zan rā bibīnad kih bī'iḥtirāmī mī'kunad ḥassāsiyyat dārad va law ajnabī bāshand ān zan." Ibid.

16. "Ḥukūmat'hā-yi vaqt, muḥākamah mī'kardih ast ḥukūmat'hā-yi vaqt rā." Ibid., 43.

17. Mahboubeh Abbas-Gholizadeh, interview by author in Persian, Tehran, August 23, 2004.

18. Gurji and Ebtekar, "The Life and Status of Fatimah Zahra," 7–19. *Farzānah* is a bilingual quarterly, and this essay was published in English.

19. For an account of the hostage crisis, see Ebtekar and Reed, *Takeover in Tehran.*

20. Gurji and Ebtekar, "Life and Status of Fatimah," 8.

21. Ibid., 7–8.

22. Ibid., 9.

23. Ibid.

24. Ibid.

25. Ibid., 10.

26. Gurji and Ebtekar write, "This event needs careful analysis from several perspectives. Fatimah Zahra displays her political insight and concern, thus indicating her role in the highest level of decision making in the society of her

time. Her position is also independent from that of her husband, who is himself an unquestionable authority on Islam. . . . As her husband, 'Ali does not impose his view upon her but he openly honors her attitude and assists her in her campaign when necessary. This historical account clearly indicates the independent status of a woman relative to her husband and also marks the political role and rights of women in Islam." Ibid., 10–11.

27. The sources Gurji and Ebtekar cite include Ghazvini, *Fatimah Zahra*, 314–504; Shahidi, *The Life of Fatimah Zahra*, 121–48; Majlesi, *Bihar al Anwar*; and Firouzabadi, *Fatimah Zahra in the Sources of the Sunni Scholars*. An English translation of Fatimah's speech discussing her right to inheritance was published in its entirety in a later issue of *Farzānah*. "The Sermon of Fatimah Zahra," 29.

28. Gurji and Ebtekar, "Life and Status of Fatimah," 14.

29. Ibid.

30. Ibid., 15.

31. Ibid.

32. Ibid., 17.

33. For example, in a footnote, Harvard historian Leila Ahmad is singled out as having "taken a western orientalist position" to gender in Islam that has "overlooked the roles of women like Fatimah Zahra." Ibid., 19, n 22.

34. Shariati emphasizes two roles of Fatimah—devoted mother and advocate of social justice—the later of which is similar to Gurji and Ebtekar's argument. But it is arguably primarily her role in perpetuating the Prophet's line, through giving birth to the Imams Hasan and Husayn, that authorizes Fatimah's status for Shariati. Gurji and Ebtekar are indirectly refuting this claim through their emphasis on how she acquires social and spiritual education from her actions that are independent of her status as wife and mother. For further reading on Shariati's argument about Fatimah as a role model for Muslim women, see 'Ali Shariati, *Fatimah Is Fatimah* and Ferdows, "Women and the Islamic Revolution," 283–98.

35. Given that the publication date of Gurji/Ebtekar's essay places it in a period in Iranian politics when human rights discourse was contentious, their reference to human rights might have something to do with the fact that the article was published in English, and therefore assumed in part a western audience. Nevertheless, human rights' values as a rhetorical strategy is commonly used by a number of Iranian women in more recent writings. This was not the case, however, for Khomeini. Take, for example, the following excerpt from a 1978 speech: "All the miseries that we have suffered, still suffer, and are about to suffer soon are caused by the heads of those countries that have signed the *Declaration of Human Rights*, but that at all times have denied man his freedom." Khomeini, "In Commemoration of the First Martyrs," 213.

36. Although John Paul has used the word *co-redemptrix* to refer to Mary, he resisted making this dogma and never invoked his extraordinary papal magisterium on the matter.

37. John Paul's experience with illness, accidents, an assassination attempt, and loss of intimate friends and family connected him in an intimate way to the Virgin

Mary. One of John Paul's biographers, Tad Szulc, writes, "John Paul II is convinced, in a most mystical fashion, that he, too, has been chosen for suffering and martyrdom. He believes that the Virgin Mary, whom he deeply venerates . . . has saved his life on many occasion as well as having taught him how to suffer." *Pope John Paul II*, 30. This seems to be confirmed by the Pope's own statements. For example, after a month long hospital stay for a broken hip his first public comments are "through Mary I would like to express my gratitude today for this gift of suffering." Ibid.

38. John Paul II, *Mulieris dignitatem.*

39. Ibid., para. 3–4.

40. Ibid., para. 3. Emphasis in the original.

41. Ibid., para. 4.

42. Ibid., para. 19.

43. Ibid., para. 5.

44. Ibid., para. 4. Emphasis in the original.

45. Ibid., para. 5. Emphasis in the original.

46. Ibid., para. 18.

47. Ibid. In addition to making women more nurturing by nature, this ability to engage others on a personal level has very important ethical meaning given John Paul's personalistic understanding of faith and the moral life: women seem to be more naturally endowed with gifts to make them successful in the moral life.

48. Ibid., para. 4.

49. *Womanist*, a term originally coined by Alice Walker, is used by some minority feminists as an alternative to feminist.

50. She continues, "Sexism is not the only issue; rarely is it the most important issues. Rather, it is the intertwined evil emanating from the multiplicative effect of all of these which act to restrict her and her community that are the cause for her concern." Hayes, *And Still We Rise*, 140. Hayes identifies Dolores Williams, Jacquelyn Grant, Katie Cannon, Emilie Townes, Renita Weems, Cheryl Saunders, and Kelly Brown Douglas as Protestant womanists, and Shawn Copeland, Jamie Phelps, Toinette Eugene, and herself as Catholic womanists. Ibid., 141.

51. In 1452, Nicholas V gave permission to the kings of Spain and Portugal to enslave pagans. Alexander VI extended this to the Americas in 1493. As late as 1866 the magisterium declared that slavery was not contrary to natural law. It was not until Vatican II, in *Gaudium et spes,* that the magisterium declared that slavery violated human dignity, and not until 2002 that John Paul II made a public apology for the church's role in justifying the slave trade. The ordination of black men and their leadership in other forms was not encouraged until the twentieth century, demonstrating internal institutional racism. Davis, *The History of Black Catholics.*

52. Hayes, "And When We Speak," 113–14. Hayes has made similar statements elsewhere about Mary, most recently in "Black Catholics in the United States: A Subversive Memory," 57.

53. "The Madeleva Lectures series annually commemorates the opening of the Center for Spirituality of Saint Mary's College, Notre Dame, Indiana, and honors the memory of the woman who inaugurated the college's pioneering program in theology, Sister Madeleva, C.S.C." Hayes, *Hagar's Daughters*, frontmatter.

54. Ibid., 6.

55. Frymer-Kensky, "Hagar, My Other, My Self," 225–37.

56. "The angel of YHWH said to her, 'Return to you mistress and be oppressed under her hand.'" Genesis 16:10.

57. Hagar is a particularly interesting role model given the comparative nature of this book, because Hagar also holds an important place in Islamic narratives. Hagar, or Hajār in Arabic and Persian, founds the Islamic civilization in Mecca by bringing Ishmael there and finding him a wife. Muslims consider Ishmael a fully legitimate son of Abraham who inherited his line of prophethood; the Prophet Muhammad is a direct descendent of Ishmael and Hajār.

58. Hayes, *Hagar's Daughters*, 6.

59. Ibid., 6–7.

60. Ibid., 8.

61. Ibid., 7.

62. Genesis 12.

63. Hayes, *Hagar's Daughters*, 6.

64. Hayes, "And When We Speak," 108.

65. "All too often in that struggle [to find myself], my greatest challenge came from my own—Black men and women or white women—who distrusted my efforts and sought to impede my self-emancipation for reasons of their own. Thus, my struggle was two-sided. It involved the white world, that dominant structure which sought to label and thereby suppress my voice and my own world, that of African-Americans, who often saw me as a traitor to the race, as well as to Protestant Christianity." Hayes, *Hagar's Daughters*, 43–44.

66. Ibid., 60.

67. Ibid.

68. See Hayes, "And When We Speak," 113; "To Be Black, Catholic, and Female," 52–62; "My Hope Is in the Lord."

69. Hayes, "Black Catholics in the United States," 55.

70. Hayes, *Hagar's Daughters*, 33–34.

71. Cannon, *Black Womanist Ethics*.

CHAPTER TWO

Surprises from the Laps of Mothers

Leveraging the Gaps in Procreative Virtues

That clerics in these two traditions devote enormous rhetorical energy toward instructing women on the issues of reproduction and procreation is a sign of the times. Contemporary worldviews demand that women have some say in their own fertility. Motherhood has become increasingly understood as a choice rather than a strict duty (to husband, family, or community). This in turn requires that religious leaders interested in shaping the virtues of procreation and child rearing direct rhetoric toward women. In some communities reproduction is most often discussed in relation to the moral permissibility of certain actions (contraception, abortion, assisted fertilization) within specific circumstances (danger to the life of the mother or fetus). In other contexts the emphasis is on the moral virtues of women after birth. Catholics in the United States, for example, have taken a prominent role in the public debate about abortion rights and funding. In Iran, however, abortion is legal in a number of shari'a-approved circumstances, contraception is readily available, and its use supported by the Islamic regime. In postrevolutionary Iran, the conversation about procreation focuses on its role in making women into mothers, what defines a good mother, and the significance of motherhood for nation building. Despite these differences, in both contexts clerics and women invoke the virtues of procreation in their discourse about women's public roles.

As in the other chapters, I do not focus here on the usual themes in feminist ethics related to procreation (abortion and contraception) or direct rebuttals of clerical logic. Instead I consider how women use the clerical logics of motherhood, childbearing, and child rearing in their own moral discourse. How do the women shift the clerical meaning of motherhood? How is the topic of reproduction used to address an embodied dimension of feminist politics? What subjects beyond childbearing and child rearing do the logics of procreation give women an opportunity to discuss?

In this chapter I consider John Paul's rhetoric on natural family planning and then theologian Lisa Cahill's response, which shifts the conversation to the problem of clerical nonpersuasiveness on sexual ethics. I then explore Khomeini's prioritization of the role women play as mothers and how his logics were cited by women in the 2003 campaign to reform Iranian custody laws.

NATURAL FAMILY PLANNING AS NUPTIAL CHASTITY

Scholars often focus on John Paul's most authoritative documents on procreation: the encyclical *Evangelium vitae* and the apostolic exhortation *Familiaris consortio*. By contrast, I focus here on his more informal addresses because these are more indicative of rhetoric aimed at and heard by common Catholic women. Between July and November 1984, John Paul delivered sixteen general audiences reflecting on Paul VI's encyclical *Humanae vitae*. In these audiences John Paul elaborates the biblical and personalist aspects of this encyclical, covering a number of issues, including contraception and abortion as evil acts, and the meaning of responsible parenthood. Because many excellent studies have already been done on these aspects of John Paul's moral teachings,[1] I focus in this section not on what the pope prohibited, but rather what he saw as permissible—natural family planning—as elaborated in two general audiences.[2]

In these addresses, John Paul uses the teachings of Paul VI as a pedagogical opportunity. He focuses on how Paul VI prohibited all forms of conventional contraception—including barrier (condom or diaphragm) and hormonal (oral or derma contraceptive methods)—but allowed family planning through periodic abstinence, or what John Paul calls "the natural regulation of fertility."[3] The specific claim in John Paul's addresses is that "the moral evil of contraception" and the permissibility of natural regulation of fertility are consistent on two grounds. First, periodic abstinence is licit because it is natural and thus "established by the Creator."[4] In contrast, "artificial contraception" (as John Paul defines it) is illicit because it seeks to obstruct nature. This ground is authorized by John Paul's understanding of the existence of intrinsically evil acts that obstruct nature. Every act, according to John Paul, "possesses its own intrinsic moral qualification, either positive or negative."[5] Abstinence is a positive act because of the normative value put on celibacy by the Roman Catholic Church; contraception is a negative act because of the properly procreative dimension of sexuality.

The second ground for why family planning through periodic abstinence is permissible is that it intends to enact a virtue that Paul VI calls conjugal chastity. John Paul traces the doctrine on chastity to Galatians 5:25 and declares that this is the "real reason" that Paul VI allowed natural family planning.[6] This ground of conjugal chastity is authorized by John Paul's understanding that the ethical dimension of a practice is found not only in the positive value of the act (abstinence), but also in the general virtue required for the act (chastity, nuptial commitment). In this way he suggests that periodic abstinence habituates virtue.[7] Conventional contraception, however, is used strictly to limit family size. The goal—fewer children—may be the same, but natural family planning is motivated by more than this. John Paul uses a possible confusion in *Humanae vitae* to explain this point: "My predecessor Paul VI states that 'in each case married couples, for acceptable reasons, are both perfectly clear in their intention to avoid children'. . . . In these words the document admits that even those who use contraceptive practices can be motivated by 'acceptable reasons.' However, this *does not change the moral character which is based on the very structure of the conjugal act as such*."[8]

John Paul uses two backings to defend his warrants (intrinsic evil acts and the habituation of virtue). First, although his goal is to prove the logical validity of *Humane vitae*, he relies in part on the authority of that encyclical as backing for his claim. The second backing is his theology of the body, especially original unity of the sexes, which is discussed in detail in chapter 3. John Paul thus deepens and reinforces Paul VI's argument through reference to the total self-giving of man and woman in marriage as an expression of *imago dei*. But in the case of birth control, this theology emphasizes a particular interpretation of natural law that assumes the magisterium has rightly linked the morality of a given sexual act (contraception or abstinence) with the virtues necessary to the physical structure of that act (nuptial chastity). John Paul signals his reliance on this form of natural law with phrases like *biological regularity*, which expresses "the providential plan of the Creator . . . exhorts competent persons to study [and] apply it in a still deeper way."[9] I do not mean here to enter into the heated debate over charges of physicalism (intention does not effect an act) made against John Paul and vehemently denied by his defenders.[10] Rather I intend only to point out John Paul's particular combination of nature and freedom means that for him will and virtue have physical dimensions and biology has a role in determining freedom.

John Paul provides one strong modal qualifier for the permissibility of natural family planning. "It might be observed at this point that married couples who have recourse to the natural regulation of fertility, might do so without the valid reasons."[11] In other words, even natural family planning is a good act only if it is based on valid reasons. Given Catholic teaching of responsible parenthood, a couple should not abstain from sex during fertile periods to prevent pregnancy without first taking into account how an additional child might positively or negatively affect their family, society, and even the church.[12] This qualification can also be seen as reinforcing the importance of the combination of the two grounds (natural form and ethical motivation): abstinence is not enough to justify natural family planning unless it is combined with the virtue of conjugal chastity. In other words, responsible parenthood is a necessary criterion for permissibility of periodic abstinence, but by itself is not enough.

John Paul's purpose in this address is to respond to one of *Humanae vitae*'s possible rebuttals, mainly that natural family planning is not consistent with the Catholic Church's teaching against all forms of contraception. But his rhetoric on the subject creates new possible responses. For example, his use of *Humanae vitae* as backing in an argument about *Humanae vitae* opens the door for a challenge of circular logic. Second, despite an attempt to balance the nature of the act with the intention behind it, John Paul still emphasizes the discrete action, requiring each act of conjugal love to be the expression of complete self-giving. This opens him up for critique that he neglects a holistic view of the physical relationship of spouses, where holding hands or giving a back rub all contribute in different ways to the physical self-giving in the relationship. It also privileges as natural the physical aspects of nuptial union over the emotional ones. Finally, John Paul creates a possible response with his slide from biology to natural law, from *is* to *ought*. For example, he asserts, rather than argues, that periodic abstinence can be seen as more a part of God's plan than other forms of contraception. His distinction between natural and artificial family planning is at stake here, particularly when periodic abstinence involves checking temperatures, tracking ovulation, and so on, which are not clearly any more natural than a barrier method.

MAKING A CREDIBLE CASE FOR NATURAL LAW

The magisterium teaching on contraception in the mid- and late twentieth century, articulated by Paul VI and John Paul II, has met with some backlash in the United States. Despite papal prohibitions, American Catholics continue to use contraception. A 1968 Gallup Poll taken just weeks after Paul VI released his *Humanae vitae* found that 65 percent of Catholics agreed with "it is possible to practice artificial methods of birth control and still be a good Catholic."[13] That number was up to 82 percent by 1993.[14] And according to a 2005 Harris Poll, 90 percent of Catholics (versus 93 percent of all respondents) support access to contraception. Widespread public dissent from papal teaching on contraception has created what some have called a crisis of magisterium authority in the American Roman Catholic Church.[15] Lisa Cahill addresses the reasons behind this backlash. In her argument analyzed here, she is concerned with pontifical rhetoric rather than natural family planning per se, and she thus essentially changes the subject.

Cahill is a self-described moderate, professor of theology at Jesuit-run Boston College, and former president of the Catholic Theological Society of America. Her work puts in dialogue feminist theory and Christian teachings on women and sex. The rhetoric I analyze here was first delivered as a John Murray Forum Lecture at Fordham Law School in 1993. The written version was published as "Abortion, Sex and Gender: The Church's Public Voice" in the national Catholic weekly *America*.[16] The speech and its corresponding essay respond to John Paul's rhetoric by critiquing the logic of his argument for natural family planning as well as suggesting ways in which the papal teaching authority can be more persuasive in general within the American political context.

Cahill claims that John Paul's simultaneous support of natural family planning and prohibition of contraception is ineffective because it has what she calls two internal logical gaps. These two gaps serve as grounds in her argument and she summarizes the first as follows: "It is not at all clear why, if it is permissible to intend sexual union without intending to conceive, the link of intentionally nonprocreative sex acts with the parental meaning of sex has to be maintained by constraints on the physiological structure of those sex acts themselves, rather than through the place of all sexual acts in the total relationship of the spouses, for whom some acts if not others may be procreative."[17] Cahill seems to be attempting to remind the audience of the contemporary shift in magisterium teaching, which now acknowledges not only procreative but also unitive value (e.g., love and intimacy) in intercourse. Put another way, allowing natural family planning means accepting the premise that the intention to conceive is not required to make sex an authentic human act. Cahill gently suggests that this shift has implications that the Vatican has not realized. Mainly, if the unitive qualities of sex are valuable, there is no logical requirement for insisting that each act of intercourse must intend procreation. Instead, we should consider an openness to procreation within the overall sexual life of a couple. At the same time, the unitive meaning of sex suggests to Cahill that the focus should not be only on the virtues of physical-biological dimensions of sex because the unitive qualities of sex are not created solely by these physiological structures.

The second logical gap in John Paul's rhetoric, according to Cahill, is that he neglects how the welfare of the marital relationship depends on gender equality within that relationship: "The equal and reciprocal love relation of the partners is the fundamental moral context for both sexual expression and parenthood. But neither the welfare of the marital relation as a whole, nor the full equality of the woman in family and society, is officially accepted as a rationale for seeking the most secure means possible of promoting the affirmed goal of 'responsible parenthood.'"[18] Cahill shows here her frustration that, despite the lip service paid to the nuptial relationship and the equality of each partner, John Paul's calculus for assessing responsible parenthood is based solely on procreation and chastity. For Cahill, the movement from these grounds (unitive nature of sex and full equality within marriage) is warranted by a holistic view of sex within relationship. John Paul, on the other hand, isolates each act of intercourse as a total self-gift, which Cahill refers to as a very romantic depiction of sex.[19] Cahill's rhetoric is backed by the experiences and subsequent beliefs of Catholic couples, who do not find birth control to corrupt their relationship with their partner.[20]

In addition to the specific claim about the logical gaps in John Paul's message, Cahill makes a more general claim that the Roman Catholic Church is not persuasive on issues related to sexual ethics in the United States. She describes this state of affairs with reference to the abortion debate as follows: "To the extent that we perpetuate this family feud instead of looking for common ground with cultural values that could support abortion alternatives, we also run the risk of sectarian isolation from the 'real world' of social institutions and politics in which we think our views should be heard. Deeply disturbing to me is a crusade mentality on the part of certain self-defined champions of Catholic orthodoxy who seem to be arming true believers for a battle aimed at total obliteration of the enemy, rather than building consensus about a more humane common life."[21] Note how Cahill criticizes a form of Catholic discourse that is about demolishing the opponent (dialectic) rather than about building consensus or attempting to persuade the audience (rhetoric). Her point is that rhetoric in a classical sense is better suited for discursive teaching about the moral life and that the Vatican has neglected this.

Her grounds for the Roman Catholic Church's general lack of persuasiveness are also specific suggestions for how to shift clerical rhetoric to make it more effective. The first is that "the natural law argument should . . . be accompanied by the realization that the expression and protection of values is always a historical task with culturally variant results."[22] Cahill urges a less static view of natural law, one that sees it as received moral knowledge refined within a specific sociocultural context. The current use of natural law (exemplified by John Paul) is inefficient, according to Cahill, because it assumes itself to be neutral and self-evident, which she argues (as a warrant for this first ground) misunderstands how public discourse functions.

Cahill's second ground is that the Vatican fails to see how, for a given audience, issues are interconnected. She uses the example of abortion to illustrate this point: "For instance, it will be of little practical use to proclaim the right to life of the unborn without addressing that message to high-profile cultural concerns about women's equality and economic pressures on families. A single-issue focus on the rights of the unborn ends by marginalizing the pro-life message. It makes that message as unintelligible in the public philosophical, moral and political debates as if it were written in Latin or based solely on Scripture."[23] Cahill reminds us that the abortion issue in the U.S. context is not just about the right to life of the fetus. The pro-choice movement has made women's equality central to their rhetoric and these issues are interrelated in the public mind. To ignore this, to focus only on the component of the debate the church thinks is the most significant, makes the Catholic message unintelligible.

The third fact that grounds the Catholic message's nonpersuasiveness is its failure to act tactically: "The public recognizability of the Catholic message on any social issue depends on its success in pinpointing problems in the culture around which there is a receptivity to the challenge of Catholic moral ideals." Cahill argues that to make arguments that will be effective, the Roman Catholic Church must not begin with its own teachings, but with what a given audience understands to be the pressing moral problems. She suggests that, in the case of sexual ethics in the United States, this might include "the quest for sexual meaning and for the renewal of family life in a new era of gender equality."[24]

Two warrants in Cahill's response move the three grounds (contextualized natural law, acknowledgement of the interconnection of themes, and identification of receptivity) to the claim (the Catholic message is not persuasive). One warrant is that the Catholic message has something to contribute to the American conversation about sexual ethics. Because Catholic teaching on sex "comes out of a religious tradition is not enough to disqualify it from the public arena, since all moral discourse has a history and an agenda of some sort."[25] The second warrant is that criteria exist for reasonable debate specific to the American context. One criterion is related to an assumption of gender equality; another is a local sexual morality.[26]

Cahill demonstrates these warrants as being reliable in the way she understands discourse to persuade. Rhetoric, not dialectic, is the most effective way to contribute to the public discourse in the United States: "The way to engage those who are ambivalent is not to blast them as stupid or immoral (a self-defeating 'sectarian' move)."[27] Her advice to the Vatican is to move beyond bully pulpit tactics to attend more specifically to the intended audience of moral teachings.

Cahill directly engages John Paul's claim that natural family planning is permissible by carefully looking at the logical structure of his rhetoric. She agrees that the full meaning of sexuality for the moral life is not widely understood. She shares with John Paul a belief that Catholicism has something to add to an ongoing conversation about contraception and abortion in the American context, particularly in its affirmation of a universal value of life and its focus on the unitive meaning of sex. Finally, she agrees that natural law is an important source of the moral life.

Cahill's rhetorical performance also shifts John Paul's arguments about family planning and nuptial chastity. By not engaging components of his rhetoric, such as his assumption of intrinsically evil acts (which functions as a warrant), or the virtue of conjugal chastity (which functions as a ground), she moves the conversation away from these aspects to focus on her concern about making a credible Catholic case for sexual ethics in U.S. public discourse. Most significantly, she uses rhetoric surrounding contraception to argue that the Vatican is not as successful in convincing Americans about the truth of its message as it might be. She suggests three ways in which Catholic teachings, including papal teachings, could be more persuasive. At their core, these three suggestions are ways to attend more closely to the particularities of the given audience.

MORAL CITIZENS SPRINGING FROM THE LAPS OF MOTHERS

For anyone who has spent substantial time in Iran, the intensity of maternal relationships with sons and daughters is unmistakable. This value can be historically traced to the manuscripts of the national Persian epic poem, the *Shahnameh* (Book of Kings). Written in the late tenth and early eleventh centuries by the poet Ferdowsi (935–1020), the *Shahnameh* drew on a mixture of existing oral and written sources.[28] Mothers often appear in the epic to protect their children, such as Katayun's warning to her son Isfandyar.[29] The case of the mother of the main hero of the epic (Sohrab) is particularly interesting. According to Dick Davis, in the oldest manuscripts of the poem she appears only for the conception of Sohrab, and therefore is primarily a lover, not a mother. In later versions of the poem, however, her role is considerably expanded to protector of Sohrab and eventual mourner of Sohrab at his death. These episodes are not Ferdowsi's, but they are nonetheless aspects of the *Shahnameh*'s cultural legacy for motherhood in Iran. In contemporary Iranian culture the emphasis on motherhood, as well as the apparent joy a woman takes in fulfilling this duty, endure as a cultural value. In Iranian films such as *Ten* (2002, Abbas Kiarostami) and *Children of Heaven* (1999, Majud Majidi), non-Iranians can observe the special emphasis put on mothers' relationships with children.

In a 1979 speech in Dezful, Iran, Khomeini addressed a group of women on the issue of motherhood.[30] Khomeini begins his remarks as follows: "You ladies have two very virtuous vocations. One vocation is to train your children, which is the highest vocation"[31] (as a mother). He later mentions the second vocation, which "is a vocation to develop human beings"[32] (as a teacher). It appears that Khomeini is encouraging two roles for women: mother and teachers. But a closer look at the context and content of these remarks provides a better understanding of Khomeini's underlying claims, which are related to what he means when he says teacher.

A first step is to consider the makeup of the audience he addressed, described as a group of ladies from Dezful. It would be a stretch for us to assume that Khomeini thought that the majority of the listeners would be teachers in formal school settings. More likely is that he assumes all these women are, or are potentially, child bearers and child rearers. And in this way even the statement that women have a special occupation as teachers is arguably an extension of their motherhood duties: they provide education for their children.

This moves us from identifying the idea Khomeini foregrounds in the speech as "women should be mothers and teachers" to "women should be mothers, which includes a teaching component." But though this is the meaning of Khomeini's opening statement, his actual claim, or the precise action he is trying to persuade women to enact, is to be full-time mothers. In other words, not only should "women be mothers," "women should only be mothers" and not work outside the home. This is not to say that Khomeini never spoke of a role for women in the workforce. He did in fact address this issue a number of times. However, given the logical structure of this speech, his primary aim is to persuade women to reconsider their roles outside the home, or at least to order their vocations so that motherhood is clearly the most important.

The first ground for why motherhood is the primary occupation of women is found in Khomeini's critique of the situation of women during the period of *ṭāghūt*, or the Pahlavi regime's non-Islamic rule of Iran: "Unfortunately, during the government of *ṭāghūt*, they wanted to take this vocation [motherhood] away from these mothers."[33] Khomeini goes on to criticize the Pahlavi period of rule for importing a type of Western modernity that deemphasizes traditional values. He is thereby attempting to invoke a particular Iranian value of motherhood and attribute an opinion (motherhood is not valuable) to Western modernity as a way to mark it as un-Islamic.

Often Khomeini assumes that a link to *ṭāghūt* or the West is adequate evidence to persuade his audience that a particular action or belief is immoral. But in the case of motherhood Khomeini adds another two grounds by referencing a child's welfare and psychology. He asserts that children need mothers more than other adults: "They are influenced more by their mothers than by their fathers, teachers, or professors."[34] The final ground can be seen in Khomeini's equating an orphanage with day-care nursery: "When a child is raised in an orphanage, without a mother, and with strangers, and without any affection from her mother, this child will obtain a psychological complex."[35] All three grounds are warranted by the idea that for women to fulfill their duties as mothers, they need to be with their children.

Notice how the warrant has brought us back to the first ground about the rule of *ṭāghūt*, which Khomeini now argues is the direct result of mothers not making motherhood their primary vocation: "Much of these corruptions which appear in the society are caused by these children who have a complex and by these adults who have grown up with a complex."[36] As women were being encouraged by the Shah to join the workforce, they forgot or disregarded the value of motherhood. Their children felt abandoned and developed "complexes," which contributed to society's overall immorality. Khomeini goes so far as to argue that the responsibility for an immoral child rests on a mother's shoulders: "If somehow, God forbid, this child does not come out right from your moral training [literally, from your lap], then it is possible that this child would make society corrupted, and you will be responsible."[37]

The most frequent backing used in this speech is the historical facts of the period of *ṭāghūt*, which Khomeini offers as rationale for why the neglect of motherhood has severe ramifications. A concern for children's psychology also backs his rhetoric, which is significant because this argument is first introduced by the pro-establishment women's movement under the Shah. References to children's psychology are therefore a case of Khomeini citing women's rhetoric, reconstructed for his own aims. We see how the cycle continues in the next section when we analyze how women use this backing to make a claim unanticipated by Khomeini.

The most striking aspect of Khomeini's speech is his lack of qualifiers. He does not qualify women's role as mothers with discussion of their other vocations; he does not qualify a mother's special role with any discussion of fatherhood; and he does not put any limits on the responsibility of mothers for the moral lives of their children.

Nevertheless, possible responses are created by the logical form of Khomeini's rhetoric on motherhood. He uses, for example, cultural sensitivities connected to a woman's role as mother to make his argument about the moral duties of women more persuasive—a particular form of affectivity. But in doing so he creates a rhetorical space in which women's arguments and actions as mothers have priority, a space that will be discursively exploited by Iranian women. Second, in these remarks he speaks directly about women's responsibility for the moral education of children: "You must pay attention that these children who are being educated by you obtain a religious and moral education."[38] This implies that women are responsible, ultimately, for all immoral behavior in society because an individual who acts badly was raised improperly by his mother. By making women morally responsible for their children's actions, Khomeini raises the stakes immensely on women's ability to provide a proper Islamic moral education. He also creates a possible response that his logic unfairly burdens women with all of society's moral failures. Third, because Khomeini assumes that the quantity of time a woman spends with her child is the linchpin to proper motherhood, some of the other roles he will want women to perform, especially in terms of political activism during the Islamic Revolution, will need to be sacrificed. This understanding of a priority of motherhood also conflicts with other Shi'i teachings codified in Iranian law, such as automatic custody for fathers at the time of divorce. This conflict is the basis for the women's rhetoric about custody reform in Iran we consider next.

CONFIRMING GENDER ESSENTIALISM IN DEBATE OVER THE CUSTODY OF CHILDREN

There are certainly direct rebuttals to Khomeini's claim for the priority of motherhood, most notably in the actions of the women who were closest to him before and after the Islamic Revolution. Despite their rhetoric, these women left their children at home to be raised at least in part by others. In fact, arguably, none of the *khaṭ-i imāmī* women active in the women's movement make motherhood a priority in the way Khomeini's rhetoric tried to convince them was necessary. Khomeini's rhetoric is also directly contested in a number of studies by Iranian scholars that look at the effects in Iran of working mothers on the development of children. These studies argue that a child does quantifiably better in school, both academically and socially, if their mother works.[39] Positive effects of working mothers on girls are especially emphasized. Rather than these direct rebuttals, I consider in this section how the building blocks of Khomeini's rhetoric are reiterated by women to justify the 2003 campaign to reform custody law in Iran.

The 2003 reform is seen by many Iranian activists as one of the most remarkable achievements of the contemporary women's movement.[40] I was told this over and over during interviews in Iran, and found this claim at first odd given what I knew to be a minor change made to the custody law in 2003. To understand the significance of this reform, it is necessary to place it within the context of the history of the status of Islamic family law in Iran as well as against the discursive context of Khomeini's rhetoric.[41]

Generally speaking, marriage is conceived as a contract in Iran, and children, as a by-product of the marriage, belong to the father. Custody is actually the combination of two distinct concepts in traditional Shi'i jurisprudence: *vilāyat* (guardianship or legal custody) and *ḥiżānat* (fostering or providing necessary care). *Vilāyat* of children is the right of the father after divorce, and *ḥiżānat* is usually assumed to be the right of a mother, especially for small children. These two distinct concepts of custody were codified in the Iranian Civil Code in the beginning of the twentieth century, but the Family Protection Law of 1967 combined both legal and physical aspects of guardianship into a single concept of custody. Under the Family Protection Law, the fitness of the parents, not just their assumed natural capacities as men (providers) and women (nurturers), was used in courts to determine custody. After the 1979 revolution, the Family Protection Law was abolished and the Civil Code reverted to distinguishing between two types of custody. At this time, *vilāyat* of a child went automatically to the father or the "paternal grandfather, in case of the father's death. *Ḥiżānat* of young children went to the mother: for boys until the age of two and girls until the age of seven."[42]

Two reforms related to custody preceded the 2003 reform and provide additional background for how ideas of child welfare and parental suitability from the Family Protection Law have become reincorporated into the Iranian Civil Code.[43] The first occurred in 1985, when the Majles effectively amended Article 1181 of the Civil Code to give the right of *ḥiżānat* to the mother instead of the paternal grandfather in the event of the death of the father.[44] This was in response to the protests of war martyrs' widows over losing their children at the death of their husbands, which became a national controversy. Note that this reform took place while Khomeini was still supreme leader and was done with his blessing. Another amendment to Article 1173 of the Civil Code limited the *ḥiżānat* rights of a father who was addicted to drugs, mentally ill, abusive, or corrupt.[45]

The 2003 reform campaign targeted Article 1169 of the Civil Code, in a section titled "On Maintenance and Education of the Children," which read as follows: "A mother has preference over others for the fostering [*ḥiżānat*] of the child for two years from the birth. After this period, fostering will go to the father, except in the case of a daughter who will remain with the mother till seven years."[46] This law explicitly differentiates based on gender. First, it ties a parent's duty and right to aspects of fostering and legal custody to their gender. Fathers always have legal guardianship of children, and get automatic physical custody of children above a certain age (two for boys, seven for girls). A mother's fostering is conceived of as a temporary measure, necessitated, presumably, for biological needs of the child (such as breast feeding). Second, it differentiates between children based on their sex, with boys having two years of guaranteed residency with their mothers and girls having seven.

Given that a reform to this law is seen by many as one of the most important successes of the Iranian women's movement since the Islamic Revolution, it may be surprising for the reader to learn that the reform did not make the custody law gender neutral (equal access to guardianship and fostering by both parents). Rather it merely raised the age of fostering for mothers of boys from the age of two to seven.[47] In this way it eradicated the gender distinction between the children, but not the overarching gendered assumptions about adult men and women within the law.

While in Iran, I had the opportunity to interview Leila Arshad, director of the Society for Protecting the Rights of the Child (SPRC). According to its mission statement, SPRC seeks to promote the principles of the United Nations Convention on the Rights of the Child and played a large part in lobbying for custody reform on the basis of child welfare. A translated excerpt from our conversation follows:

> Question (Bucar): I understand that in November 2003, legislation raised the age of boys who women get *ḥiżānat* of from two to seven. What was the argument made by advocates for this reform?
>
> Answer (Arshad): Well first, I want to say that our ultimate goal is to get judges to give *ḥiżānat* to whichever parent has more resources to support the child: emotional and financial resources, independent of age. The argument for raising the age of boys was made based on the needs of the child, especially his emotional needs. It has been psychologically proven that a mother's occupation is more necessary than a father's. . . . The feelings of a mother are special. Fathers cannot feel in the same way. Men just do not have the same emotionality. The problem is the judges do not currently weigh the emotional needs of the child as strongly as the economic needs.[48]

Two claims can be seen in Arshad's response. One directly engages my question about the justification for raising the age to seven for boys: Arshad argues that women should have physical custody of young children, independent of gender, because of the needs of the child. Note how similar her grounds are to those of Khomeini. The first is identical: a child needs their mother more than their father. The second is only slightly different: instead of focusing on the complexes of children not raised by mothers, Arshad builds on the ground that a child suffers emotionally and psychologically if separated from their mother. A third ground is that women have a higher emotional capacity than men, which leads to a special connection between mothers and their children. This is a strict gender differentiation that not even Khomeini made.

The move from these grounds to her claim uses the same warrant that Khomeini did: mothers need to physically be with their children for as many hours as possible to nurture them. For Arshad, this warrant is not qualified and is backed by the trauma of the break of the maternal bond, which has been proven by "scientific studies."[49] In addition, her claim is backed by her authority based on her running an organization focused on "the general living conditions and the physical, mental, and emotional, and social growth of Iranian children."[50] In this way her advocacy and rhetoric on the issue of custody is an extension of her role as caregiver of children.

This first claim, that mothers should foster their young children, was a direct response to my question about the justification for the custody reform campaign, but Arshad is also making a second claim about custody, indicated by her remark: "our ultimate goal is to get judges to give custody to whichever parent has more resources to support the child: emotional and financial resources, independent of age." Reconsider this statement in terms of her assertion that women are better able to connect with a child emotionally. Even under circumstances where men are more financially capable, this capacity can be easily transferred (through generous child support), but the emotional capacity, as Arshad understands it, cannot. In this way, Arshad's rhetoric encourages specific judicial rulings—giving women physical custody of older children and giving women generous child support—based on women's innate emotional connection to their children.

From this analysis, it can be seen how a campaign to change the custody laws draws on a number of components of Khomeini's rhetoric. On the subject of gender, Khomeini argues that in Islam, women and men are spiritually equal, but different in material ways that give them different rights and duties in the moral life. The coalition that worked on the custody reform also assumed that gender difference under the law is required for justice. In fact, the idea of women's innate emotionality that Arhsad uses is a stronger case of gender essentialiam than Khomeini's idea of the priority of motherhood. Arshad does not seek equal access to custody. She argues for the necessity of a women's legal right to foster her young children.[51] In this light, the custody campaign was a move to make the Civil Code more just for women by more perfectly ensuring their unequal rights.

Khomeini privileges the importance of mothers over fathers for the welfare of young children in his citation of prerevolutionary rhetoric of the women's movement. This is cited again in Arshad's rhetoric. Drawing on Khomeini's claim that children raised by people other than their mother develop complexes that are detrimental to society, Arshad's entire justification of the custody reform is made based on the common good and not only on a mother's right. Because according to Khomeini women are responsible for their own actions and the actions of their children, they have a double responsibility for the success or failure of moral life of the community. This makes it all the more imperative to act when they observe a problem in the law. In a similiar way, the custody campaign is justified by women's experience that their Islamic duty of motherhood is impeded by a purportedly Islamic civil code that denies them fostering rights.

Although some of the logics and norms of the custody campaign are found in Khomeini's teaching on women, the custody campaign itself is unanticipated by his rhetoric. The Civil Code that is the subject of reform is the one reinstated on Khomeini's watch and he presumably did not find the custody provisions problematic. Women used his teachings creatively in ways he might not have approved. Arshad shifted Khomeini's emphasis on the duty to raise their children into the necessity of the right to physical custody after a divorce. She argues that in the case of motherhood, correct Islamic practice in the private sphere necessitates certain publicly guaranteed rights. Finally, and perhaps most important, Arshad moves the conversation about custody from a man's right to his children as a product of the marriage (*vilāyat*), to the nature of the relationship between a mother and her children, and its proper effect on *ḥiżānat*. This allowed something that had previously been impossible in the name of women's rights: a reform of codified shari'a law.

SUMMARY OF CREATIVE CONFORMITY

The women's discourse discussed works with the clerical logics of procreation, as can be seen even at the level of components of argumentation. Arshad argues for the same claim (priority of motherhood) and does so using several of Khomeini's grounds (female distinctiveness and women's bond with her children). Both Cahill and Arshad use the same warrants as the clerics to authorize the move from their grounds to claims (the contribution of Catholic teachings to sexual morality and mothers need to physically be with their children) and backings similar to John Paul's (natural law) and Khomeini's (the welfare of children).

But despite these similarities, the women's discourse is structured differently than the clerical rhetoric. Although Cahill uses backings similar to those of John Paul, she adds human rights and feminist discourse on women's equality to radically shift the content of her claim about sexual ethics. And though Arshad is on one level arguing for the priority of motherhood like Khomeini, she does so to encourage a practical political change that is unintended and unanticipated in Khomeini's rhetoric.

In addition to the existence of a relation between the clerics' and women's argumentative components (claims, grounds, warrants, and backings), the women's arguments can also be understood to engage in logical tactics when compared with the clerical rhetoric on themes related to reproductive virtues. This metalevel of discursive interplay among the clerics and women shifts the function of motherhood and reproduction in moral discourse within the community.

First, we observe a tactical engagement through the logic of resolution: a logical tension is identified in clerical rhetoric and resolved in a response. For example, Cahill identifies two logical problems in John Paul's prohibition on contraception (neglect of nonphysical virtues of sex and importance of equality within marriage). Her arguments become suggestions of possible correctives to these conundrums, which moves the conversation about sexual ethics into new territory. For Arshad, the clerical tension related to reproduction is an acutely practical one: by affirming the role of mothers and denying mothers' physical custody after divorce, Khomeini had created an unresolveable tension for women. Arshad works to demonstrate how this tension can begin to be resolved through modification in the civil code.

The women also use the logic of recombination: selecting components of clerical rhetoric to unpack into a different argument or recombine to argue for a different claim. Arshad uses this tactic when she builds an entire argument for woman's right to *ḥiżānat* from the priority of motherhood. Cahill uses it to engage John Paul as well, taking his rhetoric for natural family planning as an opportunity to critique the Roman Catholic Church's ability to be persuasive in American public discourse.

Arshad and Cahill use the logic of specification: applying specific logical requirements to an argument. In both cases the women specify a particular political and cultural audience from which to engage the clerical rhetoric. Cahill's arguments about the unpersuasiveness of Vatican teachings on sexual ethics are the result of considering this rhetoric from within the specific context of contemporary U.S. politics and in particular the public debates over abortion and women's rights. Arashad does not shift the geographic context of Khomeini's rhetoric, but does bring it forward in time. If Khomeini was concerned with justifying an Islamic Revolution and the subsequent stability of an Islamic government, women in the last fifteen years (since Khomeini's death) have been concerned with the imperfect implementation of Khomeini's vision and the challenges faced by operating an Islamic Republic in the geopolitical context of the twenty-first century. Arshad uses the logical strategy of specificity to pose a set of contemporary questions to the Islamic Republic: How can reform on gender issues take place? What is the public dimension of the responsibility of motherhood?

There is the logic of praxis: reworking theoretical arguments into practical ones. This is the logical strategy behind Arshad's leveraging Khomeini's rhetoric against some of its practical applications in the Islamic Republic that impede women's ability to fulfill their moral duties as mothers. Cahill uses an interesting logic of indirection through her engagement with John Paul's rhetoric at a metalevel. Although she begins her argument with natural family planning, in essence she uses the topic of procreation as an opportunity to critique the pope more generally on his moral guidance.

Finally, the women's engagement of the clerical logics of reproduction involves a logic of connectivity: drawing logical connections between different arguments. Cahill highlights how the tendency of some clerics to isolate the physical structure of the act of sex neglects the other dimensions of its virtue (emotional, interpersonal, social). She also emphasizes connectivity in her assertion that we do not think about actions in isolation but rather as situated within a network of actions, beliefs, and reactions. This is why, for Cahill, equality cannot be neglected as virtue within discussions of sexual ethics. Arshad uses the logic of connectivity to link the virtues of motherhood to the rights of physical custody to argue for a necessary reform of civil law based on this intimate connection.

Although Cahill and Arshad share logics in their responses, it is important that not only do the paradigms they offer for motherhood and procreation differ, the types of gaps they tactically leverage are different as well. John Paul is concerned with procreation as it relates to the role of prophylactics within his vision of the ideal family. His focus, therefore, is on conception, and particularly the physical dimensions of reproduction. These predominately biological concerns lead Cahill to question his vision of when women become mothers. She is specifically concerned with the neglect of the unitive dimension of sexuality within the context of the overall sexual life of a couple. In contrast, Khomeini focuses on the sociological implications of procreation, particularly on how child rearing affects the stability of an Islamic Republic in Iran. His central concern is in what ways women can be good mothers. Arshad leverages a gap related to praxis found in his rhetoric: if women are primarily responsible for the moral upbringing of children, custody laws based on shari'a should not give physical custody to fathers after divorce.

THE TACTIC OF FEMINIST PROCREATION

The role of mother is an important reality for many women, and both clerics and women engage this theme when discussing the ethical lives of women. In this chapter I have explored how clerics and women argue about various dimensions of procreation, including how one becomes a mother and the ways in which a good mother is judged. My focus has been on how the arguments interact at the level of informal logics.

Although the women agreed that motherhood is an important topic for moral discourse, they also identified how clerical rhetoric on this issue created a number of tensions. First, this is an issue of definition. In the women's arguments, the discursive import of motherhood is significantly different than that in the clerics'. For John Paul, being a mother is actually a number of behaviors and actions, and his ethical reflection on motherhood is thereby a consideration of the good or bad of discreet acts such as natural family planning. For Khomeini, a mother's moral education of her children is central. For Cahill and Arshad, motherhood is discursively important in different ways.

For one, they add to John Paul's biological concern and Khomeini's sociological concern a focus on the interpersonal dimensions of procreation. For Cahill this is through the relationship of spouses and for Arshad through the relationship of a mother to her young children. In fact, they use the acutely interpersonal embedded nature of motherhood as a discursive advantage: a mother, as embedded within a number of relations (wife-husband, mother-child, daughter-parent), has a unique perspective on interpersonality of the moral life. Cahill's position as a mother and wife become an important source of the production of knowledge, as does Arshad's role as an advocate for children's rights.

Mothers are also understood in a wider context in the women's discourse. Clerics emphasize the importance of the moral education of children. Women extend this, so that the experience of motherhood, or perhaps even the capacity to give birth, gives women access to special ethical knowledge. The role of women as mothers is also metaphorically extended to caregiver on a discursive plane: Cahill and Arshad "care for" the audience by considering its discursive and practical needs. This expands the meaning of mothers as moral teachers: women, as metaphorical mothers, become teachers of the community on a wider scale.

Women use the clerical logic of female essentialism (such as women are more emotional), but twist it for a different effect. For Arshad, women's emotionality is affirmed, but then applied to the legal case of custody. In so doing Arshad has built her argument on a priority of women's custody over men's that can be leveraged in shari'a courts. Women's emotions thus become connections to divine law, one that is missing in clerical *fiqh* and that should be reinserted to guarantee justice. This is no small movement: Arshad has effectively used emotionality to justify a reform of divine law. For Cahill, emotionality is emphasized to thicken our understanding of an action like intercourse: she pushes the clerical rhetoric past its view of the virtues of the physical structure of an act to a consideration of the virtues of emotions related to the act as well. In this way procreation becomes an opportunity to discuss the complexity of all actions.

This leads to a final shift: toward a greater consideration of the complex matrix of ethical issues within which women find themselves embedded. On the one hand, the ethics of motherhood and family can be discussed in isolation, as family values. The women's arguments vehemently deny this approach. For them, motherhood is an example of the acute interdependence of moral issues (equality, chastity, responsibility) and how rights and duties depend on one another and on the rights and duties of others. This makes procreation more complex in moral discourse. It is not just a biological act to be policed. Mothers are not just the caregivers of children. Instead, reproduction and motherhood have symbolic meanings related to pedagogy, emotionality, and the interdependence of moral discourse.

Cahill and Arshad by no means agree on the goals of feminist tactics of procreation. Each argues for a different paradigm for mothers and about a different practical issue. They share, however, in their tactics of procreation an engagement and citation with the clerical logics of motherhood. In both cases there is also an identification of gaps: for John Paul, this gap is logical; for Khomeini, it is practical. But even for the women to leverage these gaps in their own rhetoric they have to accept to some extent the paradigms the clerics work within.

Cahill and Arshad do not deny the ideal of motherhood for women, in fact, they expand the moral importance of this unique embodied experience by arguing that it gives access to ethical knowledge to women. Through their creative conformity the women thus receive traditional norms about motherhood and procreation through clerical rhetoric and use them for their own ends.

NOTES

1. See, for example, Curran, "Marriage, Sexuality, Gender, and Family," 160–201; Cahill, *Sex, Gender & Christian Ethics*.

2. John Paul II, "Faithfulness to the Divine Plan," 395–96; "A Discipline That Ennobles," 399–401.

3. John Paul II, "A Discipline That Ennobles," 399.

4. Ibid., 400.

5. John Paul II, "Faithfulness to the Divine Plan," 396.

6. John Paul writes, "Even though the periodicity of continence in this case is applied to the called 'natural rhythms,' the continence itself is a definite and permanent moral attitude. It is a virtue and therefore the whole line of conduct guided by it acquires a virtuous character." "A Discipline That Ennobles," 400.

7. This ground is also warranted in part by natural law, especially as it related to human desire, and reason's ability to discipline the self: "the virtuous character of the attitude which is expressed in the natural regulation of fertility is determined not so much by fidelity to an impersonal natural law as to the Creator-Person." Ibid., 401.

8. Ibid., 395. Emphasis in the original.

9. Ibid.

10. For an overview of this debate through analysis of the writings of Richard McCormick and Martin Rhonheimer, see Pinches, *Theology and Action*, 59–73. Pinches makes a persuasive case that despite some ambiguous use of the word *intention* in John Paul's *Veritatis splendor*, he can be read as maintaining the importance of human will to the human act that would deny that the object of an act is completely described by "a series of physical movements." Ibid., 69. Nevertheless, John Paul does maintain an important place for the physical structure of acts.

11. John Paul II, "Faithfulness to the Divine Plan," 395.

12. John Paul II, "Responsible Parenthood," 402.

13. Gallup Poll, September 11, 1968, as quoted in Buckley, "Contraception."

14. Gallup Poll, August 11, 1993. Ibid.

15. See, for example, Curran, *Contraception*.

16. Cahill, "Abortion, Sex and Gender," 6–11.

17. Ibid., 10.

18. Ibid.

19. Cahill explains this overly romantic notion of sex as follows: For *Humanae vitae* (and John Paul by extension), "Every act of sexual intercourse is invested with the full weight of the couple's love and relationship, and that weight is pinned, not on the emotional or pleasurable aspects of the act, but on its procreativity, reduced to pristine biological format. . . . The idea that each act is a total self-gift depends upon a very romanticized depiction of sex, and even of marital love. . . . In the *most* ideal of circumstances, human beings rarely if ever accomplish 'total self-gift.'" *Sex, Gender and Christian Ethics*, 203.

20. "I am confident that most Catholic couples would be incredulous at the proposition that the use of artificial birth control necessarily makes their sexual intimacy selfish, dishonest, and unfaithful. Nor is their valuing of parenthood based on their experience of isolated sex acts as having a certain 'procreative' structure. Rather, married love, sexual sharing and shared parenthood are intertwined in a lifetime project that requires sacrifice yet brings bountiful satisfactions and joys." Cahill, "Abortion, Sex and Gender," 10.

21. Ibid., 7.

22. Cahill continues, "For instance, human life is respected cross-culturally, but societies make different exceptions. . . . this means that, while the basic value of life should be unquestioned, there will be unavoidable differences in the way cultures institutionalize protection of life." Ibid., 11.
23. Ibid.
24. Ibid.
25. Ibid.
26. Cahill describes general American sexual morality as follows: "Our culture is not without a sexual morality of its own, and we will need to recognize and reinforce it before we move on to something more complete. Cultural standards of sexual responsibility include consent, communication, respect, honesty, well-deliberated choice about conception and birth, and health." Ibid., 10.
27. Ibid., 11.
28. Davis, *Shahnameh*, xviii–xx.
29. For a summary of the account in English, see Davis, *Shahnameh*, 375–79.
30. Khomeini, "Bayānāt dar jam'-i gurūhī," 150–152.
31. "Shumā khānum ́hā dū tā shughl-i bisyār sharīf dārīd. Yakī shughl-i tarbiyat-i farzand kih īn az hamah-i shughl ́hā bālātar ast." Ibid., 150.
32. "Shughl-i shumā shughl-i insān ́sāzī ast. Mu'allim insān durust mī ́kunad, hamān shughl-i anbiyā' ast." Ibid., 151.
33. "Ma'al-asaf dar ān ḥukūmat-i ṭāghūtī īn shughl rā mī ́khvāstand az īn mādar ́hā bigīrand, tablīgh kardand bih īnkih zan chirā bachchah ́dārī bikunad. Īn shughl-i sharīf rā munhaṭṭash kardand dar naẓar-i mādar ́hā." Ibid.
34. "Ānqadrī kih taḥt-i ta's̲īr-i mādar hastand, taḥt-i ta's̲īr-i pidar nīstand, taḥt-i ta's̲īr-i mu'allim nīstand, taḥt-i ta's̲īr-i ustād nīstand." Ibid.
35. "Vaqtī bachchah dar parvarishgāh va bidūn-i mādar bā ajnabī bikhvāhad sar va kār dāshtah bāshad va muḥabbat-i mādar az sar-i ū kam bishavad, īn bachchah 'uqdah paydā mī ́kunad." Ibid.
36. "Bisyārī az īn mufsidah ́hāyī kih dar jāmi'ah vāqi' mī ́shavad, az īn bachchah ́hāyī hastand kih 'uqdah dārand, az īn insānhāyī hastand kih 'uqdah dārand." Ibid.
37. "Agar chunanchih Khudā-yi nakhvāstah īn bachchah az dāman-i shumā durust az kār dar nayāyad, az taḥt-i tarbiyat-i shumā kih mu'allim hastīd durust az kār dar nayāyad, mumkin ast yak bachchah yak jāmi'ah rā fāsid bikunad va shumā mas'ūl bāshīd." Ibid., 152.
38. "Va bāyad tavajjuh dāshtah bāshīd kih īn bachchah ́hāyī kih pīsh-i shumā tarbiyat mī ́shavand, tarbiyat-i dīnī bishavand, tarbiyat-i akhlāqī bishavand." Ibid.
39. For examples of such sociological studies, see Biabangard and Hatami, "A Study on the Effects of Working Mothers," 11–20; Halimeh Enayat, *The Effects of Employed Mothers*.
40. See, for example, Ebadi, "Reforming Iran," 13.
41. For an in-depth study of Islamic family law, focusing on divorce and marriage, see Mir-Hosseini, *Marriage on Trial*, 54–83.
42. A detailed account of custody law in Iran can be found in Paidar, *Women and the Political Process*, 294–97 and Kar, "Women's Strategies in Iran," 180–1.

43. Paidar, *Women and the Political Process*, 294.

44. *Civil Code of Iran*, Art. 1181.

45. Ibid., Art. 1173: "If the physical health or moral upbringing of the child is endangered by lack of care or moral degradation of the father or the mother who is the custodian, the court may, on the request of the child's relatives, his or her guardian or the public prosecutor, take whatever decision appropriate for the child's custody."

46. Ibid., Art. 1169. Author's translation.

47. The process of reform of this law was by no means easy. In 2001 parliament passed the law after a protracted campaign by a coalition of women's organizations. But, "the Guardian Council, which sits above the legislature, vetoed the bill. The reformists in parliament objected, so it was sent to a higher council, the Expediency Council, for arbitration. The law remained pending there for two years. . . [then] was passed within 15 days." Ebadi, "Reforming Iran," 13.

48. Leila Arshad, interview by the author, Offices of the Society for Protecting the Rights of the Child, Tehran, August 3, 2004.

49. Interestingly, Arshad invoked "scientific studies" numerous times, but when pressed was unable to provide me with copies or citations. The actual existence or nonexistence of such reports is not as important as the fact that Arshad draws on them to strengthen her rhetoric. Similar reports are referenced in note 39.

50. SPRC's mission statement, in English at www.irsprc.org/english.

51. Under the current civil law, mothers have fostering rights, and thereby physical custody, of their children until the age of seven. A child is defined in Article 1210 as one who has not reached puberty. The legal age of puberty is nine years for a girl and fifteen years for a boy. As a result, a girl is in her father's physical custody for only two years, a boy for only eight. This means mothers currently have a right to much longer physical custody of girls, and almost equal length of custody of boys.

CHAPTER THREE

Scripture, Sacred Law, and Hermeneutics

Exploring Gendered Meanings in Textual Records

Sacred texts have a special place in the ethical discourse of communities. For Christians and Muslims they contain road maps for moral living by recording the Word of God or other forms of revelation. For the longevity of a community they become important references for moral continuity and flexibility: although texts themselves remain the same, they must be reinterpreted in the context of modern living. Texts are thereby living archives for the proper practices within a community and opportunities for rethinking these practices in light of new circumstances.

Many texts dealing with ethics assume a fundamental difference between men and women, or what ethicists refer to as a gendered moral anthropology. For this reason, rereading various canons is a strategy women use to transform discursive parameters in traditions. It occurs in the secular academy as major philosophical figures are reconsidered from feminist perspectives.[1] With regard to the foundational scriptures in the Abrahamic traditions, Christian, Muslim, and Jewish women have all engaged in "the theoretical exploration of the exegetical and sociocultural presuppositions of" sacred texts to discover more woman-friendly meanings. [2] This is an example of feminist hermeneutics as a direct strategy. Its goals include correcting biases of male authors, highlighting women's narratives, and building new analogous meanings.

Although the strategic aim of revisiting texts from a woman-centered perspective is to some extent well studied, the concern of this chapter is different: How do women engage textual interpretations on the logical grounds of others? How do authoritative hermeneutics provide opportunities for women to argue for new ideas and practices? In this way, I focus not on how texts are interpreted, but rather on how the logics of textual interpretation are used discursively to form new epistemologies. What ruses are texts engaged for?

This chapter considers clerical rhetoric focused on two sacred texts, the Bible and the codified version of the shari'a in Iran. The two texts are very different: one is understood as the record of Christian revelation and the other is a written national civil and penal code based on interpretation of divine law. They are put into conversation here not as similar genres of texts, but as examples of written ethical codes interpreted using particular methods. It is the method of understanding, not the text, that will become important in identifying women's creative conformity.

It should also be noted that to call any text "shari'a" is misleading. Shari'a best translates as divine law, something that can never be perfectly understood, recorded, or followed. Contemporary Iran, however, is exceptional on this point: in Iran, the constitution, civil code and penal law are all attempts to codify shari'a for a modern nation state. To some extent shari'a has become a written text in Iran in that it has a textual life in politics through its official interpretation and codification by clerics.

The clerical rhetorics analyzed in this chapter do not line up: John Paul focuses on the creation narrative in Genesis 1 and 2, Khomeini on a more general argument about the shari'a and an Islamic Republic as beneficial for women. What they share is a display of textual hermeneutics in their rhetoric, even if the texts and method of hermeneutics are different. Their rhetoric also shares an underlying practical concern—divorce. The Catholic Church prohibits divorce. Shi'i Islam discourages divorce but gives the right exclusively to the man. But divorce is also an interesting way to explore feminist politics for another more conceptual reason. In both traditions marriage is understood as the natural embodiment of sexual complementarity. Divorce becomes significant as a moment of unanticipated and undesirable separation of men and women after a marital state of unity. Exploring rhetoric focused on divorce allows us to see the issues at stake for a given religious community when the "natural" union of a man and woman fails, why the union is important in the first place, and thereby the theological understanding of gender complementarity.

This chapter is divided into two main parts: Catholic and Shi'i. Within each part, clerical rhetoric provides discursive context once broken down into components of its informal logic (claim, grounds, warrants, and so on) and examples of women's tactical responses are described. By way of conclusion I compare the women's discourse to explore how the tactical use of hermeneutics contributes to the production of local ethical knowledge.

ORIGINAL UNITY IN GENESIS 1 AND 2

Shortly after becoming pope, John Paul delivered a series of weekly speeches on the subject of the theology of the body.[3] These general audiences are homiletic, informal, and directed to the common believer rather than to bishops or cardinals. Understood from the position of a woman in the audience or one who read the version later published by the Vatican, these homilies contribute to a discursive context for feminist politics. In this section I consider not only what, but how John Paul argues for a particular gendered anthropology.

John Paul's general audience on the theology of the body can be divided into three thematic groups of meditations of biblical passages: creation, fall, and redemption.[4] The two audiences discussed in this section are from the first group (creation) and they interpret Genesis 1 and 2 in light of Matthew 19:3 and Mark 10:2 to make an argument about the indissolubility of marriage.

John Paul sets the context for his teaching on gender and creation by beginning with Christ's response to the Pharisees' question, "Is it lawful to divorce one's wife?" Christ responds, "Have you not read that he who made them from the beginning made them male and female."[5] John Paul points out how, with this response, Christ effectively shifts the ground of the discussion: "Christ did not accept the discussion at the level at which his interlocutors tried to introduce it. In a certain sense he did not approve of the dimension that they tried to give the problem. He avoided getting caught up in juridico-casuistical controversies. On the contrary, he referred twice to 'the beginning.' Acting in this way, he made a clear reference to the relative words in Genesis."[6] John Paul uses a similar move, claiming that in order to understand why divorce is not permissible, we should reflect on Genesis as the beginning of the theology of the body.

For the sake of rhetorical analysis, this section focuses on the audiences of November 7[7] and November 14[8] in 1979, which reflect on the order of creation of man and woman. For this reason they are especially helpful for considering John Paul's theological, anthropological, and scriptural understanding of gender. Even in these two brief addresses, at least three claims are layered on each other. First, John Paul makes the claim that despite conventional interpretations that Adam is created first in Genesis 2, this text actually discloses that man and woman taken together constitute the image of God in a theology of gender complementarity. In this way John Paul works to rehabilitate the Genesis 2 account of creation from interpretations that see it as either inconsistent with Genesis 1 or as demonstrating the ontological hierarchy of men and women based on their order and manner of creation.

One of John Paul's grounds for this claim (Genesis 2 is consistent with Genesis 1) is that the language in Genesis 2:21–22 (Eve as created from Adam's rib) is an "archaic, metaphorical, and figurative way of expressing the thought."[9] He therefore rereads the account of Eve's creation from Adam's rib allegorically. It is significant, for example, that Adam falls asleep to wake up male and female or *ish* and *ishah*. John Paul suggests that "the analogy of sleep indicates here not so much a passing from consciousness to subconsciousness, as a specific return to non-being. . . . That is, it indicates a return to the moment preceding the creation."[10] In terms of gender, this is a radical suggestion: Adam, man, has no gender. Man must elapse into nonexistence through a metaphorical sleep to be reborn as *ish* and *ishah*, male and female.[11]

Christian women have problematized Genesis 2's account of Eve as created from Adam's rib, arguing that this makes Eve a lesser being because she is formed from a part of Adam's body. The rib is glossed by John Paul, however, as an "archaic, metaphorical and figurative way" of expressing the "homogeneity of the whole being."[12] John Paul thus moves away from the idea that Eve is made from only a part of Adam, and therefore a lesser body, to the idea that the rib represents human embodiment, a characteristic that Adam and Eve share equally.

A second claim John Paul makes in these addresses is that, taken as a whole, Genesis's theology of the body implies an original unity of the sexes, even as it maintains the complementarity of bodily difference. The grounds for this claim are found in a dialectical reading of Genesis 1 and the now reinterpreted Genesis 2. John Paul's informal logic relies here on the warrant that the Bible is internally harmonious and should be read holistically. Therefore, the differences in the two creation accounts point to different aspects of our embodiment. He writes,

> In the first chapter, the narrative of the creation of man affirms directly, right from the beginning, that man was created in the image of God as male and female. The narrative of the second chapter, on the other hand, does not speak of the "image of God." But in its own way it reveals that the complete and definitive creation of "man". . . . is expressed in giving life to that *communio personarum* that man and woman form. In this way, the Yahwist narrative agrees with the context of the first narrative. If, vice versa, we wish to draw also from the narrative of the Yahwist text the concept of "image of God," we can then deduce that man became the "image and likeness" of God not only through his own humanity, but also through the communion of person which man and woman form right from the beginning.[13]

Reading these chapters together, John Paul argues that Genesis 1 is about the creation of human as distinct from other animals, and Genesis 2 explains the two ways of being human in a body: male and female.[14] In this fashion, John Paul emphasizes both what he calls *somatic homogeneity* and *difference in constitution* of creation.[15] Corporation is the same, sexuality is different, and the nature of our true creation is through the unity of both.

This connects to the third claim about a specific action John Paul is trying to motivate his audience to perform as part of the Christian moral life. He argues that the theology of the body "in the beginning," as recorded in Genesis 1 and 2 (claim 1), which has both an ontological original unity and duality (claim 2), has "an axiological meaning" (claim 3).[16] In practice, ontological unity is why marriage is a sacrament and indissoluble. It is only through our union with the opposite sex that we are able to fully participate in the meaning of humanity; it is only as married that we reflect an embodied image of God.[17] At the same time, sexed bodies make a difference for the moral life and John Paul slides between sexuality and gender freely in these addresses. This means that some duties will be woman specific, tailored, for example, to the specifically feminine gifts (gendered) of female bodies (sexed).

This move from ontology to axiology is not explicitly warranted in the text of the addresses, but relies logically on John Paul's understanding of natural law.[18] Drawing on Thomas Aquinas and magisterium teachings, John Paul describes natural law elsewhere as the eternal law, or God's plan, "inscribed in the rational nature of the person."[19] John Paul equates natural law with human nature, which is given ontologically, not historically. This means for John Paul, our nature, if we can discern it, has moral value. This is why Genesis's account, as an account of our original nature, is an insight into God's plan for us.

The first two claims are layered one on top of another in these addresses: original duality and unity. The third claim argues from ontology to morality. What these three claims have in common is that all are warranted by a specific method of biblical interpretation. The Bible, John Paul writes, "must be read in context."[20] He refers to two contexts: an external context (sociocultural context in which it was written and in which it is interpreted) and an internal context (abrogation of passages by passages in different books and chapters). John Paul's calling Genesis 2 a "Yahwist text" demonstrates reliance on historical studies of the Bible, which inform his conception of an author of scripture who uses words metaphorically, as well as the existence of different authors for different texts such as Genesis 1 and 2.[21] There is also an aspect of creativity on the part of the interpretation, which is marked by John Paul's claim that Genesis 2 "in its own way" agrees with the content of Genesis 1. Finally, John Paul's method of biblical hermeneutics is based on the idea that the biblical teachings are holistic and therefore the passages are ultimately reconcilable and not contradictory.[22]

The claims are backed three ways. John Paul's invocation of Christ's response to the Pharisees lets Christ's teaching authority stand as backing for John Paul's entire rhetorical performance. John Paul's use of the Bible is also backed by its central place among the sources of Christian ethics. Last is the Christian tradition's emphasis on natural law, which legitimizes John Paul's use of this source for his gendered moral anthropology.

In terms of qualifications, the theology of the body that John Paul reconstructs might not be a theology for all bodies. It is based on married couples, and it is less clear how it would apply to single men and women, much less widows or widowers, or gay and transgendered individuals. In addition, John Paul's own method of biblical hermeneutics seems to qualify his claims about sacred text. The method requires John Paul to read aspects of Genesis allegorically, and it is unclear why some aspects of the Bible are still being read literally. In fact, John Paul assumes Genesis 1 is much less mythical than Genesis 2 but never gives us a reason. This functions as a logical qualification that the creative work required to use the Bible could lead to mistakes.

Possible responses are created by the internal logic of these rhetorical performances as well. For example, the method of biblical hermeneutics is never fully explained but instead simply deployed. This creates an opportunity for a different reading of Genesis 1 and 2 based on a different method. The same can be said of John Paul's particular understanding of natural law. Finally, because an interest in shoring up the indissolubility of marriage frames John Paul's entire discussion, to some extent he uses the Bible to explicate his vision of the moral life. The process of biblical study does not seem to shift his theology of the body, but is rather an opportunity to assert it. This creates a possible response that would bring to the text a different ethical concern and thereby adopt John Paul's tactic of persuasion without accepting his specific claims.

REVISITING CONSCIENCE THROUGH LATINA LIBERATION

The author of this section's discursive practice is Ada María Isasi-Díaz, an activist-theologian. Isasi-Díaz was born in Cuba and brought up in a Catholic home. She left Cuba as a political refugee in 1960, entered a convent, and later traveled to Peru as a missionary. After earning a master's in divinity and a doctorate in Christian ethics at Union Theological Seminary, she became active in the Las Hermanas, a U.S. Latina-based Catholic group.[23] In 1998, with the national coordinator of Las Hermanas, Yolanda Tarango, Isasi-Díaz published the first book on American Latina theology, what Isasi-Díaz would later name *mujerista theology*. According to a definition Isasi-Díaz publishes in English and Spanish on her website, "A *mujerista* is someone who makes a preferential option for Latina women, for their struggle for liberation. . . . Mujerista theology, which includes both ethics and theology, is a liberative praxis that has as its goal liberation."[24]

Isasi-Díaz has said definitively that John Paul is not a direct source for mujerista theology. She is emphatic, in fact, that papal teachings are not relevant to Latina women. But she has also said that "the magisterium influences mujerista theology in so far as it influences me and I usually submit the teachings. . . to the main criterion of mujerista theology: liberation/fullness of life/flourishing of Latina women."[25] There is thus an engagement with, if not a deference to, clerical rhetoric. In this section I am concerned with understanding what happens to clerical logic when it is submitted to mujerista criteria.

To put Isasi-Díaz into conversation with John Paul, this section focuses on her biblical study of Genesis 1:26–2:3, which she delivered orally at the Tenth International Christian Women's Fellowship Quadrennial Assembly in 1994.[26] John Paul in not expressly invoked in her study, but the subject matter is similar to his homily on Genesis 1 and 2. In some ways focusing on Isasi-Díaz's biblical hermeneutics is a circuitous way to analyze mujerista ethics because she has argued that the Bible is not a central source for *mujerista* theology because Latinas "seldom read the Bible and know instead popularized versions of biblical stories—versions Latinas create to make a point."[27] Yet at the 1994 event she delivered four substantial biblical reflections.[28] In an attempt to read her rhetoric through her assertion that the Bible is tactically referenced by Latinas, I focus here on how Isasi-Díaz invokes biblical stories to make a point.

In her study of Eve, Isasi-Díaz builds three interconnected claims. The first is that "in our woman-ness we image God . . . not only in what we share with men: intellect, will, intelligence, soul. We also image God in our bodies."[29] Thus, like John Paul, Isasi-Díaz makes the existence of sexed bodies theologically significant. However, in contrast to John Paul, she emphasizes original sexual difference, not an original unity.

Her ground for this claim is the creation of men and women in Genesis 1. She considers the original Hebrew, as John Paul does with Genesis 2, to refute that women were created as an afterthought, derived from men, and thereby somehow lesser. According to Isasi-Díaz, the reference to male and female (*zakhar u-neqevah*) in Genesis 1 is a clarification of God's creation of humankind (*adam*), not an account of a second action on God's part.[30]

As in John Paul's rhetoric, the move from grounds to claim is warranted by an approach to biblical hermeneutics. In Isasi-Díaz's rhetoric, this is an expressly *mujerista* biblical hermeneutic,[31] the legitimacy of which is the subject of a second claim Isasi-Díaz makes in 1994: scripture should be submitted to the needs of Hispanic women. She writes, "we use the Bible when we need it, for what we need it, in the manner we need it."[32] The method of biblical hermeneutics in Isasi-Díaz's study of Eve takes the perspective of Hispanic women readers as its starting point: "On this, the first full day of the assembly, we look at Eve, or rather, we look at how we look at Eve. When we read the stories of Eve, what do we want to know? Why do we read the story of creation, the story of Eve? What do we see? Who is Eve for us? What does she say to us today?"[33]

Because of her focus on the Latina reader, Isasi-Díaz's conceptualization of the Latina reality can help us understand what to expect from her reading of Genesis. Latina reality, she asserts, is marked by *la lucha*, the struggle for survival and liberation of a Latina woman for herself and her community, and the lived experience as *mestizaje* (mixture). This *mestizaje* is an integral aspect of Latina "racial/ethnic cultural reality."[34] It is experienced as a difference from the dominant culture in the United States, and sometimes as a negation of the specificity of Hispanic women.[35] Because these two Latina realities (*la lucha* and *mestizaje*) ground *mujerista* biblical hermeneutics, Isasi-Díaz reads the Bible with a particular eye toward struggles for liberation, as well as different sorts of women encountering different sorts of realities.[36]

The move from the grounds (*la lucha* and *mestizaje*) to the claim for a mujerista form of biblical hermeneutics is warranted by the assumption that the practice of mujerista biblical interpretation contributes to the process of Latina moral agency. As Isasi-Díaz puts it, "For mujerista theology the enablement and enhancement of moral agency go hand-in-hand with a process of conscientization, an ongoing process of critical reflection on action that leads to a radical awareness of oppressive structures and their interconnectedness. In this critical process the Bible should be used to learn how to learn."[37]

The use of the Bible here is not to learn what to do, but to learn how to learn what to do. If John Paul uses Genesis to develop a theology of the body, Isasi-Díaz approaches it as an opportunity for posing questions that might help a Latina expand the boundaries of what she is able to do as a moral agent. This warrant is also the third claim in Isasi-Díaz's rhetoric: the priority of Hispanic women's conscience over other sources of moral truth.[38]

Isasi-Díaz rhetorically prioritizes conscience based on one ground: it is a Hispanic woman's direct access to moral truth. It is therefore ultimately women's conscience, what Isasi-Díaz calls the Word of God in Us, that is reliable, more so than external, textual, institutional, or clerical teachings about the moral truth.[39] She thus attempts to theorize a direct relationship between the human and the divine through conscience.

Isasi-Díaz is an interesting test of the range of actions that can be categorized as creative conformity because she is not only or ever primarily responding to John Paul's rhetoric. Creative conformity is only one form among others of her feminist politics. Nevertheless, we can identify how she draws on and shifts components of John Paul's logic through partial citation to transform his vision about the moral life for Catholic women. Despite her statements elsewhere that the Bible is not an important source of mujerista ethical understanding, her biblical study of Genesis is on its surface a conventional way to reflect on the moral life of Christian women. Like John Paul, Isasi-Díaz uses the first woman, Eve, and the Genesis account of her creation as the starting point for her reflection. She makes at least one claim almost identical to a claim of John Paul: Eve is not created after Adam, and therefore it is incorrect to deduce an order of creation, or a cosmic inequity between the sexes from the Genesis account. At stake for both John Paul and Isasi-Díaz is that women participate equally and fully in the image of God and that Genesis must reflect this. They share a concern for the ontological distinction between the sexes, and its significance for the moral life. Isasi-Díaz also relies on one ground similar to John Paul's—Genesis 1—and warrants her move from this ground to her claim with a method of biblical interpretation. Her method has in common with John Paul's its attention to the original Hebrew of the text. She shares with John Paul a moral vocabulary as well as an audience. Finally, they both bring practical concerns to the biblical text: John Paul is motivated by the issue of divorce, Isasi-Díaz with Latina struggle.

We can see how Isasi-Díaz's rhetoric is similar in its logical form to John Paul's. Because both rhetorical performances focus on the Bible, we might assume that the Bible is the primary source for their visions of the moral life. In truth, John Paul is arguing for the magisterium mediation of the biblical message, and Isasi-Díaz for the place of the Bible in the process of Latina conscientization. The Bible is primary for neither. For John Paul, Roman Catholic tradition is primary, especially as found in natural law, and for Isasi-Díaz it is Latina *lucha*. The Bible is merely an opportunity for both to showcase their visions of womanhood. So, despite Isasi-Díaz's claim that the magisterium and John Paul are not sources for mujerista ethics, her use of scripture in rhetorical argument is very close in form to John Paul's, even if very different in content.

Despite these commonalities in their reflections on Genesis, their rhetoric is different in several ways. For example, Isasi-Díaz moves from John Paul's claim about women imaging God in union with men (original unity) to a discussion of how women alone image God. This stems in part from her practical concern with Latina struggle for liberation versus John Paul's concern with the practical issue of divorce. But it also means for Isasi-Díaz, even more than for John Paul, that sexual difference is ontologically significant.

Isasi-Díaz completely ignores Genesis 2's account of Eve being created from Adam's rib, in contrast to John Paul, who spends substantial time harmonizing the Genesis 1 and Genesis 2 accounts. This highlights a significant difference between John Paul's and Isasi-Díaz's biblical hermeneutics. John Paul assumes internal harmony of the text, and reads Genesis 1 and 2 dialectically, with the help of Roman Catholic teachings on natural law. For Isasi-Díaz, biblical harmony is a nonissue. She approaches the text from the perspective of reflecting on what meaning it might have for a Latina woman in the context of her search for fullness.

John Paul uses Genesis 1 and 2 to elaborate an ontological meaning of gender in order to say something axiological about it.[40] Isasi-Díaz works in exactly the opposite direction: she explicitly starts with an axiological concern, affirming and contributing to Latina's moral agency, and looks to Genesis for ontological grounding. At every point of her study of Genesis 1:26, Hispanic women are her touchstone.

Isasi-Díaz's third claim, that women's conscience should be prioritized over the Bible, transforms John Paul's rhetoric. A deeper look at conscience within Catholic moral theology will make Isasi-Díaz's shift more clear. Conscience is sometimes taken as a synonym for morality, or even morality according to the super ego, in the popular mind.[41] However, the term *conscience* in Catholic moral theology is considerably more complicated. Catholic moral theologians like Dennis Billy, James Keating, Timothy O'Connell, Germain Grisez, and even Thomas Aquinas conceptualize conscience as a threefold capacity, process, and judgment.[42] Conscience as a capacity is the universal human sense of value and differentiation of good and bad.[43] For John Paul, this capacity is a marker of our human dignity.[44] In other words, one dimension of conscience is as God's law written on our souls. A second dimension is related to the human process of practical moral reasoning because each believer exercises their habituated conscience in light of empirical knowledge and social context.[45] Rather than being universal, this dimension of conscience is different among various individuals. Finally, conscience entails an event of final judgment about the concrete norms that guide a person's action. It is the moment we express our free will. The judgment of conscience is true (*vera*) if it corresponds to the objective truth; erroneous (*erronea*) if it does not. Consider the relationship between the three dimensions of conscience in the following paragraph of *Veritatis splendor*: "Although each individual has a right to be respected in his own journey in search of the truth [process], there exists a prior moral obligation [capacity], and a grave one at that, to seek the truth and to adhere to it [judgment] once it is known."[46] In this way, the colloquial admonition to "follow your conscience" means a human being who knows there is right and wrong (capacity), must constantly search for what is right (process), and ultimately do what she judges to be right (judgment).

At first blush, Isasi-Díaz's understanding of conscience may seem consistent with John Paul's understanding. However, a closer look reveals that Isasi-Díaz actually proposes a radical transformation. First, she rejects an understanding of conscience as an innate human capacity.[47] She proposes instead what she calls a wholistic view of conscience as awareness of one's own moral agency.[48] In terms of conscience as a process, Isasi-Díaz moves away from John Paul's understanding of the magisterium's role in assisting believers in understanding and reasoning about the moral law to an internal process in which the agent works to develop her own moral consciousness. In this way, Isasi-Díaz refutes what she calls attempts to "subordinate conscience to obedience to Rome" that "disempowers Hispanic women in our attempt to strength our moral agency."[49] Finally, whereas for John Paul the judgment of conscience is accountable to moral truth, for Isasi-Díaz conscientization aims to strengthen Latina moral agency to assist their struggle against oppression.[50] Conscience thus conceptualized is accountable to Latina liberation and nothing else. This means conscience is something very different for Isasi-Díaz than for John Paul: an awareness of subjective agency versus an awareness of objective moral truth.

GENDER COMPLEMENTARITY AND THE CODIFICATION OF DIVORCE

One of the common themes in Khomeini's rhetoric is women's status in Islam, which he often links to their status in shari'a. Take, for example, an address Khomeini gave at his home in Qom on March 6, 1979.[51] His comments on that day were brief, and once transcribed, fill only two pages. In a telltale sign of epideictic rhetoric, Khomeini begins with praise of women's participation in the Islamic Revolution: "Beloved and courageous sisters, you fought shoulder-to shoulder with the men and ensured the victory of Islam."[52] He calls these women "lion-hearted" and declares, "I take pride in all the courageous deeds accomplished by the women of Iran."[53] This praise is a clever setup to the explicit claim of the speech, mainly that women have a duty to ensure the success of the Islamic Republic: "Just as you have participated in our revolutionary movement, indeed played a basic role in it, now you must also participate in its triumph, and must not fail to rise up again whenever it is necessary."[54] Because Khomeini is trying to shore up general female support for the Islamic Revolution, his primary ground for persuasion is that Islam is beneficial to women: "Islam made women equal with men;

in fact, it shows a concern for women that it does not show for men."[55] It is therefore in women's own interest to support the Islamic Republic, whose constitution, penal law, and civil code all derive from shari'a.

However, Khomeini's conception of equality between the sexes in shari'a law is quite different from what equality means in mainstream secular-liberal discourse. His understanding draws from the work of the prominent Ayatollah Murtaza Mutahhari. In 1975 Mutahhari wrote,

> In Islamic doctrine, man and woman are both human beings and enjoy equal rights, but what matters to Islam is that since man and woman are not by creation or nature the same, they also vary in regard to some rights, duties, and punishments. Today the western world is trying to make man and woman equal with regard to all rules, regulations, rights and duties disregarding the innate and natural differences between them. Therefore, the dispute in our country between those who support Islamic rights on the one hand and those who are for western systems on the others, is over the uniformity and similarity of the social roles of women and men rather that women's rights. And the phrase "equal rights" is a deceitful term which had been chosen to suggest the parity of roles in society.[56]

Khomeini dismisses identical rights and duties for men and women as a Western idea, foreign to Islam. Within the shari'a, Khomeini argues, women and men are equal insofar as justice demands. But this equality is not to be confused with similarity. Making them the same under the law would be unjust.[57]

Using a Sufi anthropology of sorts, Khomeini argues that Islam is good for women because it both acknowledges their spiritual equality and their material difference, thereby providing appropriate legal rights and duties for the moral life.[58] The secular-liberal argument that there should be no difference between women and men as legal entities, according to Khomeini, is observably false. Men and women are physically different and these material differences correspond to different moral responsibilities. In spiritual terms, however, men and women are the same. Both can spiritually evolve and are equal in the eyes of God. In this way, even if gender is morally neutral for Khomeini (men are not better than women), the moral life is gendered because gender is the marker for material difference.

Khomeini authorizes the step from "Islam is good for women" to "the Islamic Republic is good for women" with the warrant that Islam must be institutionalized in the form of a government for all its benefits, including those for women, to be fully enjoyed. This warrant is also the explicit claim argued for in his major treatise, *Islamic Government*.[59] However, in the 1979 Qom speech, delivered to a group of women who supported the

Islamic Revolution (at least to an extent that they were invited to the Ayatollah's home), Khomeini does not state this warrant directly. He is, however, explicit about the backing for this warrant: the Iranian experience has demonstrated that the collusion of Islam and politics creates transformations that benefit women. He provides two examples. Referring to the situation of women in pre-Islamic Arabia, Khomeini reminds the audience of the status given to women by Muhammad in the early years of Islam, and the roles in public life that women enjoyed in the early Muslim community: "In the earliest age of Islam women participated in wars together with the men."[60] Second, Khomeini refers to his favorite rhetorical strawman, the Shah, to show how women are better off under the Islamic government: "The repressive regime of the Shah wanted to transform our warrior women into pleasure-seekers, but God determined otherwise."[61]

This 1979 speech contains a secondary claim, which is signaled by the phrase "there is one particular question to which attention should be paid,"[62] and to which Khomeini devoted almost a third of his remarks that day: women have a limited right to divorce in shari'a. His comments on divorce are particularly interesting because this theme is less common in his addresses than the status of women in shari'a or the importance of women supporting the Islamic Revolution. This uniqueness suggests that it is most likely the primary claim made in the speech.

At this point an overview of Shi'i teachings on divorce and Iranian divorce law is helpful to isolate Khomeini's particular vision of the norms for marriage. Generally speaking, the *Ithnā 'Asharī* (Twelver) school of Shi'i law is followed in Iran, within which marriage is conceived as a contract, and the right to terminate held predominately by the man. The extra-juridical right of divorce, called *talāq* (repudiation), is based on the Qur'an (2:229–2:230), and historically did not require a judge at all. A man needed simply to declare to his wife "I divorce you," three times and the divorce was enacted.[63] In this way a simple discursive practice could create a major rupture between the assumed natural union of a woman and man.

Until the beginning of the twentieth century, all family law, including divorce and marriage, was administered by shari'a courts in Iran. In these courts Islamic jurists decided cases, and family law during the period was not codified. The first codification of laws related to marriage and divorce was initiated by Reza Shah Pahlavi. Between 1928 and 1935, an Iranian Civil Code was written that attempted to follow the jurisprudence used in the shari'a courts, changing only slightly things like the age of consent to marriage (from nine to thirteen for girls). But the form of the law was radically changed with codification, from a fluid, flexible, and unpredictable procedure to a fixed and predictable written code.[64] It is ironic that after

is also behind the title of the journal *Farzānah*, which is the feminine noun meaning *a wise person*, implying that essays published within will reflect the special wisdom of women.

This second claim (that women have access to special religious knowledge) is most explicit in final paragraph of the editorial: "One final word. *Farzānah* is a prophet and a messenger to the intellectuals. We also expect the intellectuals will correct us in their writings. . . . We invite the great people in the world of religion and knowledge to our strange land [of women's studies]."[91] Here she asks for advice and critique from religious leaders but also invites them to enter the unfamiliar space of feminine epistemology of which women are pioneers. A bold claim is implied: clerics have something to learn from women's studies.

With this second claim, the meaning of grounds and warrants identified in the editorial also changes. The ground that women have a lower status is shifted to the ground that conditions that would make women's flourishing possible are not currently realized. The ground that women's lower status has a negative impact on the Islamic Republic in the context of the secondary claim means that the community's morality is jeopardized by its treatment of women. The ground that current perceptions of women's nature are distorted can be seen in light of the second claim as an implicit critique of the primary expositors of women's nature: the clerics. If Iranian Shi'i perceptions of women's nature are wrong, they are wrong because those who have been in charge of conveying knowledge have misinterpreted Islam. The ground that women's studies must be local is morphed slightly in the second claim to imply that women themselves are the best sources for knowledge about women. The warrant for the first claim was simply that research focused on women can produce knowledge about women's nature. In the second claim this becomes the assertion that women's studies is religiously and ethically important.

Abbas-Gholizadeh's first claim (the necessity for women's studies) is not qualified. Here she is on the safe ground of pure research: women's studies as important scholarship is not particularly contentious. Her second claim (women's special religious knowledge) appears qualified given its obtuse presentation. But the actual logical structure of the secondary claim does not include modal qualifiers: Abbas-Gholizadeh is emphatic that women do have something to offer to religious and ethical reflection.

Consider now Abbas-Gholizadeh's rhetoric as a response to Khomeini's claim for the importance of women supporting the Islamic Republic and their responsibility in ensuring their Islamic rights. Abbas-Gholizadeh's first claim (the necessity for women's studies) does not map perfectly onto Khomeini's rhetoric, but it does respond to his argument that Islam supports women and women thereby have a duty to support the Republic. Abbas-Gholizadeh implies that Islamic teachings on women are being misinterpreted in regards to women, thereby making a distinction between Islam and cultural patriarchy that has affected how shari'a is codified. Moreover, she argues that because the Republic is hurt by misperceptions about women's nature, women's studies is actually an activity that supports the Republic. In response to Khomeini's secondary claim that women need to ensure their own rights, Abbas-Gholizadeh suggests a concrete way to do so: women's studies and research.

Khomeini's presumption about gender complementarity is also shifted by this editorial. Abbas-Gholizadeh grants that equality does not necessarily mean identical treatment of women and men, but rejects the clerical reasons offered for the different treatment and provides her own. One important premise of women's studies is that women are different from men, but Abbas-Gholizadeh turns this differentiation into a justification for women's special wisdom and women's studies as a way to access and grow this wisdom. Once Islam becomes the public standard for all truth and knowledge in Iran after the Islamic Revolution, all academic endeavors, including women's studies, fall within its arena of concern. If gender-based research is to be judged by Islam, Abbas-Gholizadeh argues that it also contributes to our understanding of Islamic teachings, especially on women. This can be seen to foreshadow her argument in later work for the importance of drawing on extrareligious sources for *ijtihad*: women's studies bring new scholarship into public discourse, under the umbrella of Islam, which encompasses all truth. Because according to Abbas-Gholizadeh women's studies are also interdisciplinary, she bridges the religious and secular worlds by arguing that both sacred and profane sources contribute to the production of ethical knowledge important for Muslim women.[92]

SUMMARY OF CREATIVE CONFORMITY

The women analyzed in this chapter use logical components in their rhetoric that are similar to those John Paul and Khomeini used. We saw Isasi-Díaz argue for the same claim (women are created in the image of God) and both Isasi-Díaz and Abbas-Gholizadeh use some of the grounds of the clerics (Genesis 1 and female distinctiveness). Isasi-Díaz uses the same warrant as John Paul to authorize the move from her grounds to claim (a method of biblical interpretation). Both women deploy the textual backings of the clerics (the Bible and shari'a as codified in Iran). A further similarity between the structure of Khomeini's and Abbas-Gholizadeh's rhetoric is the layering of arguments within arguments. In Khomeini's rhetoric, claims are either unstated or buried in his speech; Abbas-Gholizadeh also presents a two-part argument, making one direct claim and another indirect one.

Although the women do draw on specific components of clerical rhetoric in their responses, they also shift the logical form of that rhetoric on two levels: logical structure (architectonics), and logical tactics (logics). At the level of architectonics (claim, grounds, warrants, backings, and qualifiers), the women rearrange and reconceptualize components of clerical rhetoric. When Abbas-Gholizadeh incorporates the same grounds as Khomeini, such as gender complementarity, she does so for different aims. Although Isasi-Díaz begins her reflection on women as created in the image of God with a Genesis account of creation, unlike John Paul, she is unconcerned with internal biblical harmony.

In addition to these issues of architectonics, the women's creative conformity shifts the conversation about the gendered moral life in several logical ways. In the introduction, I defined the analytical category of logics as the general tactics of discursive practice within a community, which I argued was necessary to get at the intellectual coherence of women's creative conformity. They can be used at this point to understand women's discourse as not merely linguistic or argumentative actions, but as also transformative of the tradition. Although the specific content of these shifts is decisively different for Isasi-Díaz and Abbas-Gholizadeh, who are engaging different clerics, on different themes, in different contexts, the categories of tactics they practice are surprising similar. I identify five.

In the women's discursive practice we can observe the use of the logic of specification: applying specific requirements to an argument. This was the logic behind the shifts to the Latina context and the post-Khomeini Iranian context. Where John Paul's rhetorical performances assume a more universal Catholic audience, Isasi-Díaz's is articulating a vision of the gendered moral life in the United States for Latina women. This requires her to focus on a number of issues, unanticipated by John Paul's rhetoric, including *la lucha* and *mestizaje*. Abbas-Gholizadeh uses a similar tactical logic in her specification of contemporary Iran. If Khomeini was concerned with justifying an Islamic Revolution and the subsequent stability of an Islamic government, Abbas-Gholizadeh is concerned with the imperfect implementation of Khomeini's vision and the challenges faced by operating an Islamic Republic in the geopolitical context of the late twentieth century. Abbas-Gholizadeh's use of the logic of specification means she is able to interrogate the official shari'a stance on women's rights and duties while considering a larger role of women in informing this stance.

A related tactic is the logic of redefinition: redefining a concept central to the moral reasoning on a particular issue. Isasi-Díaz uses this approach in redefining conscience, which allowed her to move discussion from the role of the magisterium in the formation of conscience to the actions of

Latinas as expression of conscience. Isasi-Díaz understands conscience to be our direct access to divine truth, the Word of God in us. This is a radical reconceptualization of the human-divine relationship when compared with John Paul, who emphasizes the importance of the Roman Catholic Church in making God's Word intelligible to believers. For Abbas-Gholizadeh, women's studies are redefined as politically and religiously necessary science that will help correct the past shortcomings of government in Iran. Through defining women's studies, she also implies a radical redefinition of shari'a as something that should be informed by interdisciplinary scholarship, not just mullah-driven interpretation of the classical sources.

Both women use a logic of perfection to counter moral guidance that they perceive to be bad for women. Because God (and by extension the true message of Catholicism or Shi'i Islam) is perfect, God's moral teachings for us would never command something antithetical to women's flourishing. This logic provides a way to reject patriarchal teaching as cultural innovation and is behind Abbas-Gholizadeh's insistence on a distinction between Islam and culture patriarchy. Khomeini argues that Islam supports women, benefits women, and guarantees women's rights. Abbas-Gholizadeh accepts this presumption and applies it to a formal logical syllogism: if (A) Islam is good for women and (B) something exists that is not good for women then (C) that thing is not Islamic. This allows her to indirectly critique ways shari'a has been codified in Iran.

Another logic used is the logic of distinction: establishing a clear division between two or more concepts central to moral reasoning on a particular issue. For Isasi-Díaz, the central distinction is one of Latina difference, or *mestizaje*. This tactic allows her to assert that Latinas will have a different moral perspective than that of the dominant culture in the United States, thereby making *la lucha* an important source for feminist politics.

We see in both women's arguments the logic of reversal of order: turning the order of the logical structure on its head. Instead of moving from ontology (original unity) to axiology (no divorce) like John Paul, Isasi-Díaz begins with axiology (*la lucha*) and develops an ontology (women are created in the image of God). For Khomeini, the logical order is from shari'a to women's proper action. For Abbas-Gholizadeh, the reversal is quite daring: her argument for women's studies is based on the logic that shari'a can be informed by women's experience.

Finally, central to both women is the logic of praxis: reworking theoretical arguments into practical ones. For Isasi-Díaz, the logic of praxis means a shift in attention to *la lucha*; for Abbas-Gholizadeh, it is a shift to women's studies, which focuses on women's lived experiences, as a way to abrogate shari'a. This shift is manifested in the types of grounds both the women use (women's experiences), their warrants (women as moral agents, priority of individual conscience), as well as their moral concerns.

THE TACTIC OF FEMINIST HERMENEUTICS

The tactic of feminist hermeneutics contributes to the production of ethical knowledge on a number of levels. At the practical level, women's discourse does not envision divorce as a rupture or as creating a situation of anxiety in the same way as the rhetoric they are responding to. For clerics, divorce becomes significant as a moment of unanticipated and undesirable separation of men and women after a martial state of unity. Women's discourse for the most part ignores the issue of divorce and the conception of ontological significant gender and sexual difference the clerics tie it to. Instead, women focus on the clerical methods of textual interpretation, which, as discussed, they critique and reform. To the extent that they deal with similar practical issues as the clerics, it is on how the separation of men and women allows us to better isolate women's unique ethical voices, whether through *mujerista* theology or women's studies. This ignores the clerical and predominantly ontological concerns for what the women see as more pressing axiological ones.

A significant shift takes place in women's tactics of feminist hermeneutics with the relationships of text, reading, and interpretation to moral knowledge. Clerics view texts as depositories of moral knowledge, and engage them in attempts to understand the lessons a specific text can provide for a given situation: whether the meaning of the sacrament of marriage or the parameters of divorce. But the purpose of the text for feminist politics seems markedly different. For Isasi-Díaz and Abbas-Gholizadeh, the sacred texts are not only or even primarily depositories of moral knowledge. Instead they become vehicles to engage women's moral praxis.

There is also a shift in how the women "read" the texts. For Isasi-Díaz, reading the Bible is a practice aimed at how to learn about the moral life. For Abbas-Gholizadeh, the codified shari'a is one source of moral knowledge among many, to be critically correlated with women's studies. Women's engagement with the texts is not to uncover what they say, but rather is an opportunity to test the tradition's canon through women's experiences. This means that ultimately feminist hermeneutics interpret not written texts, but women's experiences. The depository of moral knowledge is women's practice, and the sacred texts are merely ways to help us understand that practice. This is why the clerical interpretations may be misinformed: they can neglect *la lucha* or overlay cultural patriarchy onto the tradition.

Finally, the feminist tactics of hermeneutics discussed in this chapter imply that women's moral knowledge is beyond codification in a fixed textual form. It is the clerics, not the women, who are the writers and keepers of the sacred texts of the traditions. In this way, men's moral knowledge is codified in text. In the tactics of feminist hermeneutics, the women privilege knowledge beyond the confines of the written page through an ongoing process of searching for moral truth.

NOTES

1. See, for example, the Re-Reading the Canon series published by Pennsylvania State University Press. This series consists of edited collections offering feminist interpretations of major figures in the Western philosophical tradition, including Aristotle, David Hume, Immanuel Kant, Jacques Derrida, Michel Foucault, Plato, and Theodor Adorno.

2. Schüssler Fiorenza, *But She Said*, 20. Although certainly women have always read the Bible, prominent feminist biblical scholar Elisabeth Fiorenza argues that this reading had historically been done within the "theological or spiritual frameworks articulated by elite men." Ibid.

3. John Paul's general audiences took place in 1979 and 1984. Some of these preceded *Familiaris consortio* (1981), and can be thereby understood as a more informal working out of the moral anthropology behind this later document. The addresses can be read as a complete collection in John Paul II's *The Theology of the Body*.

4. These three groups of meditations correspond to three sets of biblical reflections: Matthew 19:3 and Mark 10:2; The Sermon on the Mount (Matthew 5:8); and Future Resurrection (Matthew 22:24–30; Mark 12:18–27; Luke 20:27–36).

5. John Paul II, "The Unity and Indissolubility of Marriage," 25.

6. Ibid., 25–26.

7. John Paul II, "The Original Unity," 42–45.

8. John Paul II, "By the Communion of Persons," 45–48.

9. John Paul II, "The Original Unity," 44.

10. Ibid.

11. Although John Paul translates the Hebrew *ish* and *ishah* as male and female, they are more commonly translated as man and woman. The Hebrew used in Genesis 1, *zakhar u-neqevah,* is commonly translated as male and female.

12. John Paul II, "The Original Unity," 44.

13. John Paul II, "By the Communion of Persons," 46.

14. John Paul writes, "Their unity denotes above all the identity of human nature; their duality, on the other hand, manifests what, on the basis of this identity, constitutes the masculinity and femininity of created man." Ibid., 45.

15. John Paul II, "The Original Unity," 44.

16. John Paul II, "By the Communion of Persons," 45.

17. John Paul writes, "This structure is presented right from the beginning with a deep consciousness of human corporality and sexuality, and that establishes an inalienable norm for the understanding of man on the theological plane." Ibid., 48.

18. For an overview and critique of John Paul's theory of natural law see Curran, *The Moral Theology*, 112–22. For an excellent study of natural law and feminism, see Traina, *Feminism and Natural Law*.

19. John Paul II, *Veritatis splendor*, para. 5.

20. John Paul II, "The Original Unity," 44.

21. Ibid., 43.

22. John Paul II's method of biblical interpretation is greatly influenced by St. John of the Cross, the subject of his first doctorate. The method is grounded on the conviction that God's grace is unchanging and univocal, which leads to an understanding of the internal harmony of scripture as well as the enduring nature of its message. See Ahern, "The Use of Scripture," 11–12.

23. Latinos make up at least 40 percent of the American Catholic church, but are underrepresented in the official leadership, making up only 3.8 percent of American priests. Las Hermanas attempts to respond to this marginalization as "a network of women's groups united to empower themselves and others to participate actively in prophetic, loving transformation of Church and society through sharing riches of Hispanic culture, language, spirituality, and traditions." Las Hermanas USA Mission Statement, as printed on registration form for the Las Hermanas 25th National Assembly, "Dichosa Mujer," October 7–9, 2005, San Antonio, Texas. Las Hermanas engages clerical policy and teachings out of "a keen awareness of the influence of Catholicism on gender expectations within Latino cultures." Medina, *Las Hermanas*, 10.

24. From the definition of *mujerista* published in English and Spanish on Isasi-Díaz's website, http://users.drew.edu/aisasidi/Definition1/htm.

25. Ada María Isasi-Díaz, correspondence with author, May 7, 2006.

26. The written form of the studies are cited here, published as Isasi-Díaz, *Women of God, Women of the People*, 11–30.

27. Isasi-Díaz and Tarango, *Hispanic Women*, 66.

28. In addition to the study of Eve discussed in this section, this collection includes three other studies: "A Widow Who Believes in Herself: Luke 18:1–8;" "The Woman with the Flow of Blood: Matthew 9:20–22; Mark 5:25–34; Luke 8:43–48;" and "Mary—Woman of God, Woman of the People: Luke 1:46–55." Isasi-Díaz, *Women of God, Women of the People*.

29. Ibid., 27.

30. Ibid., 26–27. Isasi-Díaz quotes Phyllis Trible, her former professor at Union Theological Seminary in this passage. Trible, *God and the Rhetoric of Sexuality*, 15–21.

31. Schüssler Fiorenza identifies ten approaches to feminist hermeneutics. Three are exemplified by the rhetorical performance analyzed in this section: (1) text and translation; in which the texts are retranslated, or compared to other manuscripts, all out of a concern with the androcentric character of biblical texts; (2) imaginative identification, in which biblical stories where women are silenced or not present at all get retold in ways that help women to personally identify with them; and (3) women as subjects of interpretation, in which how gender, race, and class affect the way we read is emphasized. Schüssler Fiorenza, *But She Said*, 21–37. *Mujerista* hermeneutics is concerned with retranslation, as we saw operative in the

first claim, but also with personal identification of Latinas with the biblical stories, as well as how Latinas as readers of the texts affects the way they interpret the text.

32. Isasi-Díaz, *Women of God, Women of the People*, 14.

33. Ibid., 25–26.

34. Isasi-Díaz, *En la Lucha*, 186.

35. Ibid., 188.

36. This last point is particularly interesting given the subject matter of this study (the Genesis 1 account of woman's creation). Given Isasi-Díaz's commitment to *mestizaje*, the vision of human creation as simply two-part, man and woman, is itself problematic, as she asserts a crucial diversity within the category of woman. Yet this tension is never addressed in her biblical study.

37. Isasi-Díaz, *Women of God, Women of the People*, 18–19.

38. Isasi-Díaz refers to this elsewhere as "Hispanic Women's Moral Truth-Praxis." Ibid., 186. The issue of ethnic and racial moral relativism was discussed in chapter 1 through Diana Hayes's rhetoric. A similar assumption of difference in Hispanic women's moral lives is made by Isasi-Díaz in her claim of a form of moral praxis specific to Latinas.

39. Isasi-Díaz is forthcoming that for her truth is concrete and subjective: "In claiming *mestizaje* as a symbol of our moral truth-praxis we are saying that we do not believe in abstract notions of truth." *En la Lucha*, 195. She also expresses a concern over what she sees as magisterim interference with moral consciousness. Ibid., 142.

40. It should be noted that although John Paul presents his rhetoric as if he begins with ontology in Genesis, like Isasi-Díaz he is concerned with a specific practice: divorce. Where they differ on this is how they present their argument for a practical issue: Isasi-Díaz thinks her *mujerista* stance will make her more persuasive to her audience, while John Paul tries to make his practical interest seem subordinate to his theological reflection in the performance.

41. Isasi-Díaz, *En la Lucha*, 103. For a discussion of erroneous conceptions of conscience that do not correspond to the moral truth see Grisez, *The Way of the Lord Jesus*, 73–75.

42. O'Connell uses the terms *conscience/1*, *conscience/2*, and *conscience/3* to refer respectively to these three dimensions of conscience. O'Connell, "Conscience," 110–13. Grisez uses *awareness of principles of morality*, *process of reasoning from principles to conclusions*, and *moral judgments* to describe the dimensions. Grisez, *The Way of the Lord Jesus*, 76. Thomas Aquinas uses *synderesis*, *practical reasoning*, and *conscience* to describe what we now often refer to collectively as conscience. Aquinas, *Summa Theologiae*, I, q. 79, aa.12–13; 1–2, q. 94, aa. 2, 6. The language I adopt here (capacity, process, judgment) is from Billy and Keating, *Conscience and Prayer*, 12.

43. O'Connell, "Conscience," 110.

44. "According to Saint Paul, conscience [capacity] in a certain sense confronts man with the law, and thus becomes a '*witness' for man:* a witness of his own faithfulness or unfaithfulness with regard to the law, of his essential moral rectitude or iniquity." John Paul II, *Veritatis splendor*, para. 57.

45. According to John Paul, there is "a *role of human reason* in discovering and applying the moral law [process]: the moral life calls for that creativity and originality typical of the person, the source and cause of his own deliberate acts." Ibid., para. 40.

46. John Paul II, *Veritatis splendor*, para. 34.

47. Isasi-Díaz, *En la Lucha*, 154.

48. Ibid.

49. Ibid., 142.

50. Ibid.

51. Khomeini, "Address to Women in Qom," 263–64.

52. Ibid., 263.

53. Ibid. Special reference to the ladies of Qom is also made.

54. Ibid., 263–64.

55. Ibid., 263.

56. Mutahhari, *Nizām-i huqūq-i zan dar Islām*, 15. Translated in Kar, "Women's Strategies," 186.

57. Ziba Mir-Hosseini has labeled the particular conception of gender found in Khomeini's rhetoric neotraditionalist. From my own experience interviewing women leaders in Iran and informal interactions with Iranians, the conception, whether traditionalist or not, is certainly the most rhetorically prevalent in Iran today.

58. A Sufi anthropology assumes ontological equality, but material difference. For an elaboration of this argument see Sa'diyya Shaikh's "In Search of al-Insan."

59. Khomeini, "Islamic Government," 27–166.

60. Khomeini, "Address to Women in Qom," 264.

61. Ibid.

62. Ibid.

63. Although *talāq* is permissible, it is morally discouraged, based on a tradition of the Prophet calling it lawful (halal) but hateful to God.

64. For the effect of codification on shari'a in a different cultural context, see Messick, *The Calligraphic State*.

65. In 1967 Khomeini gave his opinion on Family Protection Law in the following ruling: "The law that has recently passed the two houses of the Majles (which [in their present composition] are illegal and contrary to the shari'a) on the orders of the agents of the foreigners, the law designated the 'Family Law,' which has as its purpose the destruction of the Muslim family unit, is contrary to the ordinances of Islam. . . . The divorce of women divorced by court order is invalid; they are still married women, and if they marry again, they become adulteresses. Likewise, anyone who knowingly marries a woman so divorced becomes an adulterer, deserving the penalty laid down by the Sharia." Khomeini, "Tawzīh al-masā'il (Legal Rulings)," 441.

66. Changes included requiring the registration of marriage with the state, increased grounds for women to request a divorce, and making divorce the jurisdiction of civil rather than shari'a courts.

67. This act was followed by the 1975 New Family Protection Law, basically the same as the 1967 version except it increased the age of consent to marriage again (from fifteen to eighteen for girls) and allowed courts to decide cases of custody and divorce without any reference to shari'a.

68. I am indebted to Ziba Mir-Hosseini for the insight that Article 1133 of Civil Code was softened in the Special Civil Courts Act in Article 3/2 using a Qur'anic reference. The article reads as follows: "The divorce provisions are those contained in the Civil Code and shari'a. But if a husband wished a divorce in accordance with Article 1133 of the Civil Code, the court must first refer the case to arbitration, in conformity with the Holy verse: 'If you fear a breach between the two, bring forth an arbiter from his people and from her people an arbiter, if they desire to set things right; God will compose their differences; surely God is all-knowing, All-aware.' Permission to divorce shall be granted to the husband, if reconciliation between the spouses has not materialized." As quoted by Mir-Hosseini, *Marriage on Trial*, 55–56. Mir-Hosseini writes, "Thus the new act, by requiring a man to obtain a court decree in order to be able to exercise his right to talaq, has in effect altered its extra-judicial nature; although it has not interfered with its unilateral nature. Men are still not required to provide grounds, whereas women can obtain a divorce only upon establishment of certain grounds." Ibid., 56.

69. Khomeini, "Address to Women in Qom," 264.

70. Ibid. Emphasis added.

71. The only case for which Khomeini thinks warrants divorce independent of contract stipulations is mistreatment. Ibid.

72. Whether or not women can formally attain the rank of *mujtahid* is a controversial issue in Iran, although a female *mujtahid* is not without precedence. Banu Amin of Isfahan informally claims the rank and to have an *ijāza* (license) from Ayatollah Marashi Najafi, among others. Michael Fischer argues that women can become *mujtahidūn* insofar as this means they can follow their own *ijtihād*, but they cannot become a guide for others. *Iran: From Religious Dispute to Revolution*, 163, 175, 279 n. 18.

73. Community-based organizations (CBOs) are by far the most numerous; they tend to be religiously based and focus on providing services to a specific community. But they are for the most part led by men. In contrast, especially since the Islamic Revolution, women have founded grassroots and research organizations. These are places where women can hold leadership and decision-making roles. I refer to civil society organizations rather than nongovernmental organizations because since 1979, funding by international or private foundations has not been a significant part of the Iranian civil society financial support, which has led to the criticism that Iranian NGOs are not actually NGOs at all, because they are dependent on government grants and must be licensed by the Ministry of the Interior. For further elaboration see Bucar, "Women, Gender, and Non-Governmental Organizations: Iran," 99–100.

74. Some within Iranian civil society criticize research organizations as focused on issues important only to the intellectual elites.

75. I was a fellow at the IWSR during the summer of 2004.

76. The course was cosponsored by IWSR and the House of Culture and Sustainable Development.

77. Mahboubeh Abbas-Gholizadeh, interview by the author, Tehran, August 23, 2004.

78. For more information about this incident, see a statement by Abbas-Gholizadeh and a collection of articles on the arrest by Lawyers Committee for Human Rights, Amnesty International, and Reporters Without Borders, www.ngotc.org/ennews.asp.

79. According the human rights group Front Line, Abbass-Gholizadeh was held for over a month on three separate charges: "acting against national security," "holding an illegal assembly," and "confronting the security forces." She has since been released but there are unconfirmed reports that she was rearrested in late 2009. Front Line Protection of Human Rights Defenders, "Fear for the Safety of Two Women Human Rights Defenders Still in Detention," (March 14, 2007), www.frontlinedefenders.org/node/217.

80. Abbas-Gholizadeh, "Chirā Farzānah?" 3–8.

81. As of 2003, four colleges and universities, including Tehran University, had women's studies majors. Afray, "The Human Rights," 119.

82. Abbas-Gholizadeh writes, "In all the sciences that discuss human beings one can find aspects of the subject of women. The resulting correct and wrong perceptions, often contradictory, could be gathered and corrected under a singular methodology in order to finally establish knowledge of 'women's studies'. . . as a science among other disciplines" (Dar kulliyah-i 'ulūmī kih bi-naḥvī az insān baḥs̱ bih miyān āmadah ast, ṭayf´hāyī az mawżū'āt-i "zan" rā mī´tavān yāft: daryāfthāyī durust va ghalaṭ va aghlab nā´hamāhang kih mī´bāyast taḥt-i mitudulūzhī-i vāhid taṣḥīḥ va munsajim shavad va sar´anjām dānish-i 'Zan´shināsī' rā sāmān bakhshad . . . bih 'unvān-i yak 'ilm-i miyān rishtah´ī). Abbas-Gholizadeh, "Chirā Farzānah?" 6.

83. "Ammā takvīn-i nā´muta'ādil-i īn javāmi', har bār 'avāriż-i jānabī va mushkilāt-i uṣūlī padīd āvardah ast." Ibid., 3.

84. "Dar kuntrul va ta'ādul-i istrātizhīk´tarīn masā'il-i jahānī mānand-i: jamī'at, maṣraf, tawsi'ah va bihdāsht va darmān, naqsh-i 'umdah´ī bih 'uhdah dārand." Ibid., 4.

85. "Ṭabī'at-i zanānah ast kih 'adam-i shinākht-i ṣaḥīḥ-i ān, mawjib-i paydāyish-i talaqqīhā-yi ḥuṣūlī-i nāqiṣ gardīdah va hamīn shinākht-i nāqiṣ-i ḥusūlī nīz bih ṣūrathā-yi gūnah´gūn dar raftārhā va sunan va qavānīn nahādīnah shudah ast." Ibid., 4.

86. "Ulgūhā-yi mā mī´bāyast az baṭn-i khvīshtan-i farhangī-i khvud-i mā, ẓuhūr va burūz yābad." Ibid., 8. Abbas-Gholizadeh writes earlier, "Even though women's issues are global, presentation of a universal solution is not the way to cure the problem. The cultural and indigenous characteristics and the values of each country present an obstacle for a singular formula for solving the problems of women. Different assumptions that result from defective perceptions of woman's nature in each corner of this world are based on indigenous beliefs, culture, and customs. . . . The problem is local. The problem of a woman is specifically her own" (Dūrnamā-yi jahānī-i mas'alah-i zan chunīn ast; ammā dar 'ayn-i hāl irā'ah-i ulgūhā-yi vāḥid va pīchīdan-i nuskhah´hā-yi mushābah nīz rāh-i 'ilāj nīst. Vīzhagīhā-yi farhangī va būmī va arzishā-yi 'aqīdatī-i har marz va būm, māna' az irā'ah-i furmūlhāyī vāḥid barā-yi ḥall-i mas'alah-i zan ast. Talaqqīhā-yi gūnah´gūn kih nāshī az idrāk-i nāqiṣ-i ḥuṣūlī az vīzhagīhā-yi ṭabī'ī ast, dar har gūshah az īn 'ālam bih tanāsub-i i'tiqādāt va farhang va sunan-i būmī. . . . Mushkil hamīn jāst. Mas'alah-i zan khāṣṣ-i khvud-i ūst). Ibid., 5.

87. In the same way, she claims that "Farzānah is not based on interpreting western ideas for the indigenous situation" but through translation the gain is mainly "research method and methodologies of other nations" (Farzānah banā-yi ān nadārad tā tarjumān-i būmi dādah´hā-yi gharbī bāshand. . . shīvah´hā-yi taḥqīq va ḥassāsiyyathā-yi 'ilmī-i zan´pazhūhān-i milal-i dīgar). Ibid., 7.

88. Abbas-Gholizadeh mixes very "old words," particularly Arabic ones, such as *ta'ammul* (deal) with words more recently incorporated to the Persian language.

89. This second claim arguably requires more extrapolation from the editorial, and this process is made easier once I share the topic of Abbas-Gholizadeh's lecture the day I met her. As I mentioned, I first met Abbas-Gholizadeh as part of an international course on Islam and human rights. Her lecture focused on feminism in Iran. Feminism, which she defined as theorizing about the women's movement, takes two major forms in Iran: Muslim and Islamic. Although Islamic feminists work within the traditional *fiqh* framework, and thereby consider the Qur'an and hadith as the sources of Islamic ethics, they insist that women's experiences present new issues for *ijtihād*. Muslim feminists agree, but in addition to the traditional *fiqh* sources, consult sources outside this framework, such as philosophy of religion (Abbas-Gholizadeh referenced Habermas, Marx, and Foucault). In both cases, women lobby a *mujtahid* to produce a ruling or decree that more closely reflects women's current experiences, a process Abbas-Gholizadeh calls dynamic *ijtihād*, among others (for example, Mehranguiz Kar or Zohre Safayi [aka Zahra Safati]). During her lecture in 2004, Abbas-Gholizadeh self-identified as a Muslim feminist, but since her arrest that fall she no longer publicly does so. For a report of the course in Persian, see Hosseinkhah, "Guftugū va shunūdhā'ī darbārah-i."

90. "Mawżū'āt va maqālāt-i 'Farzānah' gustardah ast va bih kulliyah-i yāftah´hā va i'tiqādāt-i basharī dar ṣāhat-i dīn va farhang va 'ulūm tavajjuh dārad. Bidān sabab kih chunīn 'ināyatī lāzimah-i takvīn va takāmul-i dānish-i 'Zan´shināsī' bih 'unvān-i 'ilmī miyān´ rishtah´ī ast." Abbas-Gholizadeh, "Chirā Farzānah?" 8.

91. "Sukhan-i ākhir ānkih, 'Farzānah' dā'ī va payām´āvar-i farhīkhtagān ast va ham az īnān inṭizār-i tahẕīb va naqd-i nigārishha va nigarishhā rā dārad. . . . Dīgar buzurgān-i sāḥat-i dīn va dānish rā bih īn khiṭṭah-i gharīb mī´khvānīm." Ibid., 8.

92. "In history, religion, art, philosophy, literature, laws, economics, political science, and social sciences one can find powerful spokes of the wheel of the knowledge of 'women's studies.' The same is true in the empirical sciences and all branches of the medical sciences, especially those that have specialized in the biological issues of women" ("Dar tārīkh va dīn va hunar va falsafah va adabiyāt va ḥuqūq va 'ulūm-i iqtiṣādī va siyāsī va ijtimā'ī, ragah'hā-yi nīrūmandī az dānish-i 'Zan´shināsī' rā mī´tavān yāft va nīz dar 'ulūm-i tajrubī va kulliyah-i inshi'ābāt-i 'ulūm-i pizishkī, fuṣūl-i 'umdah´ī bih masā'il biyūlūzhīk–i zanān ikhtiṣāṣ yāftah ast"). Ibid., 6.

CHAPTER FOUR

Performance beyond the Pulpit

Presenting Disorderly Bodies in Public Spaces

✦

Veiling is often offered as evidence of Muslim gender-based discrimination; in the Roman Catholic Church it is the prohibition of women from the priestly vocation. These two practices offend prominent secular-liberal sensibilities, and certainly women within each tradition argue against clerical opinions on them. This chapter takes a slightly different approach. I consider whether and how the logics of veiling and ordination are taken up by women in their discursive practices. I thereby test the dimension of my thesis that all clerical rhetoric provides possibilities for creative conformity. Is it possible that even rhetoric about veiling and exclusion from the priesthood is a discursive resource for feminist politics?

The issue of ordination has been central to the Catholic reform movements in the United States, and there are various types of responses to clerical rhetoric on the issue, including two direct rebuttals. One argues for entry of women in the priesthood based on gender equality (confirmed through baptism) and historically support for women's ordination in church tradition (women have been ordained into the deaconate, most recently during the communist period).[1] A second response moves beyond ordination to a new understanding of "the church" that emphasizes what Elisabeth Schüssler Fiorenza calls "the discipleship of equals."[2] This rhetoric aims to change the hierarchy of the Roman Catholic Church, not merely inject women into the level of priests, citing that ordination of women in other denominations has not removed all barriers to women's equal participation or prevented sexist teachings on moral matters. Some women in this camp have focused on establishing alternative women's liturgy groups.[3] I find both these arguments rich, but as direct responses they are strategic rather than tactical insofar as they try to refute, rather than work within, clerical logic. In this chapter I focus on a different sort of response to the ordination from the right that affirms a male-exclusive priesthood. I argue that even this tactical response reworks some of the clerical logics of the ban on women's ordination, even if not intentionally.

Privileging specific forms of women's dress is something the two traditions in this book share: for example, the nun's habit, at least visually, is similar to some forms of head covering used in Iran, such as the *miqna'ah*. What is significant about Islamic dress, referred to as hijab in Persian, is that it is now legally obligatory for all Iranian women, even non-Muslim women. Although some women do oppose the duty to wear hijab,[4] I focus in this chapter instead on an argument that, while supporting public veiling, highlights another dimension of hijab: how women's dress is used discursively in nationalist ideology. It is women's engagement with this public role, versus that of habituating or conveying virtue, that becomes an opportunity to make innovative arguments about moral freedom and women's proper role in the embodied production of moral knowledge.

What about the ethics of veiling and ordination warrants their being considered together in this chapter? On one hand, they are hot-button issues: both are read by secular feminists as evidence of the dominion of men over women. The veil is seen as a symbol of men's control of women through segregation and an emphasis on modesty, and the ban on women's ordination is seen as evidence of the male-controlled hierarchical structure of the church. But hijab and ordination also have commonality beyond secular perceptions of them. They are public and embodied performances. As public they move us away from discussions of women's roles in the family as mothers and wives. The veil is necessary only outside the home, and the ban affects women's leadership roles in the church. The clerical positions on these issues also reflect the importance of gendered bodies in the religious life of both communities. In the Roman Catholic Church, priests literally embody Christ as his representative while leading mass. Veiling is meant to hide women's gendered bodies from the gaze of men to protect the social dignity of an Islamic society and nation-state.[5] The possibility of ordaining women or unveiling women creates similar moral unbalance and disorder within the clerical logics of moral embodiment. For these reasons this chapter explores the veil and ordination, not as the complex, multidimensional practices they are, but rather only through their role in discursive practices. In other words, it considers how clerics and women use gendered logics of embodiment rhetorically to make arguments that raise theological and moral issues related to the public conceptualization, display, and work of women's bodies.

WOMEN'S EXCLUSION FROM PRIESTHOOD

In 1994 John Paul issued *Ordinatio sacredotalis*, an apostolic letter directed explicitly to bishops.[6] However, given the content of the letter, and its reference to the fact that "at the present time in some places" the issue of ordination of women is "still open to debate," it seems clear that John Paul was also addressing those who thought women should be ordained.[7] I consider the letter from the point of view of this implied audience.

From this vantage point John Paul makes two claims: that the Roman Catholic Church does not have the authority to ordain women[8] and that women's exclusion from the priestly vocation is not a form of discrimination.[9] With the first, John Paul has already shifted the focus of the conversation about ordination from "should women be priests?" to "could the church ordain women, even if it wanted to?" He articulates three primary grounds, which he calls "fundamental reasons," for this first claim, drawing from Paul VI's earlier statement on the issue: one, the first apostles were all men; two, the Roman Catholic Church has always ordained only men; and, three, the Roman Catholic Church has always taught that only men can be ordained. John Paul adds a fourth: the Eastern Church does not ordain women.

A number of warrants help connect these grounds to the claim. For example, the Roman Catholic Church has the authority to do only what it has done before: what Christ has done, what the church has practiced and taught. Therefore, because the priesthood is a continuation of the apostolic tradition, what the apostles were in the beginning (male), as well as the tradition of ordaining priests to serve the function of apostles, becomes evidence for why women cannot be ordained. Another warrant is the importance of Catholic unity. This is implied when the fact that the Eastern Church does not ordain women is used as a ground for why the Roman Catholic Church has no authority to do so. A final warrant John Paul explicitly offers is that his grounds indicate some of the contours of "God's eternal plan," that a plan must be followed to the extent it can be understood.

John Paul's backing for these warrants is located in the scriptural record of Christ's selection of only men as his apostles, the writings of Paul VI,[10] the Congregation for the Doctrine of the Faith,[11] the Catechism of the Catholic Church,[12] as well as his own moral teaching in *Mulieris dignitatem* and *Christifideles laici*. The use of his own authority as pontificate is not uncommon in John Paul's rhetoric, but because his rhetoric in this case is backed by a limitation of institutional authority (to ordain women), it is particularly significant that he ends the letter as follows: "Wherefore, in order that all doubt may be removed regarding a matter of great importance, a matter which pertains to the Church's divine constitution itself, in virtue of my ministry of confirming the brethren (cf. Luke 22:32) *I declare* that the Church has no authority whatsoever to confer priestly ordination on women and that this judgment *is to be definitively held* by all the Church's faithful."[13] This is not an explicit *ex cathedra* (infalliable) statement, but the language works to remind the audience of papal authority. Ironically, of the five rhetorical performances considered in this book, it is at this point, when John Paul is trying to deny the ban on ordination is based on his authority, that he relies most heavily on this authority.

A second claim in the letter seems even more explicitly aimed at women: women's exclusion from the priesthood is not a form of discrimination. It is grounded, like the first claim, in the fact that Christ selected only male apostles. The move from ground to claim is warranted by the presumption that Christ's example is an egalitarian one. If Christ did not select female apostles, such exclusion cannot be discriminatory.[14] This is a clever rhetorical move on John Paul's part, because he is able to shift the content of a possible rebuttal from "the church is discriminatory" to "Christ is discriminatory." John Paul assumes that his intended audience of Christian women, who have long pointed to the egalitarian nature of Christ's teachings, would necessarily reject such a rebuttal. He thereby defuses a possible response with his own premptive rebuttal to it. Anticipating another response, John Paul offers a warrant-related disclaimer: "Christ's way of acting did not proceed from sociological or cultural motives peculiar to his time," but was part of God's plan.[15] This warrant is meant to undermine any argument that Christ's selection of apostles was influenced by the gender discrimination of his cultural context.

Second, John Paul offers the fact that the Virgin Mary was not selected as an apostle as a ground that "clearly shows that the non-admission of women to priestly ordination cannot mean that women are of lesser dignity, nor can it be construed as discrimination against them."[16] He argues that Mary's nonclergy status proves that an exclusively male clergy "is to be seen as the faithful observance of a plan to be ascribed to the wisdom of the Lord of the universe," a plan that has distinct roles for faithful based on gender.[17]

Finally, women's exclusion from the priestly vocation is not discriminatory, John Paul asserted, because the "hierarchal structure of the church is totally ordered."[18] Here he draws a firm distinction between male hierarchy and the discrimination of women. In a Holy Thursday Letter one year later, he put this as follows: "Certainly the question could be put in these terms if the hierarchical priesthood granted a social position of privilege characterized by the exercise of 'power.' But this is not the case: The ministerial priesthood, in Christ's plan, is an expression not of domination but of service! Anyone who interpreted it 'domination' would certainly be far from the intention of Christ, who in the Upper Room began the Last Supper by washing the feet of the apostles."[19] This part of the argument has a number of layers. There is the warrant that hierarchy is not problematic, but instead necessary for the proper function of the church. The hierarchy involved in ordination is to be understood as a hierarchy not of power, but of service to the church. For example, although Christ is technically "higher" in the hierarchy of discipleship, he nevertheless washes the feet of the others to demonstrate his equality with them.

John Paul does not offer qualifiers for either claim discussed. Quite the opposite: his language is forceful and certain, as we saw in his closing comments where he used phrases such as "I declare" and "definitively held." This letter is meant to remove all doubt on the issue of women's ordination.

Responses that can be identified at this point have to do with the historical nature of the grounds and warrants offered in the rhetorical performance. For example, because the ground of Christ's selection of only male apostles is so central to both claims in John Paul's letter, the existence of a female apostle, perhaps in the apostolic activities of Mary Magdalene, could refute both claims. In addition, the historical record of the church as having never ordained women creates another possible factual rebuttal: what if it were discovered that a woman had in fact been ordained at some point in history? This would weaken the assertions that both the church practice and teaching on this issue have been entirely constant or consistent. In the section that follows, however, I demonstrate that even an affirmation of the ban on women's ordination can change the practical moral guidance for women resulting from this position.

IMPLEMENTING MORAL LEADERSHIP BEYOND THE PULPIT

If Isasi-Díaz in chapter 3 is the ultimate test of my hypothesis from the left (even dissenting rhetoric is obedient as citational), then this section tests my hypothesis from the right (even obedient rhetoric is partial in some way, and thereby creative). The author of the rhetorical performance I focus on, Helen Hull Hitchcock, affirms the prohibition of women's ordination but also heads an organization that operates as a women-centered resource for ethical guidance, a justification of which requires the tactical shifting of John Paul's logics of male leadership.

This section's discursive practices are found in *Affirmation for Catholic Women*, a statement of "fidelity to church teachings,"[20] which Hitchcock and six other women drafted in 1984, and in Hitchcock's essay "Women for Faith and Family," which describes the process of turning this statement into a petition, and the activities of the organization that resulted.[21]

Hitchcock is a former Protestant journalist who converted to Catholicism in 1984, the same year she founded Women for Faith and Family (WFF) and helped draft the *Affirmation*.[22] Hitchcock describes the impetus for drafting the *Affirmation* as follows:

> In September 1984, six St. Louis women gathered around a dining room table to discuss responding to the American bishops who were planning to write a pastoral letter on "women's issues." The bishops said they wanted to hear the concerns of Catholic women, and had initiated a process of gathering this information through "listening sessions" to be held in all dioceses of the United States. We were concerned that these sessions would not give the bishops an accurate picture of Catholic women. First of all, only a small minority of Catholic women would be able to attend them, and secondly, the sessions seemed designed to elicit maximum expression of disaffection and complaints from women who did attend and to discourage participation from those who supported church teaching or who were critical of any aspect of feminism.[23]

The *Affirmation* and the listening sessions it sought to contribute to are premised on the importance of women's response to clerical rhetoric: women are assumed to have a valuable take on women's issues that will differ from the bishops' perspective. Hitchcock conceives of the *Affirmation* as a particular type of discursive performance to counter the responses of leftist Catholic feminists, whom she characterizes as elite women, who have enjoyed a high level of publicity, resulting in the erroneous assumption that women who do not dissent to papal teaching are antifeminists.[24]

The statement Hitchcock and others drafted pledged their "wholehearted support to Pope John Paul II" and affirmed "his apostolic teaching concerning all aspects of family life and roles for men and women in the Church and in society."[25] Hitchcock formed WFF to collect signatures of support for this statement, and in 1985 ten thousand names were presented to John Paul. This number doubled by 1986, and is currently at fifty thousand, although all references to John Paul were changed to Benedict XVI in 2005.[26]

The *Affirmation* includes a paragraph supporting the Roman Catholic ban on ordination, which is the first claim I consider. The relevant paragraph reads as follows:

> We therefore also reject as an aberrant innovation peculiar to our times and our society the notion that priesthood is the "right" of any human being, male or female. Furthermore, we recognize that the specific role of ordained priesthood is intrinsically connected with and representative

> of the begetting creativity of God in which only human males can participate. Human females, who by nature share in the creativity of God by their capacity to bring forth new life, and, reflective of this essential distinction, have a different and distinct role within the Church and in society from that accorded to men, can no more be priests than men can be mothers.[27]

Although issued ten years before John Paul's apostolic letter, the claim is nevertheless the same: women cannot and should not be ordained. But, unlike John Paul, who draws to a large extent on Paul VI's grounds for women's exclusion from the priesthood, Hitchcock focuses on two different grounds in the *Affirmation*. First is the ground that ordination is not a right based on competence or merit, but instead a vocation bestowed by God. Women do not have a right to any vocation. This is an implicit critique of some feminist's use of rights-based language in attempts to reform theological issues, an enterprise Hitchcock finds inappropriate. The second ground she provides is that a priest must be a man because only a man can represent the "begetting creativity of God." In contrast, women represent the "birthing creativity of God." This draws on a strict vocational gender distinction based on the embodied physical differences between the sexes.

Hitchcock relies on two warrants in her rhetoric. One is the general importance of conserving Catholic tradition in a current atmosphere of dissent.[28] A second is the necessity of supporting John Paul's moral teaching as a good Catholic. Her argument is backed by the sheer number of women who signed her petition. She writes, "no petition of dissent in the postconciliar era, including the highly publicized statement of dissent from *Humanae vitae* in 1968, has attracted comparable response."[29] This marks the *Affirmation* as grassroots, in contrast to the elite Catholic dissenters in the United States, countering the impression that Catholic dissent is more widespread than adherence. Her claim is also backed by John Paul's acceptance of the statement and petition. In her organization's newsletter, Hitchcock writes that she delivered the *Affirmation* and petition to John Paul during a 1985 papal audience and that, on receiving the packet, John Paul said, "God bless the women of the United States."[30] It is noteworthy that John Paul is rhetorically invoked both as a warrant and backing.

Before demonstrating how Hitchcock, perhaps unintentionally, shifts John Paul's rhetoric on ordination, I want to consider a second claim in Hitchcock's essay about her organization. This claim can be found in the organization mission statement: "to serve as a channel through which questions from Catholic women seeking guidance or information can be directed."[31] Although Hitchcock uses the word *channel* to describe WFF's activities, its actual work makes it more of a source than channel: WFF answers letters and mail directly, organizes volunteers to conduct any necessary research, and provides referrals to other individuals or organizations with specific expertise.[32] What I find intriguing in Hitchcock's description about this dimension of her organization's work is that there is no attempt to link it to papal or other magisterial teachings about women. The reason WFF's activities shift from the petition to direct response to Catholic women on moral issues is that women approach WFF and ask for such advice. Hitchcock writes,

> What began as a way to show support by Catholic women for church teachings about women and family quickly grew beyond this relatively limited goal; response to the needs of women led to a continually expanding set of initiatives. It soon became apparent to Women for Faith and Family's organizers that its original aim—to communicate information from Catholic women to the bishops—was only one means of serving the church and women . . .Women for Faith and Family receives many letters and telephone calls from women requesting assistance and information of various kinds, as well as advice and encouragement. These communications typically ask for help in addressing problems with religious and/or moral education affecting their children in Catholic schools or raise questions about church doctrine and discipline which affect the life and worship of every Catholic; but there are also many requests for help on matters such as family, marriage, or spiritual problems.[33]

The move from the ground (women asked us) to the claim (so we needed to respond) is warranted by the assumption that laywomen are responsible to serve as resources to other laywomen and backed by the practical need for a direct service that WFF is able to provide. In Hitchcock's words, "we are sensitive to the deep desire on the part of many Catholic women for a doctrinally reliable and spiritually nourishing source of companionship and mutual support."[34]

Given the organization's other activities in regards to the *Affirmation*, the assumption behind the activity of providing advice to women on moral matters is that it is consistent with the reasons women cannot be ordained. This means that there must be something distinctly male about priestly leadership and something distinctly female about a community of "companionship and mutual support." Note how similar this is to Schüssler Fiorenza's more radical claim from the left: a discipleship of equals, women in sisterly solidarity, is an alternative and better model to the present hierarchy. My point is not that Hitchcock is making a similar claim, but rather that she shares the backing about the benefit of women-centered communities, especially on moral matters.

Hitchcock affirms the claims John Paul made: a Catholic ban on women's ordination and a critique of the interpretation of this ban as gender discrimination. Her goal in the *Affirmation* is to perfectly reiterate John Paul's teachings. She uses John Paul as a warrant and backing in her rhetoric. But, as I predicted, this reiteration is creative and shifts the logic of John Paul's rhetoric in significant ways.

One major shift is in the grounds Hitchcock provides for the ban on women's ordination. She does not link priesthood directly to the original twelve apostles as John Paul does, but instead focuses on it as a vocation bestowed by God and the theological rationale for why only men can represent the begetting of creation. If John Paul's grounds are primarily historical, Hitchcock's are theological. Although John Paul's statement on ordination is made chronologically after Hitchcock's, the source for his grounds, Paul IV's 1975 statement on the issue, was available to Hitchcock.[35] That she does not use Paul IV's historical grounds is an implicit critique of John Paul's later rhetoric. Perhaps she finds these grounds inadequate, or believes that they are vulnerable to rebuttal. Even if Hitchcock does not intend a shift, she moves the game of debate onto a different field, and opens up new opportunities for theological responses to the Catholic ban on women's ordination.

A second shift from John Paul is the slide from the ordination issue to a need to respond directly to women's moral concerns. Hitchcock's organization, founded to affirm papal teachings, evolves into a direct service organization in which volunteers read, assess, research, and respond to women's moral inquiries. This is an implicit critique of clerical moral guidance. WFF does this work because there is a need for it; women are not getting adequate advice from the official pastoral activities of the Roman Catholic Church to live fully moral lives. Through this work, they have also bypassed the need for ordination, by creating a women-centered practice of ethical reflection.[36] In some ways this can be seen as a more radical move than ordaining women because it moves ethical work from the clergy class to lay women who have no formal training and base their advice on their experiences as Catholic women. In this way Hitchcock uses the clerical logic of institutional hierarchy to make an argument about the moral guidance that is not at all hierarchical.

COMPULSORY HIJAB AS PUBLIC FREEDOM

The legal status of veiling has fluctuated greatly over the last eighty years in Iran. In 1936, as part of a set of reforms aimed at modernization, Reza Shah issued an imperial order to make veiling illegal in the country.[37] Five years later, with his forced abdication in 1941, his son, Muhammad Reza Shah Pahlavi, left it up to women to decide whether to veil. A large number of women continued to appear veiled in public, especially those from the bazaar, merchant, and lower classes, and the urban middle class continued to appear publicly unveiled.[38] But veiling remained stigmatized as unmodern.

Veiling, especially in the form of chador, had an important symbolic place in the Islamic Revolution.[39] Women wearing this distinctly Iranian form of hijab became important foot soldiers in the Islamic Revolution, an anti-Shah anti-Western symbol of a new form of Iranian politics. After the Islamic Revolution, compulsory veiling did not happen automatically, nor was it primarily a legal requirement in the beginning. In fact an attempt to impose hijab during the provisional government failed when it faced mass protest from women. But despite this early failure of legal attempts to enforce public veiling, social pressures quickly made it impossible for women to leave the house without hijab.

The first women required to wear hijab after the revolution were those who worked in or had business at government agencies, as veiling became a requirement to enter any official government space in Iran. It quickly followed that women not wearing hijab were refused entry into state-owned public spaces, including parks. Private businesses then adopted similar rules, enforced with decals on the doors of restaurants, shops, even taxicabs, reading, "for the respect of Islam, hijab is mandatory" or "hijab is necessary for service." Slogans written on the sides of buildings and billboards proclaimed, "women must be veiled or they'll be assailed," "death to the unveiled," and "my sister, your veil is more powerful than my weapons."[40] By 1981 it had become socially mandatory, and women without hijab were verbally harassed on the streets by private citizens called Hizbullah, actions that were tolerated even if not officially sanctioned by the government.

In 1983 hijab became legally compulsory when the Majles passed the Islamic Punishment Law (Iranian Penal Code),[41] which included seventy-four lashes for "lack of strict observance of Islamic hijab by women."[42] The actual legal definition of improper hijab was left ambiguous. In 1988 the Ministry of Interior passed a new regulation based on the 1983 law that included a list of what defined bad hijab: exposure of head, hair, arms or legs, use of makeup, sheer or tight clothing, and clothes with foreign words or pictures. The preferred colors for hijab were also specified as dark blue, black, grey, and brown.[43] Currently, the most important piece of legal regulation of hijab is Article 638 of the 1991 version of the Iranian Penal Code within chapter 18 titled "Offences against Public Morality." Article 638 reads as follows: "women who appear in public without proper hijab according to the shari'a will be sentenced to a period of ten days to two months or pay a fine of 50,000 to 500,000 Rials [approximately $5 to $50]."[44] Penalties in practice continue to vary. For example, when I was in Iran in 2004 rumors circulated of young girls being arrested at shopping centers for improper hijab and punished by fines, incarceration, verbal abuse, or having their feet put into buckets of cockroaches. To further complicate the issue, there is still no clear definition of hijab in the Penal Code.

Compulsory veiling was justified by the ethical teachings of clergy, like Khomeini, who believed that forced unveiling under the Shah had led to immoral behavior. But, like current Iranian legislation, clerical teachings on hijab do not necessarily clearly define what counts as hijab. For example, Khomeini in his remarks about hijab during a famous interview with the female Italian journalist Oriana Fallaci frames hijab as a choice as well as alludes to how hijab is an internal disposition, not necessary definable by articles of clothing.[45]

Hijab is often used rhetorically for a variety of moral issues that move beyond women's modesty. This is the case of Khomeini's address in Mashad on May 16, 1979, where he uses hijab to make a claim about the nature of true freedom.[46] In the address Khomeini positions his argument against several reform policies of Reza Shah and Muhammad Reza that were implemented in the name of freedom. He begins with the example of land reform, which in the government's rhetoric aimed to raise the status of the peasants. In Khomeini's opinion its true goal was "to make Iran a market for the United States and destroy her agricultural system in order to make Iran dependent on the United States for everything."[47] He then turns to women's freedom and argues that freedom to not veil, or as the case actually was, being required to disveil, is not freedom at all. His argument is summarized in the following portion of the speech:

> We all saw that during the era of this father and son there was repression that perhaps had never happened before in the entire history of Iran. No man and no woman was free. Everyone was repressed, everyone suffered. . . . examples of policies implemented in the time of Reza Shah, which followed Ataturk, were uniformity of dress and the unveiling. This uniformity and unveiling was praised with ceremonial horns and loudspeakers. . . . Then we saw that the unveiling policy was not done in the service of women. They wanted to destroy this class by imposing oppression and exerting force. They attempted to stop them from performing that glorious deed which is theirs to perform, and to prevent them from performing that most essential of services that our ladies are responsible for, mainly the education of their

> children, in whose hands the future of the country lies. . . . The plan was to take these ladies away from that great and essential role that they already had and pretend to make half of the population free.[48]

The primary claim of the address appears to be directed at the former Shah—true freedom is not what the Shah claimed it was—and the example of "presenting disveiling in the name of freedom" grounds Khomeini's argument. Engaged in his own rhetorical analysis, he points to the previous government's assertion that the law enforcing disveiling would free women. This rhetoric, coupled with the undisputable fact (according to Khomeini) that disveiling hurt women, grounds his claim that the policy to legally prohibit veiling was based on an erroneous conception of freedom.

But there is more at play here. Take Khomeini's argument that the Shah called for disveiling to gain popular support. This erroneous conception of freedom is not only the Shah's but also the common Iranian citizen's, which the Shah merely attempts to leverage. Khomeini thus directed a distinct claim to his Iranian audience: you should understand freedom as a concept that allows for obedience to religious ethical requirements, and not as the sort of freedom that the Shah espoused. Wearing hijab is a symbol that a woman correctly understands freedom.

Khomeini argues that the policy to disveil attempted to destroy women by preventing them "from performing that glorious deed which is theirs to perform." But what, precisely, is the deed Khomeini thinks is so central to womanhood? On one hand, given the context, we can infer that this deed is actually wearing hijab, and in fact on one level it is: hijab is an act of modesty and in preventing it the government limited women's ability to enact a virtue required to be good Muslim women. One backing Khomeini implicitly relies on is the tradition of hijab in the Islamic community, although he does not make specific reference to either hadith or quaranic suras in this address. That women had to be physically forced to stop veiling and other examples of women's suffering under the Shah that accompanied disveiling is also used in the address as backing.

From another perspective, however, Khomeini may not be referring to hijab at all. Consider the direction in which his rhetoric is going. Although he starts with images of women forced at gunpoint to disveil, he ends the address with a discussion of how disveiling prevents women's fundamental service to society, mainly motherhood. If Khomeini's real concern is motherhood, how does a law about veiling affect that vocation? Certainly Khomeini is not arguing that women must be modest in front of their own children? Khomeini's real concern here seems to be that unveiling accompanied women's entry into the public sphere in such a way that motherhood was no longer their primary activity. This signaled a turn from traditional Iranian values (motherhood) to Western imported values (career). In other words, a third claim is found in this rhetoric: disveiling is bad for women because the private sphere is where women's fundamental roles are and unveiling is a public symbol of an internal turn away from these roles and thereby a corruption of women's nature.

This warrant is the focus of second part of the address. Take, for example, the following passage: "Of course, there is no objection to work for women, appropriate work, but not in the way that [the Shahs] wanted. They did not have in mind work for women, but to make women like men, destroying in the process both women and men by pulling them down from the position they have and preventing the natural growth of women and men."[49]

Here Khomeini shows that he considers some types of employment more suitable for women than others. He criticizes women "who have unrealistic expectations, who have done nothing. . . . now they are coming forward, one wanting to become a minister, another a lawyer, member of parliament, and so on. They are just building castles in the air, they had better come down to earth."[50] Although Khomeini changed his mind on these issues, for example, later supporting the idea of female members of parliament, at this point he is clearly trying to shame ambitious career women. In contrast, he praises the women before him, who he considers good Muslim women, for whom motherhood is their primary role: "You class of people, may God preserve you and grant you happiness, you do not have any expectations."[51]

I have identified three claims in this address: that the Shah had an erroneous view of freedom, that Muslims should understand freedom as freedom to and not freedom from, and that the wearing of proper hijab is an outward sign of understanding that women's primary roles are in the private sphere. In terms of qualifiers, the first claim is completely unqualified, and the coupling of the second claim with the first makes it also seem more certain. Khomeini's later writings do qualify his statements about devaluing women's work in the public sphere, but the internal logic of this address does not.

The logical form of Khomeini's rhetoric on freedom and hijab creates a number of possible responses. One is through his simultaneous concern with disveiling and improper hijab. Khomeini is concerned with both nonveiling and bad veiling, though for different reasons: the first demonstrates a fundamental misunderstanding of moral freedom, whereas the second is a form of improper habituation. This creates a logical ambiguity over the purpose of hijab: is it primarily an external practice for the good of the community or an internal disposition? In this way, hijab is an embodied performance of freedom as an outward manifestation of inward submission to God, as well as a condition that creates and recreates that devotion.[52] In addition, by linking hijab to freedom Khomeini creates the opportunity to make a different sort of argument about freedom using the practice of hijab.

DEFENDING HIJAB AS MORAL RIGHT AND MIGHT

Although public veiling has been legally required in Iran since 1983, what counts as hijab is left open to interpretation within a social context that encourages the wearing of dark colors, not showing any "womanly shape," and limiting exposure of skin and hair.[53] Several articles of clothing are used by women to satisfy the legal requirement to veil, including chador or a manteau and head scarf.[54] Women use forms of hijab to make statements about Islam, politics, and modern concepts of gender. Take, for example, the use of what I call bad and good hijab, so named not because one is more properly Islamic, but because of how they are perceived by a given audience.[55] The difference between bad and good hijab depends on the context of a performance: wearing a loose manteau in a coffee shop in Vanak Square may be perceived as good, whereas painted toenails in a government office may be considered bad. Women use hijab much like I might use a power suit or a low-cut dress in different contexts to convey or disguise different aspects of femininity or embodied power. In this way, and despite secular perceptions of veiling, the practice can be an opportunity for women to visually speak out about their understanding of authentic practices of Muslim womanhood.

In this section I focus on Elaheh Koulaei's rhetoric addressing her decision to become the first female member of parliament (MP) not to wear chador in a session of parliament. When I interviewed Koulaei in the summer of 2004, she held a position as a professor of law, was active in the reform party, and was in the process of trying to get approval by the Guardian Council to be a candidate for the 2005 presidential election. Koulaei was a chador-clad participant in the Islamic Revolution and a picture of Khomeini continues to hold a place of honor on her cluttered desk at the University of Tehran. During our conversation, she conveyed her commitment to the ideal of the Islamic Republic, and her displeasure with what she understands to be a hijacking of Khomeini's vision by ultraconservative clerics since his death.

Koulaei was elected to the Sixth Majles in 2000, one of eleven women out of 290 MPs.[56] Despite threats from conservatives, she attended the inaugural session of the Majles without chador, wearing only a headscarf and long manteau. Although there is no specific regulation banning this form of hijab in parliament, no woman had ever sat in the Majles without chador, and Koulaei's action was perceived as a case of bad hijab. In a 2005 interview with *Zanān* magazine, Koulaei reflects on this experience, connecting the practice of hijab and true freedom in the moral life, just as Khomeini did in his speech.[57] She argues that the form of chador is not required by Islam: "As a woman, I believe I have this right [to choose my form of hijab] and that society has formally recognized my freedom."[58] Note that her actions in Majles in 2000, and her argument about why she was justified to do so five years later, do not oppose the requirement to wear hijab. Rather, she focuses on the issue of adequate hijab, which she believes should be left up to the discretion of each woman.

According to Koulaei, her actions were legitimately grounded in two ways. First is the issue of the proper definition of hijab: "I wanted to show clothing is not necessarily the only type of hijab. . . . in many instances, the other types of hijab can work better."[59] Koulaei does two things here with the definition of hijab. She attempts to remind the audience that despite legal requirements to wear a physical veil, proper hijab is a much deeper, internal moral issue. She also makes it clear that there is not a strict hierarchy of forms of hijab, and that in some instances, a manteau and headscarf more effectively convey the proper virtue of modesty. The second ground is that "today, all Iranian women, like all Iranian men, expect to be allowed freedom to choose their type of clothing."[60]

The move from the definition of hijab and women's desire to have free choice in clothing to Koulaei's conclusion that her bad hijab is permissible is warranted by a particular conception of freedom. It is not coincidental that, just as Khomeini's rhetoric on hijab stemmed from a particular understanding of proper freedom in the moral life, so too does the issue of hijab involve freedom for Koulaei. In the article published in *Zanān*, Koulaei introduces her understanding of Islamic freedom with an anecdote: "Of course I knew that many pressures would accompany my decision not to wear chador. Even friends said to me: 'Do not do this. It is a minefield.' But I replied, 'I walk on the mines in order to show Islam's capacity is much higher than the imposition and enforcement of obligation that have been done to the people in the name of Islam.'"[61]

This imagery of minefields is a common one in Iranian discourse, especially since the ten-year war with Iraq. Leaders of the women's movement often describe their work as negotiating minefields, and given the number of political arrests and executions since the Islamic Revolution, the metaphor seems appropriate. Here Koulaei invokes the image in order to depict her actions in the parliament as indeed dangerous, pushing against the status quo, and yet necessary to demonstrate the meaning of true freedom in Islam that includes individual choice. Koulaei's claim about true freedom in Islam is not merely discursive, but also entails a bodily aspect: free to wear certain clothing, free from imposition of someone else's interpretation of proper Islamic behavior. In her own words, she tries "to be a representative of women who are not ready to bodily submit to [enforced chador]."[62]

Her vision of Islamic freedom is grounded in three ways. First, coercion is un-Islamic:

> As an individual of the revolutionary generation, and with the hopes and dreams and rights and freedoms of women I had for Islam, I never could accept an imposition of this type, which forces people to wear a special form of hijab. I have in mind my studies of the experiences of the communist period of the Soviet Union, during which they tried to make the people into only one form. I do not want to compare, but because of political and cultural structure and frame of minds, I saw current behavior in Iran that was similar to those [Soviet] actions.[63]

Note how the incompatibility of coercion and religious freedom is warranted by the example of communist rule in the Soviet Union. Khomeini was also a harsh critique of the Soviet Union, predicting an evitable fall of communism. Koulaei backs her argument here with her own scholarship on the Soviet Union as well as her status as a participant in the Islamic Revolution, which was acutely concerned with bringing true freedom to Iran.

A second ground for Koulaei's claim about true freedom is provided in the negative example of how she was treated after she attended parliament without chador: "I faced a wide range of accusations and insults that were unfounded and which completely contradicted proper religious and moral conduct. It was difficult for me even to imagine that some people would do such things. Some of them I had even studied with twenty-five to thirty years ago. In fact, I had worn chador with them."[64] The insults she had to endure were unjustified because her accusers knew her to be a pious woman. But, more important, the behavior of her accusers was itself un-Islamic: trying to control a woman's behavior with such threats does not respect her human dignity. Remembering the discussion of *taqlīd* in the introduction, any attempt to coerce moral behavior negates its moral content. Particularly given that hijab is designed in part to protect women from unwanted public attention, unjustly accusing a woman of improper hijab is immoral.

This brings us to the third ground for Koulaei's conception of Islamic free will: the role for the common believer in discovering and assessing the true teaching of Islam. This idea is central to how in this interview she ends her discussion of hijab with a critique of the legal requirement of non-Muslims to veil.

> Is it necessary for all Iranian women to wear hijab, not only Muslims, but also Christians and Jews and followers of other faiths who are formally

> recognized in our constitution? With respect to shari'a, most believers do not think a Christian woman should be forced to wear hijab for the same reason as a Muslim woman. These are current discussions in our society. . . . If we take a wide view of all aspects of this discussion, we can strengthen that entire public sphere and we could access the insights from different spheres of influence.[65]

Koulaei suggests that the current debate over non-Muslim veiling is an example of believers grappling with difficult issues related to veiling obligations within an Islamic community. The diversity of views should be accounted for in Iranian law, she implies, because different perspectives illuminate the issue in different ways. This, in turn, might require a reform of compulsory veiling laws in Iran. Interestingly, for a primary argument that does not purport to challenge the requirement to veil—only the form of veil required—a secondary claim, when pushed to its logical conclusion, does just that.

Koulaei's arguments share aspects with Khomeini's rhetoric, such as the connection of hijab and freedom: proper understanding of Islamic freedom leads to hijab requirements in the Islamic Republic (Khomeini) and choice in veiling options comes from an Islamic understanding of free will (Koulaei). Koulaei emphasizes Khomeini's teaching of hijab as something you have, not necessarily tied to a specific article of clothing, and the impermissibility of externally judging a woman's hijab. Both agree that chador is not the required form of hijab. Both are concerned with the proper understanding of freedom within a distinctly Islamic political context.[66]

At the same time, Koulaei shifts Khomeini's rhetoric with her indirect response. First, her focus is different: whereas Khomeini is concerned with the duty of hijab, and freedom as obedience to duty, Koulaei is concerned with choice of hijab, and thereby free will within the context of obedience to duties. A shift also occurs at the level of the order of the logical connection: whereas Khomeini starts with freedom as obedience and moves to hijab, Koulaei uses the occasion of her hijab practice on the floor of the Majles to raise the issue of free will. Khomeini writes out of concern with the stability of the new Islamic Republic. Koulaei's action and justification for it occurs more than twenty years later, when her concern is not the longevity of the Islamic Republic, but rather its compatibility with its original Islamic goals. In fact she worries that because Khomeini is gone, his vision for an Islamic government has been hijacked by those who misunderstand its original purpose. This allows her to leverage Khomeini's rhetoric against some of its practical applications. Finally, where Khomeini's rhetoric is very top down, Koulaei asserts the wisdom of the common believer on ethical matters. In particular, she emphasizes the importance of knowledge that arises out of diverse situated experiences. This is the logic behind her very different public role for women: as contributers to communal understanding of proper political practices. This final shift is significant because it uses the clerical logics of segregation to compose an argument for integrated political participation.

SUMMARY OF CREATIVE CONFORMITY

In this chapter I have juxtaposed women's arguments about veiling and ordination against clerical teachings on the same themes to show what women do with the clerical logics relating to women's bodies. In doing so it has become clear that the women take on some components of clerical rhetoric and shift others. Women argue for the same claims (hijab is a moral duty, women have no right to be ordained). Some of the clerical grounds are deployed (the definition of hijab, hierarchy is not discriminatory). In Koulaei's argument, the same warrant is used to authorize the move from grounds to claim (a conception of freedom warrants hijab). Both women use backings related to clerical authority: Koulaei uses her participation in the Islamic Revolution as backing, thus discursively connecting herself to Khomeini; Hitchcock uses John Paul's acceptance of her petition as backing. A further similarity between Khomeini's and the Koulaei's rhetoric is the layering of arguments within arguments. In Khomeini's rhetoric, claims are either unstated or buried in Khomeini's speech; Koulaei also presents a two-part argument, making one direct claim, and another indirect one.

At the level of logical structure, we begin to see how the women are working creatively. Khomeini tends to rely on the period of *ṭāghūt* to back his rhetoric. Koulaei introduces additional backings, such as human rights ideals, which entirely changes the focus on her discourse on hijab. Even when Hitchcock attempts to perfectly affirm John Paul's teaching on women's ordination, she offers decisively theological grounds in contrast to his historical ones.

The subject matter of this chapter has lent itself particularly well to exploring how even attempts to reenact clerical rhetoric result in changing not only the actual structure or components of an argument but also the logics on which it is based. The shift enacted by Hitchcock's affirmation of John Paul II's teaching on ordination, for example, is on one level more radical than the discursive practice of Isasi-Díaz explored in chapter 3, despite the former being "conservative" and the latter "liberal." Koulaei does not need to directly rebut clerical rhetoric on public veiling to turn it into an opportunity for feminist politics.

These shifts can be seen more precisely at the meta-level of logical tactics. For example, Koulaei uses the logic of specification, that is, applying the particulars of a given situation to an argument. If Khomeini was concerned with countering forced unveiling, Koulaei is concerned with how public veiling has become an opportunity to harass women. In this way Koulaei uses the temporal specification of the contemporary context to critique how hijab has come to be codified in Iran without a wholesale rejection of women's veiling.

There is also the logic of resolution, which resolves an apparent logical tension or paradox in the women's responses. This is the tactic in Koulaei's use of ambiguous hijab legislation to argue for women's fundamental choice in the form of hijab. Hitchcock also engages in this tactic by offering significantly different grounds for the male-exclusive clerical class, implying a logical tension in John Paul's rhetoric.

We see too the logic of reversal of order, that is, turning the order of the logical structure on its head. This is the case with Koulaei's defense of diversity in hijab practices and her link of hijab to a specific conception of freedom, as opposed to Khomeini, who begins with freedom and moves to hijab to make a different claim about both.

Finally there is the logic of praxis, reworking theoretical arguments into practical ones. Koulaei leverages Khomeini's rhetoric against some of its practical applications in the Islamic Republic. Hitchcock uses this tactic to move from her theological justification for a ban on ordination to her practical justification for her organization's direct service to women on moral issues. She makes women, and not John Paul, the source of knowledge.

THE TACTIC OF FEMINIST EMBODIMENT

A chapter devoted to hijab and ordination in a book on the feminist politics of Catholic and Shi'i women is not surprising. What is distinct about the approach here is that the male clerical rhetoric on these issues is considered beyond the specific moral codes they imply (women's duty to veil, ban on women's ordination) in order to understand the implications for embodied public participation. This allows us to see how women use the logics associated with gendered bodies to make feminist arguments.

On one hand, the clerical rhetoric on these issues focuses on controlling women's public performance: women's bodies are covered to prevent sexual tension, women are banned from the priesthood because their bodies are inappropriate in this context. But clerical arguments also open up possibilities for other discussions. In Khomeini's speeches on hijab, he moves beyond hijab as an act of piety that signals women's modesty and sexual segregation to its role in national politics and conceptions of freedom. John Paul's argument about exclusion of women from the Catholic priesthood is about not only Church leadership, but rather also ordination conceptualized in terms of a vocation to serve that reflects to some extent the longevity of a chain of male leadership back to Christ and Peter. It entails a thick meaning of hierarchy as related to theological order. In both cases the rhetoric does not merely convey a particular rule to women (you must wear hijab, you cannot be ordained). These issues are used as occasions to discuss the proper role of women's bodies in the public sphere. In both cases the clerical arguments create opportunities for women's creative conformity.

This creativity is perhaps not as initially obvious as elsewhere in this volume given a high level of conformity in the women's responses. For Koulaei, the legal mandate of hijab as a public religious duty makes her close citation of Khomeini's rhetoric a necessity. It becomes clear, though, that this citation is on one level only a matter of perception, because her argument is tactically quite different. For Hutchinson, close citation is the intention: she tries to perfectly affirm (in her words) John Paul's teaching on ordination. But here again the moral guidance is shifted because Hitchcock does not make exactly the same argument. Furthermore, her embodied performances, such as starting an NGO and giving moral advice directly to women, do not necessarily match with the primary claim of her address.

Taken together, Koulaei and Hitchcock can be seen to shift the clerical logics of women's embodiment three ways. First, the central ethical ideal of order, which hijab and ordination exemplify, is shifted. For Khomeini, hijab is about the public segregation of the sexes. Koulaei uses Khomeini's logical connection between freedom and the veil, but her central ethical ideal is not public segregation as order but rather the proper order of political action. For John Paul, a ban on women's ordination in the Roman Catholic Church is the realization of the ideal of order as institutional hierarchy. Here the stability John Paul advocates is the constancy of male leadership as the physical embodiment of Christ. Although Hitchcock cites his concept of hierarchy, her rhetoric is centered on the ethical idea of a discipleship of equals and therefore creates a form of service and leadership that is not at all hierarchical. This can be seen most directly in the advice-giving activities of her organization.

A second shift through the women's discourse takes place at the level of parameters of public actions. The clerics share a concern with placing limitations of what counts as proper public action for women by setting rules for public dress and barring women from particular leadership positions. Their limitations on the roles of women's bodies in public are both visual (through veiling) and symbolic (through a ban of women's bodies in certain capacities from the pulpit). In the clerical rhetoric, women's bodies are important sites for maintaining control, whether that control is of church tradition or a theocratic nation-state. The women, however, use these same gendered bodily logics to argue for a larger role for women. For Koulaei, the subject of veiling becomes an opportunity to argue, through the critique of national laws based on a Muslim women's experience of veiling in postrevolutionary Iran, for an expanded political role for women. Hitchcock expands women's leadership in the community to include the role as moral guides for the community. Women thereby leverage rather than overcome their bodily roles through acts of surrender and seizure, presentation and truancy.

NOTES

1. Women who make this type of argument include Joy Barnes, Mary Ramerman, Joan Chittister. For further background, see Bonavoglia, *Good Catholic Girls*, 239–52; Weaver, *New Catholic Women*, 109–18.

2. Schüssler Fiorenza, *But She Said*, 20.

3. Ibid.

4. See, for example, Fatima Mernissi's groundbreaking work, *The Veil and the Male Elite* (1991), or Marnia Lazreg's most recent work on veiling, *Questioning the Veil* (2009).

5. For example, Murtaza Mutahhari (1920–79), a prominent Iranian ayatollah, argues in seven lectures published under the title *The Islamic Modest Dress* that a community's morality depends on the veiling of its women. His argument hinges on the concept of a social dignity that veiling protects, and forms the logical basis for the justification for national laws that require public veiling in Muslim majority states.

6. John Paul II, *Ordinatio sacredotalis*.

7. Ibid., para. 4.

8. Ibid., para. 1. John Paul is here quoting Paul VI, "Response to the Letter."

9. John Paul II, *Ordinatio sacredotalis*, para. 3.

10. Ibid. and Paul VI, "Address on the Role of Women."

11. Paul VI, "Declaration on the Question of the Admission of Women."

12. Catechism of the Catholic Church, no. 1577.

13. John Paul II, *Ordinatio sacredotalis*, para. 4. Emphasis added.

14. Note that this was not explicitly part of the argument in the earlier *Inter insigniores* justification for the ban on women's ordination.

15. John Paul II, *Ordinatio sacredotalis*, para. 2.

16. Ibid., para. 3.

17. Ibid. Roles for women mentioned in this letter include "holy martyrs, virgins and mothers of families." Ibid., para. 11.

18. Ibid., para. 3.

19. John Paul II, "Women in the Life of the Priest," 754.

20. Hitchcock, "Affirmation for Catholic Women," 177–78.

21. Hitchcock, "Women for Faith and Family," 163–76.

22. Hitchcock's conversion story is published as part of a larger collection in *Spiritual Journeys* by Daughters of St. Paul Press.

23. Hitchcock, "Women for Faith and Family," 163.

24. Ibid., 164–65. She makes this point more explicit later in her essay: "One modest achievement with which Women for Faith and Family might be credited is that it is now impossible for dissenting feminists to claim convincingly to speak for all Catholic women." Ibid., 176.

25. Hitchcock, "Affirmation for Catholic Women," 178.

26. The number of signers is according to the Women for Faith and Family website, www.wf-f.org.

27. Hitchcock, "Affirmation for Catholic Women," 178.

28. Ibid., 166.

29. Ibid., 168.

30. Hitchcock, "Ten-Thousand Names," 4.

31. Hitchcock, "Women for Faith and Family," 166.

32. Hitchcock describes the work of WFF as follows: "The volunteer staff responds to these requests. In 1994, at this writing, three volunteers spend one day a week in the 'mailroom' in one woman's home, answering letters and fulfilling routine requests for WFF publications. . . . Occasionally a request may involve research and/or consultation with or referral to other individuals or organizations with appropriate expertise. Most research, when necessary, can be done in the office library or nearby university libraries, or via computer-accessible resources." Ibid., 169.

33. Ibid., 168–69.

34. Ibid., 171.

35. Paul VI, "Response to the Letter."

36. Interestingly, this is also similar to the type of work Iranian women do in the discipline of women's studies, as discussed in chapter 3.

37. This law was not supported by all women. For example, Shahla Haeri argues, "The law posed considerable difficulties for those women who did not wish to leave their homes unveiled, and for men who could not bear to allow their women to appear unveiled in public." "Temporary Marriage," 107–8.

38. Scholars have pointed out the class distinctions that ground different veiling practices. For a study focused on Cairo that links re-veiling practices to an emerging middle class, see MacLeod, *Accommodating Protest*.

39. Of course chador did not become a symbol at the time of the Islamic Revolution, rather it was an existing symbol that was deployed within a new context. In this way, hijab is not merely a religious, ethical, or political symbol, but also deeply implicated in the construction of gender in Iran. For a historical tracing of this issue, see Najmabadi, *Women with Mustaches*, 132–55.

40. As translated by Kar, "Shari'a Law in Iran," 49.

41. Ratified August 9, 1983. Referred to as *Ta'zīrāt* in Persian.

42. Paidar, *Women and the Political Process*, 342. The fact that the law focused on improper hijab and not disveiling is further evidence that by 1983 women did not appear unveiled in public.

43. Ibid., 344.

44. Sadr, "Bad hijāb dar qānūn," 44.

45. During the interview, Fallaci asked why women must hide beneath the chador. The response was as follows: "First of all, this is something that is their choice, and they have chosen it for themselves. What right do you have to deprive them of their choice? If we tell the people to come out and demonstrate their approval for Islamic dress, whether the chador or some other form, out of our population of 35 million, 33 million would come out. What right do you have to stop them? What kind of dictatorship is this you want to impose on the women? Secondly, we do not say a woman has to wear a specific type of dress, particularly in cases of women your age there are no specifications. We are concerned mainly with the younger women who when they make up and dress up draw hordes of young men after them. It is these women we are stopping. They don't need your sympathy." Khomeini, "Interview with Oriana Fallaci," 86.

46. Khomeini, "Bayānāt-i Imām Khumaynī dar jam'-i gurūhī," 265–70.

47. "Īrān rā bāzārī kunand az barā-yi Āmrīkā va kishāvarzī-i Īrān rā tabāh kunand tā muḥtāj bishavad Īrān bih Āmrīkā dar hamah chīz." Ibid., 266.

48. "Mā va shumā hamah dīdīd kih dar zamān-i īn pidar va pisar ān ikhtināqī būd kih shāyad dar ṭūl-i tārīkh-i Īrān sābiqah nadāsht, nah mard āzād būd va na zan, hamah dar ikhtināq būdand, hamah dar ranj būdand. . . . Az jumlah-i chīz-hāyī kih dar zamān-i Riza Khān bih taba'-i Ataturk anjām girift yakī ittiḥād-i shakl būd va yakī kashf-i hijāb. Ān vaqt īn ittiḥād-i shakl va īn kashf-i hijāb rā dar būq va karnā, bulandgū'hā-yi ānhā chih ta'rīf'hā-yī kardand, chih maddāḥī'hā-yī kardand. . . . Ba'd dīdīm kih qażiyyah-i kashf-i hijāb qażiyyah'ī nabūd kih īnhā bikhvāhand barā-yi khānum'hā khidmat bikunand, īnhā mī'khvāstand kih barā-yi īn ṭabaqah ham bā zūr'āzmāyī va bā fishār, bā zūr īn qishr rā ham nābūd kunad, ān ma'āsirī kih īnhā dārand, ān khidmat'hāyī kih īn qishr mī'khvāhand bih millat bikunand, ān khidmat'hā-yi arzandah'ī kih bānuvān-i mā 'uhdah'dār-i ān hastand, ān az dastashān giriftah bishavad va naguzārand īnhā ān khidmat-i aṣīlī kih bāyad bikunand va ān tarbiyat-i bachchah'hā kih ba'd'hā maqdārāt-i mamlakat bih dast-i ānhāst īnhā naguzārand kih īn khidmat anjām giriftah bishavad...az īn jahat naqshah īn būd kih īn bānuvān rā az ān maqām-i aṣīl-i buzurgī kih dārand kinār bizanand va bih khiyāl-i khvudashān nīmī az īn jam'iyyat-i Īrān rā āzād kunand." Ibid., 266–67.

49. "Albatah shughl barā-yi zan, shughl-i ṣaḥīḥ barā-yi zan hīch māni'ī nadārad lākin na ānṭawrī kih ānhā mī'khvāstand, ānhā naẓarashān bih īn nabūd kih zan yak ishtighālī paydā bikunad, naẓarashān bih īn būd kih zan rā misl-i mard'hā ham, zan'hā rā va mard'hā rā az ān maqāmī kih dārand munḥaṭṭ kunand naguzārand yak rushd-i ṭabī'ī az barā-yi qishr-i zan paydā bishavad yā yak rushd-i ṭabī'ī az barā-yi qishr-i mard." Ibid., 267.

50. "Ān tavaqqu'ʹdārʹhā-yi bījā kih hīch bih īn umūr kār nadāshtand yak nafar kushtah nadādand ānhā ḥālā āmadand yakī mīʹkhvāhad vazīr bishavad, yakī mīʹkhvāhad vakīl bishavad, yakī mīʹkhvāhad chih bishavad." Ibid., 268.

51. "Alān ham shumā ṭabaqahʹī kih Khudāvand ḥifẓatān kunad, Khudāvand sa'ādat bih shumā bidahad shumā hīch tavaqqu'ī nadarīd." Ibid.

52. For a theoretically savvy argument about the role of habituation for Muslim piety, see Mahmood, *Politics of Piety*, 1–39.

53. On the one hand, the diversity of veiling practices moves us from actual rhetoric to embodied performances, which are not necessarily justified in discourse. These performances, however, are helpful for setting the context for the rhetoric I examine in this section because they also demonstrate claims about the moral life.

54. A chador (*chādur*) literally means tent. It is a loose garment covering the entire body, often black. It is often used in the Western press to represent veiling practices in Iran. It is a traditional form of dress, going back at least as far as the tenth century. See Algar, "Chādor," 609–11. If a woman chooses not to wear chador, she will most likely wear a manteau, a coat-like article of clothing, at least knee-length, designed to disguise a woman's shape. Manteaus come in variety of colors and styles—"cowboy," "military," and "mod" manteaus were particularly popular while I was in Iran. Head coverings to wear with a manteau, or sometimes under a chador, come in a number of varieties. Two of the most common are a maghnae, a form-fitting veil that covers all hair and chin, and a *rūsarī* (on head) or *shāl*, a looser fitting head covering, tied at the throat or wrapped casually around the neck.

55. The term "bad hijab" is also used in Persian to denote improper veiling practices.

56. "Results of the 6th Majles Elections," *Bad Jens: Iranian Feminist Newsletter* (May 13, 2000) www.badjens.com/secondedition/election.htm. Despite their small number, these women were able to form an important block in the Majles through their shared focus on women's issues. They were successful in part because the Reform Party had gained control of the Majles that same year, and as a party, was more open to reforms on women's rights, for example the reform to custody law discussed in chapter 2.

57. Sherkat and Koulaei, "Iṣlāḥʹṭalabān va sukhangūyī az jins-i dīgar," 3–16.

58. "Man bih 'unvān-i yak zan īn ḥaqq rā barā-yi khvudam qā'ilam kih jāmi'ah āzādīʹam rā bih rasmīyat bishināsad." Ibid., 4.

59. "Mīʹkhvāstam nishān bidaham pūshish żarūratan yak naw'-i khāṣ nīst . . . dar bisyārī az mavārid nisbat bih anvā-i digar ḥijāb mīʹtavānad kārʹkard-i bihtarī dāshtah bāshad." Ibid.

60. "Imrūz hamah-'i zanān-i Īrānī, mis̱l-i hamah-'i mardān-i Īrānī, inṭiẓār dārand kih dar intikhāb-i naw'-i pushishashān āzād guẕāshtah shavand." Ibid.

61. "Ḥatman mīʹdānīd kih chunīn taṣmīmī chih fishārʹhāyī bih hamrāh dāsht. Ḥatta dūstānī bih man guftand: 'Īn kār rā nakun, rū-yi mīn mīʹravī.' Guftam: 'Mīʹravam rū-yi mīn tā nishān bidaham Islām ẓarfīyatash bisyār bālātar az taḥmīlʹhā va ijbārʹhāyī ast kih bih ism-i Islām dārad bih mardum mīʹshavad.'" Ibid.

62. "Namāyandah-'i zanānī bāsham kih ḥāzir nīstand bih īn vaż'īyat tan bidahand." Ibid.

63. "Man bih 'unvān-i fardī az nasl-i inqilāb, bā ārmān'hā va taṣavvurātī kih az Islām va ḥuqūq va āzādī'hā-yi zan dāshtam, hīch vaqt natavānistam īn naw'-i taḥmīl rā bipaẕīram kih insān'hā rā majbūr kunand bih shakl khāṣṣī dar 'biyāyand. Bā tavajjuh bih muṭāla'ātam tajrubah-'i dawrān-i Ittiḥād-i Shawravī rā ham dar' ẕihn dāshtam kih sa'y mī'kardand insān'hā'yī yak shikl tarbiyat kunand. Namī'khvāham muqāyisah kunam valī, bih laḥāẓ-i sākht-i siyāsī va farhangī va chārchūb-i fikrī, raftār'hā-yi rāyij dar Īrān rā shabīh-i ān barkhvurd'hā mī'dīdam." Ibid.

64. "Majmū'ah-'i vasī'ī az tuhmat'hā va tawhīn'hā-yi bī'pāyah va asās muvājih shudam kih bā raftār-i dīnī-i va akhlāqī kāmilan ta'āruż dāsht va ḥattá taṣavvurash ham dar mawrid-i ba'żī afrād barāyam mushkil būd. Ba'żī'hā ham az kasānī būdand kih 25, 30 sāl pīsh bā ānhā dars mī'khvāndam, dar vāqi' bā ānhā chādur sar mī'kardam." Ibid.

65. "Āyā chunīn ilzāmī barā-yi kull-i zanān-i Īrānī nah tanhā Musalmānān balkih Masīḥī'hā, Yahūdī'hā-yi va payruvān-i adyānī ham kih dar qānūn-i asāsī bih rasmiyat shinākhtah shudah'and vujūd dārad yā khayr. Bih laḥāẓ-i shar'ī bisyārī az afrād mu'taqidand namī'tavān yak zan-i Masīḥī rā mulzam kard kih ḥijāb dāshtah bāshad, bā hamān chārchūb'hā-yi yak zan-i Musalmān. Īnhā baḥs̱'hā'yī ast kih imrūz dar jāmi'ah-i mā vujūd dārad. . . . Agar bitavānīm yak nigah-i kalān bih majmū'ah-'i īn mabāḥis dāshtah bāshīm mī'tavānīm ān rūykard-i 'umūmī va kullī rā taqviyat bikunīm va bih maṣādiqash dar 'arṣah'hā-yi mukhtalif dastrasī paydā kunīm." Ibid.

66. This is why Koulaei is careful to make it clear that her "intention was not to weaken the Islamic Republic nor Islam itself." "Muntahā man taṣmīm-i khvudam rā giriftah būdam. Qaṣdam ham nah taż'īf-i Jumhūrī-i Islāmī būd va nah taż'īf-i Islām." Ibid.

CHAPTER FIVE

Republication of Moral Discourse

Compromise and Censorship as Political Freedom

This chapter explores how Catholic and Shi'i women produce and reproduce religious moral discourse within national and global political forums. Although male clerics envision women's proper participation in public debates about secular politics to be based on the articulation of official dogma, I consider how women apply the logics of this participation to pluralistic and democratic contexts. In doing so, they are able to intervene in the public production of knowledge in ways unanticipated by the clerical rhetoric. They thereby construct new visions of the proper role of religious citizens in secular politics as well as the role of all religious believers as public theologians.

Although all the creative conformers discussed in previous chapters of this volume are to some extent public intellectuals, I have focused so far on how their discourse shifts conceptions of the ideal woman within the family, before God, or within a particular religious community. I have intentionally postponed discussion of the ways in which their discourse is political insofar as it is situated in the pluralistic public sphere of global and national debates about a just state. I hope that by this point the reader's conception of what sort of discourse counts as feminist politics has been sufficiently expanded that I can safely address politics in a more traditional sense, as discourse aimed at public participation.

This discussion of public intellectuals is closely related to the subject matter of chapter 4 in that this is also an ethical "performance beyond the pulpit." My concern here, however, is not with religious leadership or moral guidance, but rather in what ways individuals participate in discourse at the public level, whether that public is defined as the family, the local community, the nation-state, or the world. What forms do women's voices take in public debate? How are these voices ethically or religiously conceptualized? What is their effect on the construction or maintenance of public ideology? How does this engagement form political spaces? Do religious women become full citizens by creating a nongendered political identity through gendered discourse?

Unlike those in previous chapters, the themes of the discursive practices I consider here, abortion and free speech, do not appear immediately to line up. However, the issues have several dimensions in common. Within the U.S. and Iranian contexts, both entail public debates in which religious arguments engage with more secular ones. This sort of public deployment of "God-talk" may be more familiar to the reader in the case of abortion in the United States. Free speech debate in Iran, though, involves similar arguments about the religious morality, particularly the morality of expression aimed at critiquing aspects of the Islamic Republic. These are also issues on which both men and women are assumed to have opinions. In other words, both are to some extent nongendered political issues within discourse (even if, of course, abortions are an action by women). These two themes allow us to consider when feminist politics moves past an assumed gendered subject, even if it does so through acutely gendered discourse. Finally, the feminist ethics of the women's responses to clerical rhetoric on these two issues will be shown to demonstrate a similar tactic of engagement that I am calling the feminist tactic of *republication*. The word *republication* signals the many ways in which women construct new visions for public participation such as through conceptualizing new *publics*, creating *publications*, and redefining what it means to be a *republican* all through the *republication* or reproduction of theological arguments within secular national or global political context.

The chapter begins with a rhetorical analysis of a message by John Paul on women's participation in the Fourth World Conference on Women. This message is used as clerical context for Frances Kissling's argument for compromise in the U.S. debate about abortion. Next, I consider a speech by Khomeini on ideological unity, which entails a logic of public engagement that Shahla Sherkat draws on in her argument for the virtues of self-censorship in the Iranian press. In the clerical rhetoric we see attempts to influence how women intervene in public dialogue as well as strong suggestions about what the specific ends of such dialogue should be: stability of the Islamic Republic and the eradication of abortion and contraception. The women's responses to the clerical rhetoric envision a different public role for religious women. On the one hand, they use the logics of public participation for different ends, such as establishing a role for women as the arbitrators of diversity who work for compromise within complex webs of moral discourses. On the other, they also change the form of public engagement using a feminist tactic of republication.

WOMEN'S ROLE IN HUMANIZING SOCIETY

In September 1995 the United Nations held the Fourth World Conference on Women in Beijing, China. As part of the lead up to the final meeting, John Paul II met with Gertrude Mongella, secretary-general of the conference, on May 26 at the Vatican.[1] As is customary with official papal visits, the pope presented Mongella at the end of this meeting with a written message.[2] This document is one way to access the types of subjects the pope broached with Mongella and the focus of the rhetorical analysis here.

The message begins by formally welcoming Mongella to the Vatican, and expresses appreciation for her efforts in organizing the upcoming World Conference. The themes of the conference, "equality, development and peace," are also affirmed. This praise of Mongella is an indirect endorsement of a woman's role as facilitator of reflection and action on these issues. John Paul extends this logic of appreciation to affirm all women's participation in public life: "Solutions to the issues and problems raised at the Conference, if they are to be honest and permanent, cannot but be based on the recognition of the inherent inalienable dignity of women, and the importance of women's presence and participation in all aspects of social life."[3]

In terms of the public engagement, this excerpt contains a claim for the importance of women's physical presence and active participation in all areas. John Paul calls this engagement the sharing of women's gifts.[4] Consider these two dimensions of engagement in terms of the theme of embodiment. In chapter 4 I explored the political ethics of women's embodiment, that is, their physical presence. In this chapter I focus on the second dimension mentioned in this passage: the forms and content of engagement the clerical logic envisions for women's active participation.

John Paul's argument for women's public participation is grounded several ways. First, as seen in the excerpt, women's participation is a necessary condition for finding the solutions to challenges to equality, development, and peace. This ground, in turn, is warranted by the need to recognize the dignity of women, which according to John Paul is not only backed by the Christian tradition, but also the preamble and paragraph 2 of the United Nations Charter.[5] In this way the warrant also alludes to another ground for women's full participation: if the recognition of the dignity of women requires full participation, and human dignity is the foundation of human rights, full participation becomes classified as a human right as well.

Another ground is "a recognition of *the unique role which women have in humanizing society* and directing it towards the positive goals of solidarity and peace."[6] According to John Paul, a woman's role as humanizer is warranted by her role as a mother. This can be seen in his insistence that "every new life is *totally entrusted* to the protection and care of the woman carrying it in her womb."[7] This responsibility functions logically as a backing in the message, but it also signals a shift at this point in the message to a discussion of abortion, a practice John Paul is concerned the World Conference will endorse. John Paul calls abortion a false solution to women's development needs, one that exploits women and denies the protection of the sanctity of life. John Paul's claim that women should participate fully in public life is qualified by the fact that this participation should defend the sanctity of life.

Another strong qualification of the primary claim (women's public participation is necessary) comes at the end of the message: "The challenge facing most societies is that of upholding, indeed strengthening, woman's role in the family while at the same time making it possible for her to use all her talents and exercise all her rights in building up society. However, women's greater presence in the work force, in public life, and generally in the decision-making processes guiding society, on an equal basis with men, will continue to be problematic as long as the costs continue to burden the private sector."[8]

John Paul is clear that women's private, familial duties should take a priority over her public, political ones. This qualification is so strong it becomes another claim and competes with the first: is this message about increasing women's public participation, directing it toward a Catholic conception of the sanctity of life, or constraining it? The rhetoric's logical components can be interpreted in all three ways.

This structural ambiguity is caused by the combination of John Paul's strongly gendered moral anthropology (see chapter 3) with his understanding of the proper engagement of Christians with the secular world. But it can also be understood as an intentional logical manipulation given the timing of this letter, which was released just months before the 1995 World Conference on Women in Beijing. John Paul was well aware that the draft program of actions circulating before the conference included language about access to contraception and safe abortion. His rhetoric here is explicitly directed in part to this conference's participants in order to persuade them to focus dialogue and projects on other issues related to women's development and peace.

It is also helpful to clarify what John Paul means when he says peace. In a short address titled "Women: Teachers in Peace," written to commemorate 1995 World Peace Day, John Paul provides the following clarification of his use of the word: "We are called upon to do everything possible to banish from society not only the tragedy of war but also every violation of human rights, beginning with the indisputable right to life, which every person enjoys from the very moment of conception. The violation of the individual human being's right to life contains the seeds of the extreme violence of war."[9] There is a conceptual slide here from peace, to human rights, to the right of life. In other words, peace is not juxtaposed by John Paul against armed combat but against what he calls elsewhere the "culture of death," the ideological devaluation of the sanctity of life which leads to extensive contraception use and abortion.[10]

In terms of political participation, a further point demonstrates John Paul's engagement with the realm of secular politics: he offers suggestions for how the nation-state can facilitate women's public roles though its "duty of subsidiarity, to be exercised through suitable legislative and social security initiatives."[11] John Paul does not elaborate on the exact content subsidies should take, but that their goal is to help women balance their private familial and public political duties.[12]

Many of the backings John Paul uses for his grounds and warrants are already apparent from the preceding discussion. In some of the rhetorical performances discussed in earlier chapters, he quotes the Bible more than any other source.[13] In this message, however, there is no reference to scripture. Instead he depends on formal papal documents (Paul IV's *Evangelium vitae* and his own *Mulieris dignitatem*) as well as his less formal 1995 World Day of Peace Message. The use of these sources as the primary backing shows the importance he puts on tradition as embodied in magisterium documents even for rhetoric aimed at a non-Catholic audience. But he also uses the United Nations Charter as backing, thereby acknowledging his audience's acceptance of human rights norms as codified in international law.

Qualifiers serve a central role in his rhetoric. On a general level, women's public participation, which John Paul encourages, is qualified by his insistence that their roles in the family not be compromised. On a more specific level, their freedom within the act of participation is qualified by a directive to focus their efforts on peace as defined by John Paul. In this way, the content of women's political participation is set before they engage in public life by the church.

Finally, John Paul's message creates a number of possible responses with its logics. For example, by making women's insights into peace necessary in terms of resolving conflict and by suggesting that women as women have something unique to contribute to public discourse, he opens the door to the argument that women's contribution may take a form and content unanticipated by a male cleric.

MEDIATING THE ABORTION DEBATE

The author of this section's discursive practice is Frances Kissling, who spent almost forty years "Making the Vatican Sweat" through her leadership roles at Catholics for Choice (CFC, formerly Catholics for a Free Choice).[14] She has her strong supporters, particularly in the women's rights and church reform movements. Although she by no means limits herself to domestic issues, in the national context she has been called the philosopher of the pro-choice movement and even "the pope of the Left."[15] Kissling is also infamous for her activities within U.S. conservative Catholic circles. The Catholic League for Religious and Civil Rights calls her "the most notorious anti-Catholic bigot in the nation."[16] The U.S. Conference of Catholic bishops have denounced her twice.[17] The Vatican denounced her in 2003 for her support of condoms to prevent the spread of HIV, methods of contraception, emergency contraception, and access to safe abortion.[18] But, as Kissling is fond of saying, "They haven't excommunicated me yet!"[19]

Given her organization's focus on gender, sexuality, and reproduction, she responds daily in press releases, op-eds, and speeches to the claims made by John Paul and others on behalf of the Catholic hierarchy. When I interviewed Kissling in the winter of 2004, I asked about the relationship of her work to John Paul. She answered as follows:

> Responding to John Paul II is a piece of what we do, but not the primary thing. CFC works to completely reframe religious experience. Responding to John Paul II's rhetoric is more of a political strategy for me. If I was just operating on my own I wouldn't necessarily use church documents as my touchstone. What he says is not the most important intellectual perspective, or moral perspective. But it is very influential. People pay attention to it. It deserves to be critiqued and rejected when it should be and not allowed to occupy a privileged space. To ignore it would be like a political scientist who ignores what George Bush says. John Paul's perspective becomes used by bishops and priests and becomes seen as the Catholic position.[20]

Kissling's critical stance toward Catholic hierarchy means that she makes a number of direct rebuttals to John Paul's teachings. In terms of his message analyzed in the previous section, Kissling does exactly what the pope seems to hope she would not: she attends the Beijing Conference and is a vocal Catholic supporter of access to safe legal abortion and contraceptives as part of women's development. Because my concern is with how response to John Paul's rhetoric can shift, not merely refute, his argument, this section considers three of Kissling's claims related to women's public participation in the abortion debate that act as more indirect responses: women, including potential mothers, have full moral agency; there is a value in fetal life; and mutually beneficial compromise is possible in the American abortion debate.

For the first claim, I draw from a published version of Kissling's posting on a church reform listserv that was later published in the organization's quarterly: "women are moral agents and as a matter of law should be allowed to make the decision whether or not to have an abortion with minimal state intervention."[21] This claim has also been the central tenet of CFC since its inception. In terms of John Paul's speech about motherhood, Kissling believes that motherhood as a vocation is a choice, and that no woman should be forced to carry a pregnancy to term. Her focus is on a woman's rights, which arise from a woman's status as moral agent.

It is noteworthy that even though Kissling's audience extends beyond the church to U.S. citizenry of all faiths in this rhetorical performance, her three reasons are theological:

1. There is no firm position within the Catholic church on when the fetus becomes a person.[22]
2. The principle of probablism in Roman Catholicism holds that when the church cannot speak definitively on a matter of fact (in this case, on the personhood of the fetus), the conscience of individual Catholics must be primary and respected.[23]
3. The absolute prohibition on abortion by the church is not infallible. Therefore we defend the right of Catholics to take positions on the morality and the legality of abortion that differ from that of the church.[24]

Note that although all three reasons are presented as if they are grounds, the second actually logically functions as a warrant: the move from the grounds (the fetus's status is undetermined and the teaching on abortion is an example of ordinary papal magisterium) to the claim (abortion is a permissible choice for women) is warranted by Kissling's understanding of the function of an individual's conscience in the moral life. Clerical teachings, even by the pope, on abortion are fallible and therefore, Kissling argues, dissent is possible. In terms of the discussion of conscience in the introduction, papal teaching on abortion acts to inform our human process of practical moral reasoning. But for Kissling, a woman's judgment of conscience, that is, her concrete decision, might tell her that abortion is permissible.

Compare Kissling's discursive use of women's dignity to John Paul's. For the pope, women's special gift to raise children reflects their dignity. For Kissling, women's dignity also backs her warrant, although she emphasizes how this dignity makes a woman a moral agent capable of making decisions about her moral life. In addition, Kissling backs her argument with official church documents, including *Evangelium vitae*, and American

Catholic theologians, including Daniel Maguire, Carol Tauer, Patricia Beattie Jung, and Thomas Shannon.[25]

In contrast to the majority of pro-choice rhetoric in the United States, Kissling has an important qualifier for a woman's right to make a decision about whether abortion is justified: "The act of taking a life in abortion is defensible and can have positive results, but in and of itself is not a moral good."[26] This qualification, based on fetal value, is the subject of a second claim that Kissling expanded on more recently.

In the winter of 2005, Kissling published an essay that can be seen in part as a shift from the focus of her earlier rhetoric on abortion. While continuing to defend a woman's right to terminate a pregnancy,[27] Kissling nonetheless critiques the supporters of choice for neglecting and even devaluing the fetus. "Those committed to the right to choose have felt forced to defend what appears to be an absolute right to abortion that brooks no consideration of other values—legal or moral. This often means a reluctance to even consider whether or not fetal life has value."[28]

Unlike the pro-choice movement, Kissling affirms that fetal life has value,[29] which she grounds in two ways. The first is that, independent of the debate over the moment of ensoulment, which Kissling thinks is "similar to arguments over the number of angels that could dance on a pinhead,"[30] the fetus, as alive, has value.[31] The second ground is related, but emphasizes the human dimension of fetal life. The warrants that connect these grounds to the claim of fetal value are Catholic teachings on the sanctity of life and human dignity. This is all backed, according to Kissling, by how most people feel about the fetus.[32]

Kissling, however, makes a qualification to fetal value through a distinction between merely human life (fetus) and the full personhood of a born human: "Inherent in our focus on women's rights has been our belief that fetal life does not attain, at any point in pregnancy, a value that is equivalent to that of born persons, most specifically women, infants or children who are most often cited in discussions of abortion."[33] In this way, Kissling combines these two claims (women's right to decide about abortion and value of fetal life) into a mutual feedback loop. Women are full moral agents, but abortion is not an absolute good just because a woman chooses it. Fetuses have value, but this value is not the same as that of a born person. With this logic, Kissling puts into conversation the two polar ends of the abortion debate—women's rights and fetal value—by showing how they do not negate but rather qualify each other's logic in important and meaningful ways.

At this point a third claim can be identified: it is possible, even logical, to affirm both women's rights and fetal value, what Kissling calls "walking and chewing gum at the same time."[34] Kissling suggests anti-choice legislative efforts by Senator Sam Brownback (R-KS) and Congressman Chris Smith (R-NJ) create an opportunity to express such a holistic position on abortion. If passed, the Unborn Child Pain Awareness Act (H.R. 4420 and S. 2466) would require doctors to inform women seeking abortions after twenty weeks that the fetus may feel pain and to offer fetal anesthesia. Although Kissling does not support the bill, [35] she argues that the underlying issue of fetal pain should be addressed by the pro-choice lobby. Kissling sees this as an issue on which both sides might reach a tenable compromise without legislation. If medical research suggests that fetuses might feel pain, a protocol could be established by groups like Planned Parenthood, the National Abortion Federation, and the American College of Obstetricians and Gynecologists: "Standard medical practice for abortion at the stage of pregnancy when fetal pain was a possibility would subsequently include either routine use of fetal anesthesia or the offer of anesthesia when requested by the woman following sensitive and careful counseling about the possibility that the fetus might feel pain."[36] This protocol could achieve at least a partial ceasefire to the abortion issue by combining the core claim of each side: affirming the right of each woman to decide whether or not to have an abortion and enhancing commitment to the respect for fetal life.[37]

Kissling's claims parallel John Paul's claim in an indirect, but very real way. Kissling is drawing on her humanizing gifts to intervene in the discursive "war" that has been prominent in the American Catholic community over the legality of abortion. She offers her insight on the shortcomings of both the pro-choice and pro-life factions and a concrete solution to the conflict on a specific issue: fetal anesthesia. Kissling thereby accepts to some extent John Paul's moral burden for Catholic women to participate in public debate through articulating a form of public Catholic moral theology.

However, what counts as public theology for Kissling is different. Kissling models a specific role for women as mediator in national debates on moral matters. She is making theology, not just supporting official dogma as she reframes religious ethics in more pragmatic and secular political terms.

BE UNITED IN WORD, BUT THINK FOR YOURSELF

The subject matter of Khomeini's addresses to women shifted over time, especially once the Islamic Republic was established and he faced a new set of issues as leader of a modern nation-state. For example, in an address on March 16, 1981, he indirectly takes up the themes of dissent and obedience in the community, or what I conceptualize as creative conformity.[38] At the end of the speech, after generally praising the role of women in society, the main claim of the address is revealed: women should not politically dissent. Khomeini specifies dissent as arguments that the Islamic Revolution was not successful: "There are those who tell people that this revolution has done nothing. They are people who do not count the transformation, which has taken place in you, because it is harmful to them and to destroying powers [e.g., the United States]. With their harmful rhetoric they want you to believe that nothing has happened."[39] He has a vision of a very particular sort of politically or rather apolitically good woman: one who tries "to be useful" to her country, but does not disturb the status quo.[40] Political decisions are not the concern of the masses, he argues. They should be "united and not pay attention to the issues that arise in the higher levels of governments."[41] If disagreements do arise, the women are told, "be vigilant and resolve these differences yourselves."[42]

This claim is built on the ground that dissent may actually prevent resolution: "You should remain 'united in word,' which can bring prosperity to this society, and 'disunity of word' can perhaps, God forbid, lead to the special mercy of God, that has been bestowed upon you, being taken away from you and your country becoming again that same country that has suffered for many long years."[43]

Khomeini even implies that disunity might cause Iran to lose the war with Iraq. "If differences between people arise which cause, God forbid, us to be defeated in the war or, God forbid, prolong its resolution, this sin would be on the shoulders of those who ignited differences and the caused commotions in the alleys and bazaar."[44]

The importance of ideological unity is especially warranted for women because "women, in addition to being themselves active members of society in all different spheres, also train active members in their laps."[45] We saw earlier how Khomeini argues that women inspire men and train children. In this way women get triple credit: for their own activities, those of their children, and those of the men they inspire. But they are also blamed for any wrongdoing, or at the very least their moral or immoral behavior encourages the moral or immoral behavior of others. This creates an interesting practical limitation or even disadvantage out of a theoretical advantage: because women are so important to the moral life of Iran, they must be careful not only to be good, but also to obey. Khomeini seems to say to them, you are our core, but your voice, if it is critical, does not have a place in public discourse.

Khomeini uses one more warrant for his claim that women should not dissent: God has given women special favor that could be taken away. It is tied politically to women's participation in the Islamic Revolution, but is not eternal and can be taken back for any infraction. Mentioning the possibility of special favor being revoked functions as a threat of sorts: "if you do not obey, God will punish you." Here Khomeini conceptualizes political disunity as a fundamental religious turn away from God.

Khomeini's address shows an interesting tension between a command for political unity and another to "think independently and do not follow the ideas of others."[46] Take Khomeini's use of the backing of historical precedence of *ṭāghūt.* Using *ṭāghūt* to back a claim against political dissent is odd because during this period of Iranian history pious Muslim women did politically dissent. In the 1981 speech Khomeini urges women to "pay attention so that corrupt hands, pens, and rhetoric do not deceive you and return you to your previous situation."[47] The reference to independent thinking directly follows a discussion of Khomeini's often invoked enemies (the Shah, the West, secularists). In contrast, the command to not dissent follows a discussion of the postrevolutionary Iranian state and its government officials. This placement signals that in Khomeini's mind there is no tension: women must think for themselves when others try to corrupt them in a moral sense, but it is their job to follow the leaders of the Islamic Republic, the clerics, on all political matters. Now that the 1979 revolution has established an Islamic Republic, women should be politically supportive or silent. However, the way he constructs his argument produces a powerful qualifier: women should obey, except when they think it goes against their moral duties. And in light of Khomeini's praise of women as the keepers of Islamic morality during the period of *ṭāghūt*, it is fair to assume that it is up to women to know what their moral duties are.

Khomeini's rhetoric on political unity and the danger of political dissent becomes codified with regards to the journalism in the Iranian constitution, penal code, and press law. Take, for example, the 1986 Press Law, which states that the mission of the press is to "enlighten public opinion" in different subjects including social, political, cultural, and religious matters,[48] counter disunity in the community,[49] and promote Islamic ethics.[50] Although the law does not allow explicit censorship,[51] items that "violate Islamic principles and codes and public rights"[52] are not permitted. A variety of publications are therefore prohibited, including those that address the topics of atheism and luxury; [53] argue against Islamic morals;[54] endanger the "security, dignity and interests of the Islamic Republic of Iran;"[55] insult Islam, Khomeini, or other senior clerics;[56] or commit "libel against officials, institutions, organizations, and individuals in the country or insulting legal or real persons who are lawfully respected, even by means of pictures or caricatures."[57] Violations are punished according to the Iranian Penal Code,[58] and the managing directors and license holders of the publication are particularly vulnerable, and can be personally fined and sentenced to prison time.[59]

Just as political unity is codified, so too is Khomeini's mandate to "think for yourself." Consider the Press Law again. Included among the rights of the press is the right to critique and dissent: "The press has the right to publish the opinions, constructive criticisms, suggestions, and explanations of individuals and government officials for public information while duly observing the Islamic teachings and the best interest of the community. Constructive criticism should be based on logic and reason and void of insult, humiliation, and detrimental effects."[60] This is a tenuous mandate to act as a public critic, however extremely qualified.

This leads us to a possible response created within the logical form of the 1981 speech on ideological unity: Khomeini attempts to simultaneously hold together the importance of political assent under the Islamic Republic and political dissent under *ṭāghūt*. But this keeps dissent and assent in tension, especially in a post-Khomeini Republic in which women sometimes argue that the imperfect implementation of Islamic government requires them to "think for themselves" again. This is an example of how an ever-widening rhetorical space is created by Khomeini's rhetoric now that he is gone. Because all Iranians are required to be good Muslims in order to be good citizens, the practice of public theology is the responsibility of every Iranian.

SELF-CENSORING AS A TIGHTROPE ACT

Although a number of scholars have argued that media is at the center of the Iranian women's movement, Iranian journalism in general has also been criticized for merely repeating official positions.[61] Indeed, we have seen that the press in Iran is closely regulated and subject to a number of federal laws. This restriction makes the production of moral discourse in the Iranian press a good case study to explore the possibilities for creativity under conditions of external control. In this section I demonstrate how one journalist produces innovative moral expression, not only despite, but also because of conditions of strict regulation.

Print media devoted to women's issues has existed in Iran for almost a century. Many Iranian organizations focused on women's issues publish newsletters or journals in addition their other activities.[62] Other organizations are devoted primarily to journalism about women in Iran, the most prominent being *Zanān* (women), sometimes called the *Ms. Magazine* of Iran, which at its height of popularity had a circulation of more than one hundred thousand.

In 2008, after seventeen years of production, *Zanān* had its license revoked by the Iranian Press Supervision Board. That the Iranian authorities closed the magazine is not surprising: between 2006 and 2008 alone forty periodicals were banned. What is surprising, given the feminist politics of *Zanān*, is that it survived for the seventeen years it did. Reports in English language press credit *Zanān*'s longevity to its managing editor, Shahla Sherkat, who manages "to avoid general politics" and instead focus on "women's issues."[63] These statements, however, misrepresent the nature of debate over women's status in Iran. These debates have become, certainly since at least the beginning of the twentieth century, intertwined with political debates over the status of Islamic authority in Iran and what constitutes the proper form of government in a Muslim majority state. Certainly it is not fair to say that Sherkat avoided politics when she published on contentious issues such as Western feminist theory, homosexuality, HIV/AIDS, and theological critiques of certain Iranian laws. I argue that rather than by avoidance of contentious issues, the longevity of *Zanān* is better explained through Sherkat's mastery of the tactics of creative conformity. Specifically, she has used Khomeini's logics of political unity, dissent, and obedience to fund a specific form of rhetoric in the women's press.

Shahla Sherkat participated in the Islamic Revolution under Khomeini, demonstrating in the streets against the Shah. She is now widely known in Iran as a reformist journalist and best known outside Iran as a member of the group of reformists who were sentenced to prison time (her four months were later commuted on appeal) and fines (hers was the equivalent of US$3,000) for participation in a Berlin conference in 2000, during which the Islamic Republic was criticized. *Zanān* was launched in 1991 after Sherkat was pushed out of her position as managing editor of *Zan-i rūz* (*Today's Woman*), a weekly geared toward propagating a particular conception of the post-Revolution ideal woman. In the context of increased factional conflicts at the end of the war with Iraq, Sherkat was fired after eight years with the publication because she was considered an opponent of the conservative leadership of *Zan-i rūz*.[64] According to Sherkat, unhappy with the formulaic representation of women in *Zan-i rūz*,[65] she had obtained a license to publish the monthly *Zanān* before being fired.

When Sherkat and I met in 2004, I asked her about the relationship between Khomeini's rhetoric and her current work and she mentioned two legacies. She argued that Khomeini encouraged the women's press by allowing Muslim women to be more active in public life.[66] In addition, and even more important for *Zanān* magazine, Khomeini, through the Islamic Revolution, increased political solidarity: "Before the 1979 Revolution, social participation was only for the elite or women who were married to power. But the Revolution was a mass movement, and as a result many women across social sectors became interconnected. We left the four walls of our houses and became participants in new ways."[67] Sherkat conceptualizes *Zanān* as a space in which different women, with different beliefs and socioeconomic backgrounds, can speak to each other.

Sherkat's rhetoric about the role of censorship within the women's press can be read as a form of response to Khomeini's claims about political unity. I draw from three sources of Sherkat's rhetoric: her 1991 editorial for the first issue of *Zanān*;[68] her 2004 editorial for the 100th issue of *Zanān*;[69] and a 2004 interview with Sherkat for the 100th issue of *Zanān*.[70] I focus primarily on the 2004 editorial, using the other sources to help explain Sherkat's labyrinthine and sometimes obtusely written discourse—qualities that will be shown to be discursively productive.

Sherkat's editorials are often highly poetic, and her nuanced use of language, metaphor, and allegory is difficult to convey in translation. For example, the title of her editorial "100 tāziyānah bih khātir-i ʻishqī mamnūʻ!" ("100 Lashes for Forbidden Love") is itself multilayered, invoking at one level the existence of flogging as punishment in the Iranian Penal Code for certain sexual acts, including lesbianism. But in the text the lover is God, and the practice of publishing a woman's magazine equated to a mystical journey, which has left Sherkat "with broken bones and a scarred head and face."[71] Her editorials are sophisticated, layered, and responsive to many different forms of discourse, and could easily be the subject of an entire book about creative conformity. For the most part I limit myself to the informal logic of her rhetoric, focusing specifically on her argument about the practice of self-censorship at *Zanān* on her watch.

When Sherkat speaks directly about censorship, she calls it a "bestowed blessing" that has trained Iranian journalists "to have expertise to know how to write in order to be able to continue to write."[72] Censorship as a bestowed blessing is a surprising claim from a leading publisher in Iran who has been arrested, had her publication shut down, and summoned to court, all because of articles published in her magazine.[73] Her claim is grounded in two ways. Censorship, at least in form, is self-imposed. Despite harsh press laws in Iran, Sherkat does not submit her magazine to any government agency for approval before publishing. "We have freedom of expression," she joked with me when I interviewed her in 2004, "just not freedom after expression!" So while censoring is necessary for the magazine's survival, the form of censorship is up to the editor. Sherkat takes calculated risks, determining which articles or statements should be published as a public service and which should not be because they might jeopardize *Zanān*'s ability to educate and influence public opinion.

This leads to a second ground; mainly that censorship becomes an opportunity for creative expression. Sherkat writes, "If there were no censorship, the allusive language of journalism, which has developed during the past years under censorship, would not be as rich!"[74] On the one hand, the artistic quality of the editing and self-censorship is Sherkat's literary style. On the other, the creativity goes beyond a literary art form. There is also artistry to mastering the unstated rules of the rhetorical game in Iran. Since the rules are ambiguous, Sherkat needs to be tuned into the local parameters of discourse. In terms of religion, she must constantly ask herself, what are the assumed moral principles of Islam in any given year, month, week, or even day? What are the mullahs talking and writings about? What issues do women care about, to such an extent that the risk of publishing on them is worth the cost?

Sherkat refers to this aspect of the artistry as a tightrope act: "Do you not think that a tightrope walker who walks on the high tightrope with no net has to know the steps and have the proper experience? If she falls because of one uncalculated movement, what do you make of this fall? Is this result of boldness or stupidity? In my opinion, this is the creativity of the third world journalist: because of coercion and out of necessity, she has learned when, where, and how to speak her mind."[75] Knowing when to censor and when to break the rules is all part of the skill of enacting freedom within self-censorship, and the balancing act of walking the tightrope. The assertion that self-censorship can be creative is based on Sherkat's assumption that it is possible both to be careful and say something new. In her words, she both self-censors and maintains a level of professional integrity.[76]

However, Sherkat's tightrope act is not precisely without a net, as she claims. The discursive warrants and backings in her informal argument in fact act as nets. These are what make her arguments tactical rather than strategic and allow *Zanān* to continue being published. Safety features are built into her prose, typically in citations of her local discursive context, including that of Khomeini's understanding of freedom. For example, one net used to protect her from charges of libel is the ambiguity of her writing. Sherkat is intentionally obtuse when referencing those who have caused problems for women, referring to them using the Persian pronoun *ānhā* (they), or with such complicated combinations of nouns and adjectives that it is impossible to tie her to one meaning.[77] Any criticism of leading clerics or government officials could be interpreted as libel and Sherkat is therefore careful to not name names.

A second net is her nod to Khomeini's distinction between politics and religion: Sherkat's use of Sufi language and imagery place her artistic prose firmly in the religious camp and thereby subject to Khomeini's mandate to think for oneself (rather than of political obedience). An editor's censorship takes on an even greater religious quality when we consider how, to ensure the safety of her publication and her employees, she must have a keen understanding of what counts as the unwritten Islamic principles that must not be violated. Sherkat is constantly interrogating the Iranian community's understandings of proper Muslim womanhood. She is the ultimate expert in local and current Islamic beliefs and practices.

Khomeini urges women to politically obey, which is codified in the Press Law as an obligation to counter disunity. Sherkat fulfills this duty and at the same time builds another safety net by publishing a variety of authors (secularists, Islamists, conservatives, feminists, and so on), opting for inclusion of many voices over deference to a single dominant opinion. Her editorial role ensures that this conversation produces unity. She thus morphs Khomeini's proposal that political obedience is a necessary precondition for political unity into an argument for tolerance, a concept she introduces through a driving metaphor:

> A hairpin presents the driver with two options: a decision to proceed with caution or to brazenly display driving skills and succumb to a desire for over-taking other cars and demonstrating power. Those with broken steering wheels usually do not arrive at their destination. Those who arrive later, do so in one piece. I wish every one of us would see ourselves as part of a cosmos, not in a single galaxy of individual ambition. Of course this dream will not come true with "wishes" and "ifs." It needs practice, cooperation, and tolerance of different beliefs in order for us to know the experiences, feelings, and desires of others.[78]

Sherkat here redefines the goal of unity entirely so that working toward the common good means including, versus obliterating, a diversity of beliefs.

Another safety net is created by reference to Khomeini's argument that women should think for themselves, codified as the press's duty to enlighten the public. *Zanān* fulfills this duty because it serves as a forum, as the title of her editorial of the first issue declares, for "a spring of consciousness." The range of issues Sherkat publishes on—feminism, homosexuality, botox, nose jobs, domestic violence, flower arranging—demonstrates that *Zanān* is a unique space for women to share their experiences as part of the process of developing women based wisdom. In our interview, Sherkat discussed the dialogue between women that *Zanān* fosters: "Women in general do not know each other's problems. This is one reason for the existence of *Zanān* magazine: to allow the flow between women, to allow women to know about each other's issues. It is a medium for elite and lower-class, secular and religious women to continue to unite into a common voice that funds the women's movement in Iran."

The relationship between Sherkat's and Khomeini's rhetoric is both dependent and transformative. On the one hand, Sherkat at least indirectly cites the components of Khomeini's rhetoric. She assumes the importance of placing limitations on freedom of expression. She uses, without alteration, one of Khomeini's grounds: the importance of protecting the Islamic Republic. She uses her relationship to Khomeini and the Islamic Revolution as backing for her rhetoric. Both Sherkat and Khomeini assume the interplay of individual free will and the legal, social, cultural, and religious obligations of the Iranian community.

Her citation of Khomeini is also seen in the safety nets she constructs for her tightrope act. For example, she fulfills her duty to politically obey by keeping the subject of her criticisms vague. Her role as managing editor and writer is presented as religiously motivated. Building on Khomeini's mandate for women to think for themselves, *Zanān*'s essays become educational for women in creating an opportunity for dialogue between different perspectives on gender and sexuality. Finally, Sherkat ensures political unity by redlining any references that might be politically agitating. She thus uses Khomeini's teachings to establish the religious authenticity of her argument.

At the same time, Sherkat shifts Khomeini's teachings on political dissent and unity in a number of creative ways. These transformations have been even more possible since Khomeini's death. Women can now use his rhetoric to gain religious traction in order to critique the imperfect implementation of Islamic ideals in the Islamic Republic.

Whereas Khomeini emphasizes the importance of political unity at all costs, Sherkat sees value in the diversity of perspectives on contemporary issues and posits tolerance as an important public value and path to unity through understanding. She therefore transforms Khomeini's assertion that political dissent can prevent a solution to national problems: for Sherkat, thinking outside mainstream discourse is a way to create a solution.

Khomeini assumes a distinction between religious and political actions, which Sherkat significantly changes in her discussion of censorship. On the one hand, her actions as editor are marked as religious, even when she publishes on political issues, given her religious language and the need for her to be aware of important Islamic principles and clerical teachings. But in an even more radical way, Sherkat implies that a distinction between political and religious actions is nonsensical in the context of an Islamic Republic: women must be proficient in both to be good Iranian citizens.

All these shifts are made possible by Sherkat's nets, which link her argument to the pervasive cultural values of her audience. In other words, her creative conformity is a political tactic specific to her local discursive conditions.

A final word about the possible unease the reader might feel in this discussion of Sherkat's artful argument in favor of censorship.[79] Certainly as Westerners committed to freedom of expression, it is almost impossible for us to take these arguments at face value. But what if we did? What if, following de Certeau's suggestion, we use this detour through another society to show how similar tactics of republication exist in our own society? One example might be public debates over hate speech that appeal to Christian conceptions of blasphemy or arguments over abortion rights, which draw on Catholicism, liberalism, and environmentalism. In other words, we can use the radically different conceptions of public expression in Iran as a springboard to reflect on the situation in the United States, where free speech is also not complete. My point is not that state censorship backed by coercive force is the best mechanism to moral creativity, but rather that even under conditions where the technologies of the self are backed by such force, there can be a blossoming of subtle innovation. The argument here is simple: freedom is not just the strategic rebellions against systems of control. Freedom is also the negotiations of authority, power, and liberty within such systems. In the case of Iran, it may be more obvious that such negotiation is the only option. But I would argue that radical autonomy is not possible in any context: there are always rules of discursive engagement. For moral discourse the question is how specific actions continue to play by those rules and yet shift the very nature of the game.

SUMMARY OF CREATIVE CONFORMITY

This chapter has explored two cases in which women engage clerical rhetoric aimed at forming how religious women participate in the creation and distribution of political ideology. As in other chapters, though perhaps less explicitly, the women analyzed use logical components in their rhetoric similar to those used by clerics. We saw women arguing for the same claim (the importance of ideological unity). The women use the same grounds or evidence (sanctity of life, the importance of deferring to the Islamic Republic). Kissling uses the same warrants to authorize the move from grounds to claim (women's dignity). Sherkat uses backings similar to Khomeini's (Iranian politics and a personal relationship to the Islamic Revolution). The women have tended to omit qualifiers from their rhetoric, or to use them as the clerics do to reinforce their claims (connecting two claims through mutual qualification). In particular, Sherkat's rhetoric follows the complex logical structure of Khomeini's with her careful labyrinthine presentation, which creates the illusion of qualification through the layering of arguments within arguments.

Although the women do draw on specific components of clerical informal argumentation in their responses, they also shift the logical form of this rhetoric. In terms of structure, the women rearrange and reconceptualize aspects of clerical rhetoric. Kissling and John Paul share a central concern about women's dignity. However, in the logical structure of her argument, this norm shifts from the warrant for the sanctity of life to the backing for women's conscience as the determinative factor on the morality of abortion. Sherkat transforms a paradox in Khomeini's rhetoric into a warrant: it is possible to both defer to clerical rule and freely express yourself.

In addition to these issues of architectonics, the women's creative conformity on the issue of public engagement shifts the conversation about the gendered moral life in a number of logical ways. The logic of resolution operates in both discursive performances: solving an apparent logical tension or paradox within the clerical rhetoric. When Kissling tries to harmonize Catholic teachings on fetal life and women's equality, she uses this form of informal logic. Sherkat also uses it in her engagement of Khomeini's two imperatives that appear to be in tension: a simultaneous emphasis on political deference and independent thinking. She combines the two into a coherent policy for a managing editor: self (based on individual reasoning) censorship (deference to prevalent norms). Sherkat thereby uses Khomeini's secondary claim, "think for yourselves," to abrogate his primary claim, "do not dissent" to argue that it is possible for a woman to both defer to clerical rule and freely express herself.

Both Kissling and Sherkat apply the logic of redefinition to great effect. This tactic redefines a concept central to a particular case of moral reasoning for a specific issue of ethical practice. In Kissling's discourse, she reworks the concept of peace from John Paul's definition, which links it to the culture of death, to an understanding that moves through human rights to women's agency and finally to safe motherhood. This allows her to revisit the scope of women's contributions to public discourse. Sherkat provides a redefinition of Khomeini's understanding of ideological unity so that in her discourse unity functions with an internal diversity that strengthens rather than undermines its stability.

The two women also share the logic of redaction. Kissling redacts the two extremes of the abortion debate through a process of critical correlation and compromise. Sherkat literally redacts essays for her journal *Zanān*. This is not censorship as taking away, but rather constructive censorship that can go in many directions and yield various results.

THE TACTIC OF FEMINIST REPUBLICATION

Kissling and Sherkat remain to some extent within the parameters the clerics set up for engagement in public discourse, deploying similar language and examples (abortion, free expression) to speak about women's public participation. At the same time, the women make significant changes to the clerical rhetoric. Taken as a whole, I call this creative conformity the tactics of feminist republication. The word *republication* in this context is meant to signal the many dimensions through which women construct new parameters for public discourse.

One shift is over what counts as the primary public, or audience, for women's discourse. John Paul makes it clear that women's primary roles as communicators are within the public of the family, based on their unique role in the rearing of children. The public Khomeini is most concerned with is the public of the Islamic (Re)public. In both, the discourse considered in this chapter is different than the clerical context. Kissling is concerned with U.S. legislation, United Nations' Programs of Action, and the tenor of U.S. public debate. She thereby expands the public implied in John Paul's rhetoric. Sherkat also shifts the public in her discourse from the Islamic Republic to a community of Iranian women that exists through the dialogue in *Zanān*. Although still directed to citizens within the Islamic Republic, this is a contraction of Khomeini's implied audience.

The word *republic* is embedded in the word republication as well, and the tactics of the women's discourse in this chapter has a distinct connection to the nation-state. What Kissling and Sherkat share in this aspect of their feminist tactics of republication is an unapologetic assumption that religious arguments have a place within democratic public dialogue. In contrast to some secular feminist politics, these women introduce theological logics, illustrations, and forms of knowledge into national discourse even when addressing nonbelievers. In this way they engage in a form of public theology for the sake of the republic.

The women also create new forums within which dialogue can take place. Playing with my category of republication, these publics are created literally through *publications*. Sherkat's magazine, *Zanān*, has become a new postrevolutionary space for moral discourse and thereby a way in which Iran's public space is reconstructed. Kissling's organization produces a journal as well in which her arguments on women's agency and fetal value were published. The title of this quarterly, *Conscience: The Pro-Choice Journal of Catholic Thought*, takes what might appear to an outsider as an oxymoron—pro-choice Catholic—and creates a distinct space for public conversation on this topic. By linking communication and censorship, participation and management, pluralism and diversity, the women's press creates new public spaces for women's political engagement through the writings. It also thereby shifts the production of ethical knowledge from exclusively religious institutions to a wider lay community and suggests that one component of feminist politics is the assertion that women have a particular take on how public dialogue should proceed.

The tactic of republication from another perspective is the republication of women themselves: the process by which religious women become full republicans, or citizens, of the nation-state. John Paul conceptualizes women's engagement primarily as teacher. Mothers, for example, provide moral instruction and guidance to children. For Khomeini, women's engagement is akin to a campaign supporter: holding up banners for the Republic. Kissling and Sherkat enact a different sort of position in their discourse. In the tactics of feminist republication, women insist that to be good women they must also be good citizens. This involves taking an active role in shaping the direction of public debate: rather than teacher or support staff, both women become facilitators of public dialogue. Kissling does this by trying to find a common moral ground between two sides of the abortion debate. Sherkat's facilitation is through her role as editor: she stays attuned to the local presumption about women's proper roles to better navigate which voices should be published and which should be redlined to be published within a different discursive context.

Republication can also refer to the "re-publication" as reproduction of theological arguments within more secular arenas. Through their engagement with the logical structure and internal logics of clerical rhetoric, Catholic and Shi'i women reproduce aspects of their religious traditions, even if selectively. Revision is inherent to this process. In more pluralistic forums it helps translate the official dogma to an audience that does not necessarily share all the assumptions of a believer. The process of reproduction also makes the gendered theological arguments more palatable to this audience by delivering them through a woman in her capacity as citizen versus a cleric in capacity of a spiritual leader.

Note how this tactic of feminist politics moves away from concern with a gendered moral life. Women's tactics do not focus exclusively on women, but on all religious believers through the ideal role as citizen. Although women's experience still remains central to their arguments in the context of citizenship, republication does not necessarily draw distinctions between the public engagement of male and female believers, but instead envisions a different sort of public engagement of believers in pluralistic democracies.

Finally, for both clerics, a goal for public discourse proceeds from the actual process of engagement: for John Paul this is eradicating the culture of death; for Khomeini it is ensuring the stability of the Islamic government. The women begin with less specific goals—compromise and tolerance. Although Kissling and Sherkat's engagement is on very different issues, they both work to create new meanings of engagement. Neither is sure what the result of the republication will be.

NOTES

1. Through the entity of the Holy See, the Vatican enjoys special status as a nonmember permanent observer at the UN, which affords its representatives status higher than other religions or organizations. And though the Holy See does not have a vote, it does have a place at the table with nation-states and has participated in this capacity throughout the preparatory meetings and final conference.

2. John Paul II, "Papal Message on Women's Conference."

3. Ibid., para. 2. Emphasis in the original.

4. Ibid., para. 5. John Paul quotes himself here. "Women: Teachers of Peace," para. 9.

5. John Paul II, "Papal Message on Women's Conference," para. 2.

6. Ibid., para. 5. Emphasis in the original.

7. Ibid., para 3. Emphasis in the original.

8. Ibid., para. 8.

9. John Paul II, "Women: Teachers of Peace," para. 10.

10. John Paul II first used this phrase during a tour of the United States in 1993, and later in an encylical. *Evangelium vitae*, para. 95.

11. John Paul II, "Papal Message on Women's Conference," para. 8.

12. Ibid.

13. Curran, *The Moral Theology*, 45.

14. Title of a *Ms.* magazine article on Kissling. Stan, "Frances Kissling," 40–43. Kissling joined CFC in 1978, became president and executive director in 1982. She retired in the spring of 2007.

15. Bonavoglia, *Good Catholic Girls*, 133. Quote attributed to Ada María Isasi-Díaz.

16. William Donahue, "60 Minutes Draws on Bigot to Slam Church," press release, December 11, 2000, The Catholic League for Religious and Civil Rights.

17. National Conference of Catholic Bishops, "NCCB/USCC President Issues Statement on Catholics for a Free Choice," Press Release, May 10, 2000, www.usccb.org/comm/archives/2000/00-123.shtml; "Statement Regarding Catholics for a Free Choice," November 4, 1993.

18. Pontifical Council for the Family, "Catholics for a Free Choice."

19. Frances Kissling, interview by the author, Washington, DC, December 12, 2004.

20. Ibid. The following year, after John Paul's death, Kissling wrote, "On a personal level, I always felt a certain affinity for this Polish man. He looked like most of the people in my family of Polish-American coal miners, and he seemed too often as harsh as they were. Hardened by a difficult work life and much deprivation, they were quicker to say no than to say yes and stubborn to the core. Of course, my reactions to him are largely projections, because I never saw him in person and certainly was not on his A-list, never having had a chance to engage him or be engaged by him." Kissling, "The Paths Not Taken," 12. In the same article, she questions his extraordinary status and influence on the Roman Catholic Church: "I bristle a bit at

the absence of any sense of history in the commentary on John Paul II. He was not the only twentieth-century pope with vision, charisma, mysticism and love of the poor. . . . John XXIII was as inspiring, charming, stubborn, smart and committed as John Paul II. John XXIII opened the church to the twentieth century, and John Paul II breezed through the door into the larger world. But John XXIII opened the church to internal democracy and left the church itself a better place; John Paul II, for all the bridges he built to the Jewish community, Islam, and the poor, blew up the bridges that spanned the divide between clergy and laity, men and women, right and left, gay and straight." Ibid., 13.

21. Kissling, "Abortion," 21.

22. Ibid.

23. Ibid., 22.

24. Ibid.

25. Elsewhere she further bolsters the claim with human rights discourse. Kissling writes, "I believe women have a basic human right to decide what to do about pregnancy. Other well-established human rights concepts bolster this argument including bodily integrity, the right to health, the right to practice one's religion (or not) and the right to be free from religious laws in modern democratic societies." Kissling, "Is There Life after Roe?" 12.

26. Ibid., 13.

27. Ibid., 12.

28. Ibid.

29. Kissling writes, "The fetus is indeed a wondrous part of our humanity; we are drawn to it as part of the ongoing mystery of who we are." Ibid., 15.

30. Ibid., 14.

31. Kissling writes, "The precise moment when the fetus becomes a person is less important than a simple acknowledgement that whatever category of human life the fetus is, it nonetheless has value, it is not nothing." Ibid., 14.

32. These feelings are not merely instinctual, according to Kissling, who writes, "There are scientific advances that affect the way we think about the fetus and indeed make it more present among us. For some these realities lead to a greater connection to fetal life; perhaps not as a person, but as part of the continuum of what we are, of humanity. Examples include 3-D and 4-D pictures of fetuses in utero that appear to be awake, asleep, walking, yawning—engaging in activities that are related to human identity." Ibid., 15.

33. Ibid., 11.

34. Ibid., 13.

35. According to Kissling, "The bill includes a mandated script that doctors must read to women seeking abortions and specific written consent forms they must sign. The wording of the script doctors are required to use is cruel. It is not completely accurate, is highly judgmental and completely negates the basic principles of good patient care, in which a health professional needs the freedom to decide how best to convey important information to patients." Ibid., 17.

36. Ibid.

37. Ibid., 18.

38. Khomeini, "Bayānāt dar jam'-i bānuvān," 152–56.

39. "Īnhā'yī kih dar gūshah va kinār bih gūsh-i ashkhāṣ mī'khvānand kih īn inqilāb kārī anjām nadād īnhā ashkhāṣī hastand kih īn taḥavvulī kih dar shumā paydā shudah ast chun muẓirr bih ḥāl-i ānhā va qudrat'hā-yi chapāvulgar ast īn rā chīzī ḥisāb nakunand va bā tablīghāt sū'ashān bikhvāhand bih shumā bibāvarānand, bāvar biyāvarand kih chīzī nashudah ast." Ibid., 153.

40. "Khvudatān barā-yi kishvar-i khvudatān kūshish kunīd kih mufīd bāshīd." Ibid., 154.

41. Ibid., 155.

42. "Bīdār bāshīd kih ikhtilāfāt rā khvudatān raf' bikunīd." Ibid., 156.

43. "Khvudashān tavajjuh kunand kih bā vaḥdat-i kalimah mī'tavānand īn jāmi'ah rā bih sa'ādat-i khvudash birasānand va ikhtilāf-i kalimah shāyad Khudā-yi nakhvāstah mawjib-i īn bishavad kih 'ināyat-i khāṣṣ-i Khudā kih bih shumā sāyih afkandah būd yak vaqt Khudā-yi nakhvāstah bar dāshtah bishavad va kishvar-i shumā ān shavad kih dar sāl'hā-yi ṭūlānī mubtalā-yi bih ān būdand." Ibid., 155.

44. "Agar chunānchih ikhtilāfātī bayn-i ṭabaqāt-i afrād bāshad va īn ikhtilāfāt mawjib shavad kih Khudā-yi nakhvāstah dar jang maghlūb shavīm yā Khudā-yi nakhvāstah ṭūl bikishad ḥall-i īn mushkil, īn gunāhash bih gardan-i ānhā'yī ast kih dāman bih ikhtilāfāt mī'zanand va tashannuj dar kūchah va bāzār ījād mī'kunand." Ibid., 155–56.

45. "Barā-yi īnkih zanān, bānuvān 'ilāvah bar īnkih khvudashān yak qishr-i fa'āl dar hamah ab'ād hastand qishr'hā-yi fa'āl rā dar dāman-i khvudashān tarbiyat mī'kunand." Ibid., 153. This is similar to the evidence Khomeini provided for women's special roles as mothers: the moral education of their children and ultimately their children's success or failure at living a moral life is their responsibility.

46. "Khvudatān mustaqil fikr kunīd va tāba'-i afkār-i dīgarān nabāshīd." Ibid., 154.

47. "Tavajjuh kunīd bih īnkih dast'hā-yi fāsid va qalam'hā-yi fāsid va guftār'hā-yi fāsid shumā rā bih ighfāl nakishānad va shumā rā bar nagardānad bih ḥal-i sābiq." Ibid.

48. *Iranian Press Law*, Art 2 (a) and Art 1. English translation by parstimes at www.parstimes.com/alw/press_law.html.

49. "To endeavor to negate the drawing up of false and divisive lines, or, pitting different groups of the community against each other by practices such as dividing people by race, language, customs, local traditions, etc." Ibid., Art 2 (c).

50. "To campaign against manifestations of imperialistic culture (such as extravagance, dissipation, debauchery, love of luxury, spread of morally corrupt practices, etc.) and to propagate and promote genuine Islamic culture and sound ethical principles." Ibid., Art. 2 (d).

51. Ibid., Art. 4.

52. Ibid., Art. 6.

53. Ibid., Art. 6 (iii).

54. Ibid., Art. 6 (i).

55. Ibid., Art. 6 (v).

56. Ibid., Art. 6 (vii).

57. Ibid., Art. 6 (viii).

58. Ibid., Art. 26 and 31. *Islamic Penal Code of Iran*, Book 5, Ch. 2, "Insulting the Religious Sanctities or State Officials" (Art. 513, 514); Ch. 15 "Personal Insults" (Art. 608, 609); Ch. 18 "Offenses against Public Morality" (Art. 640); Ch. 27 "Libels and Revilements" (Art. 697, 698, 700).

59. *Iranian Press Law*, Art. 27, 30.

60. Ibid., Art. 3.

61. For examples of general discussions of the women's press in Iran, see Khiabany and Sreberny, "The Women's Press in Contemporary Iran," 15–38; Keddi, *Modern Iran*, 292–94; Namazi, *Non-governmental Organizations,* 39; and Paidar, *Women and the Political Process,* 97, 125–26, 137. For scholarship focused on *Zanān* magazine see Eftekhari, "Zanan: Trials and Successes," 15–22.

62. For example, *Payām-i Hājar* (Hajar's message) is a quarterly published my Azam Taliqani's organization the Women's Islamic Institute, in addition to her other charity activities; *Pūshish* (covering) is a quarterly published by Shahla Habibi as part of her larger work coordinating women's NGOs at the Community Network of Women's NGOs in Iran; and *Farzānah* (a wise woman) is a quarterly published by the Institute of Women's Studies and Research, which showcases scholarship in the area of women's studies.

63. Ramin Mostaghim, "Iran: Zanan, a Voice of Women, Silenced," *L.A. Times Blogs* (January 29, 2008), http://latimesblogs.latimes.com/babylonbeyond/2008/01/zanan-a-voice-o.html. For a similar argument see Namazi, *Non-governmental Organizations,* 39.

64. Eftekhari, "Zanan: Trials and Successes," 16.

65. Ibid.

66. During our interview, Sherkat argued, "Khomeini stood up for women's rights in the face of other beliefs such as women should not go out in public, women should not vote. Khomeini's call for women to join the Revolution gave men permission to let women out of the four walls of their houses. Take the example of women's right to divorce. Women went to Khomeini and asked him about this issue and he said we could go to court to get a divorce in the case of abuse. At the time he said 'If I dared, I would say other things.' Given the political context, Khomeini could only do so much, but he did a lot." Shahla Sherkat, interview by the author, Tehran, September 7, 2004.

67. Ibid.

68. Sherkat, "Chashmah-'i āgāhī agar bijūshad," 2–3.

69. Sherkat, "100 tāziyānah,"4–6.

70. Sherkat and Staff, "Bā mudīr-i mas'ūl-i gūshah-'i rīng," 69–78.

71. "Bā ustukhvān´hā-yi khurd´shudah va sar va rū-yi zakhmī." Sherkat, "100 tāziyānah," 4.

72. "Kīst kih nadānad sānsūr az muqtażiyāt-i rūznāmah´nigār būdan va rūznāmah´nigār māndan dar sar´zamīn-i 'azīz-i mā Īrān ast va īn ni'mat-i i'ṭāyī

sabab-i varzīdagī va khibragī-i mā shudah tā bidānīm chigūnah binivīsīm tā bitavānīm bimānīm. Agar qavā'id na'nivishtah-'i sānsūr nabūd, kār-i rūznāmah'nigārī dar īn kishvar īn hamah jazzābīyat va hayijān nadāsht!" Ibid., 6.

73. During our 2004 interview, Sherkat discussed how she was taken to court recently over an article on homosexuality and feminism. She stated that anytime she publishes about feminism she risks a fine, magazine closure, or even arrest because of conventional beliefs that feminism is antireligion.

74. "Agar sānsūr nabūd, zabān-i īmāyī-i zhūrnālīstī-i khāṣṣ-i matbū'āt-i īn sāl'hā chunīn qavām namī'yāft." Sherkat, "100 tāziyānah," 6.

75. "Bih naẓar-i shumā yak band'bāz kih rū-yi band-i bārīkī dar irtifā'-i buland rāh mī'ravad va zīr-i pāyash ham kāmilan khālī ast, chiqadr jā-yi pā va imkān-i mānuvr dārad? Agar bā yak ḥarakat-i nasanjīdah suqūṭ kunad ism-i īn kārash jasārat ast yā ḥamāqat? Bih naẓar-i man īn hunar-i rūznāmah'nigār-i hūshmand-i jahān sivvumī ast kih bar asar-i ijbār va nīyāz yād giriftah har ḥarfī rā kay bigūyad, kujā bigūyad va chiṭawr bigūyad." Sherkat and Staff, "Bā mudīr-i mas'ūl-i gūshah-'i rīng," 78.

76. Sherkat writes, "Of course I also have a red-line for myself. Whenever I feel that my professional ethics are in jeopardy, I do not continue" ("Albatah man ham barā-yi khvūdam khaṭṭ-i qirmizī dāram. Har jā kih iḥsās kunam sharāfat-i ḥirfah' ī'am dar ma'raż-i khaṭar asat, dīgar idāmah namī'daham"). Ibid.

77. Take the following example from a section on religion in the 1991 editorial: "All of the discussion and arguments of today are on the one hand of those who care about the revival of religious thought and on the other hand of those superficial agitators of times and transformations. This shows that our religious thought has not remained immune from usurpation of wise enemies and ignorant friends" ("Hamah-'i baḥs va istidlāl-i imrūzah-'i dilsūkhtagān barā-yi iḥyā-yi andīshah-'i dīnī, az yak sū va hayāhū-yi sahl'ingārān-i zamān va taḥavvulāt-i ān az sū-yi dīgar nishān az ān dārad kih tafakkur-i dīnī-i mā az dast'andāzī-i dushmanān-i dānā va dūstān-i nā'āgāh dar ṭūl-i qurūn maṣūn namāndah ast"). Sherkat, "Chashmah-'i āgāhī agar bijūshad," 2. Sherkat refers here to the people who have caused problems for women, but given her grammatical structure and layering of adjectives, we are not sure precisely who is to blame.

78. "Sar-i hamīn pīch'hā-yi tund ast kih ādam'hā ẓarāfat-i tadbīr va nihāyat-i mahāratashān rā bā shahvat-i sibqat va namāyish-i qudrat andāzah mī'zanand. Farmān'burīdah'hā ma'mūlan bih maqṣad namī'rasand va ānhā kih mī'rasand dīr'tar ammā salāmat mī'rasand. Ay kāsh hamah-'i mā khvud rā dar yak manẓūmah mī'dīdīm na dar khalā'-i jāh'ṭalabī'hā-yi khvud. Albatah īn ārzū bā kāsh va agar muḥaqaq namī'shavad. Mumārasat lāzim dārad va kār-i jam'ī va taḥammul-i 'aqīdah-'i mukhālif, tā dīgar'khvāhī rā tajrubah va ḥiss-i maṭlub-i ān rā lams kunīm." Sherkat, "100 tāziyānah," 4.

79. My thanks to Aaron Stalnaker for pushing me on this important point.

Conclusion

Here I summarize the payoffs of a comparative case study that attempts to redefine feminist politics. Earlier in the book, descriptions of actual arguments women used helped us understand how feminist politics employ various tactics to construct ethical knowledge. The analysis broke down arguments to see better the practice of justification and the interactions of moral discourse. The aim was to see the precise production of women's creative conformity. Despite a focus on radically different issues, various feminist tactics of intellectual engagement are observed cross-culturally: symbolics, procreation, hermeneutics, embodiment, and republication.

Three tasks remain. First, we can now stand back and consider the Catholic and Shi'i women through the shared audience assumptions implied in their arguments. This allows us to identify commonalities and differences between them and their rhetoric to better explain why some politics work in one context but not in another.

Second, it is now possible to further describe the system of ethical knowledge the women participate in. I use the metaphor of a game to visualize the interplay of clerics and women to better understand how tradition is maintained and conveyed and the social aspects of authority.

Third, although the core chapters of this volume explain and describe the ways in which the religious women are creative conformers, still more can be said about these actions in terms of feminist politics. I address how creative conformity produces distinct ethical knowledge in the religious community, return to the issue of intention, and comment on the importance of comparison to identifying and understanding women's contributions to public discourse and religious norms.

THE BIG PICTURE: SHARED AUDIENCE ASSUMPTIONS

In the introduction, I discuss how rhetoric persuades through a logical form and affective logos. If the five chapters focus on informal logical form by deconstructing arguments into logical components and considering rhetorical responses, this conclusion looks more closely at how affectivity is used in women's rhetoric through their references to the value-charged ideas that a community adheres to.[1] In what follows, the five rhetorical performances of each respective community are considered together through the Perelman inspired categories of rhetorical analysis developed in the introduction (facts, presumptions, values, and hierarchies) in an attempt to identify the assumed agreements the rhetoric is built on. These agreements are the motivations already in place that women leverage for their political goals. In this way, these agreements map the contours of the discursive field the women reconstitute and give a general account of a more or less coherent religious ethical vision on the part of U.S. Catholic and Iranian Shi'i women, respectively.

Facts

I have defined facts as data that conforms to an audience's understanding of what is real. This means that attention to the facts women use in their rhetoric is an opportunity to understand local perceptions of reality. The Catholic and Shi'i women studied share three categories of facts that are important for the moral life: gender dualism, history of the religious community, and cultural origins of patriarchy. All the women studied assume the reality of the category of women and that gender dualism is an important component of the moral life. They speak about gendered duties or rights (Arshad, Koulaei, and Kissling), and the special challenges and opportunities women face for being good and living a full life as women within their respective religious communities (Isasi-Díaz, Hayes, Abbas-Gholizadeh, and Sherkat). The reality of a gendered moral life for some is ontological (Hitchcock), for others cultural and social (Hayes and Isasi-Díaz). Most women do not bother to ground gender difference at all, and yet this fact is the foundation of all the women's feminist ethics.

Both groups of women assume that early history of their respective communities contributes to contemporary ethical reflection. This can be seen in the women's use of sources such as the Bible (Isasi-Díaz and Hayes) and hadith (Gurji and Ebtekar), emphasis on the egalitarian nature of the early community (Isasi-Díaz, Gurji, and Ebtekar), and use of historical moral exemplars such as Eve, Hagar, Mary, and Fatimah (Isasi-Díaz, Hayes, Gurji, and Ebtekar).

Another fact all the women assume to some degree is the cultural origins of patriarchy. The distinction between religion and culture allows the women to affirm their religious tradition yet identify any clerical teaching they think discriminates against women as culturally, not religiously, based. For Cahill, this assumed fact becomes a way to rework Catholic teachings on natural law; for Abbas-Gholizadeh, it becomes a way to argue for the importance of women's special knowledge. Drawing from their experiences, the women work to transform problematic teachings to be more supportive of women and thereby more properly reflective of their respective religious traditions.

In addition to these shared facts, four key factual differences between the U.S. Catholic and Iranian Shi'i women's epideictic responses are evident. The first has to do with the historical legacy of their respective religious traditions. Although both groups of women assume the importance of their religious communities' traditions, the relevant facts of Catholic and Shi'i histories are of course different. The U.S. Catholic women assume the role of the Roman Catholic Church in the conquest of the New World (Isasi-Díaz and Hayes) and a legacy of social justice culminating in Vatican II (Kissling and Cahill). The Iranian Shi'i women assume Shi'i Islam as a minority sect faced with Sunni dominance (Gurji and Ebtekar), a legacy of martyrdom (Sherkat), and the failures of the Islamic Republic to successfully codify shari'a in a way consistent with women's moral duties and rights (Arshad and Koulaei).

A second difference in assumed facts relates to domestic political contexts as well. U.S. politics is the backdrop for the Catholic women studied. In some cases these facts present an opportunity to critique the content of public moral discourse in the United States, such as Hitchcock's argument against the priority given to religious dissent. In other cases, the reality of U.S. public discourse is used to try to transform Catholic teachings to make them more persuasive (Cahill and Kissling). A specific history of race relations in the United States is also invoked. For example, Hayes mentions the slave trade in her discussion of the black church, and Isasi-Díaz discusses the importance of the historic memory of Spanish conquest in the New World for the Hispanic community's relationship to the Roman Catholic Church.

Iran has its own national history. Women assume facts about Arab conquest and modern despotic and monarchical rule (Gurji and Ebtekar). In particular, the Iranian women use their participation in the 1979 revolution and war metaphors based on the ten-year war with Iraq to increase the affective impact of their rhetoric on the audience (Sherkat and Abbas-Gholizadeh). The biggest difference between the U.S. political context and the Iranian political context is the validity of religious and political dissent.

I discuss the general value put on dissent and obedience in more detail later, but in terms of political assumptions, any direct refutation of Islam or Khomeini's teachings is understood in Iran as an attempt to destabilize the government. Women in Iran therefore almost always frame their arguments in ways that make them seem to support the current regime. The consequences for not taking a pro-government stance would not only put the speaker herself at risk, but would also make it difficult for the audience to agree with the speaker.

A third category of facts that is distinct in the two communities is related to "women's nature." Despite John Paul's use of natural law as a source of moral law in Catholic theology, U.S. women tend to resist using human nature as evidence or authorization (Cahill and Kissling). Even Hitchcock, who attempts to perfectly affirm John Paul's teachings on women, does not use natural law to the extent that John Paul does. At play here is a distrust of moral arguments based on assertions about women's nature. This distrust is the result in part of the U.S. women's movement's success in complicating claims that move from observations about a woman's customary roles and attributes to proscriptions about her moral duties.

By contrast, nature plays a prominent role in the rhetoric of the Iranian Shi'i women. Note that this does not necessarily occur at the level of logical structure; natural law is not invoked by the Iranian women as a warrant. Yet an idea of women's special nature is behind Arshad's argument for women's custody after divorce and even Koulaei's argument about women's choice to veil. The distinction is that though natural law is an explicit source for Catholic clerics, in the U.S. context it is contested and therefore not necessarily persuasive. By contrast, women's natural attributes, as nurturers, mothers, reproducers, are assumed to be factual in the Iranian context and are often invoked to make rhetoric more persuasive.

The final fact with distinct ramifications in the U.S. Catholic and Iranian Shi'i reponses is the role of race and class difference in the moral life. The constraints of race and class are central to Isasi-Díaz's and Hayes's argument about Latina and black Catholics, but they also underlie Kissling's argument for poor women's access to medical procedures, and Hitchcock's against elite feminists defining what counts as women's proper roles. On the one hand, this can be seen as positive: Catholic women do not presume to speak on behalf of all women. On the other hand, it is a highly bifurcated view of women: white and black, rich and poor, liberal and conservative, prochoice and antichoice. By contrast, this sort of polarity does not operate in the Iranian women's rhetoric; the women's rhetoric tends to assume a much more cohesive group of Iranian women as their audience. Iran does not have the ethnic diversity of the United States, but it does have a substantial number of ethnic minorities, such as Kurds, Turks, and Afghans. Although issues of class arise, especially in Sherkat's writings, and certainly class was a central theme in the Iranian Revolution, race was not an issue in any of the Iranian women's responses I looked at. Without further study, it is not clear if this is because the Iranian women tend to address women as a group, rather than as groups within a group, or because the issues of ethnic minorities are neglected.

Presumptions

Presumptions are the opinions shared by a given audience, and can best be understood as what is considered to be normal or customary. U.S. Catholic and Iranian Shi'i responses share two presumptions, and differ on another two. One presumption found in the majority of the women's rhetoric is that it is customary to respond to John Paul's and Khomeini's visions of women's proper roles. In some cases this response is reluctant (Isasi-Díaz and Abbas-Gholizadeh) or strategic (Kissling and Sherkat). In most cases I studied, the response is indirect. The Catholic women acknowledge that when the pope speaks, many Catholics listen, and therefore the women engage John Paul's teachings. Khomeini does not hold a religious office, save for the one he justified for himself (*vilāyat-i faqīh*). And yet response to him is almost necessary in Iran given the political and legal status of his teachings. In other words, both groups of women acknowledge the importance of citation of their respective cleric, based on his institutional, customary, cultural, charismatic or legal authority. In both communities the individual women may or may not see the cleric as a helpful source, and yet they nevertheless respond to his teachings because they assume their audience believes clerical teachings warrant response.

As a whole, both the U.S. Catholic and Iranian Shi'i women think their cleric's vision is imperfect, that their leader's teachings can benefit from "a woman's touch." In some cases this presumption is based on women's experience (Hayes), in others on women's access to special religious knowledge (Abbas-Gholizadeh), and in yet others, on women's special dignity (Arshad). But even the women who affirm clerical teachings (Hitchcock and Gurji) presume that it is possible to make the clerical message on womanhood more clear and that women can and should take up this task.

The two groups of women differ in two assumed presumptions of their intended audience. For example, the U.S. Catholic and Iranian Shi'i women assume different opinions about liberal feminism, especially in terms of its belief in absolute equality between men and women. A number of the U.S. women made it clear in their rhetoric that they believe women's equality is a key presumption in U.S. public discourse (Cahill and Kissling). They attempted to make the most this presumption, even if, as in the case of Hitchcock, they thought it was flawed. The equality of men and women is theologically based on creation (Isasi-Díaz) and human moral agency (Kissling).

In the context of Shi'i Islam in Iran, the presumption is gender equity, not gender equality. Gender equality in the Iranian context means sameness between men and women, whereas equity denotes difference but parity. Independent of what the Iranian women might themselves think, they build arguments around the presumption that men and women have different duties and rights in the moral life (Arshad). Politically, this is why feminism is sometimes considered a dirty word in public discourse (Habibi): it is assumed to prioritize women or men, rather than understanding each in their proper relation to the other. Equity is theologically based on a distinction between materiality (body) and spirituality (soul). In Khomeini's and other clerics' rhetoric, men and women are equal spiritually, but their material embodiment makes them different. This means that in the embodied moral life, only equity between men and women is appropriate because true equality is possible only in a purely spiritual realm.

Another important difference in presumptions is over the role of religion in public life. In Iran, since the 1979 revolution, the law, the government, the constitution, and even citizenship itself, are expressed in Islamic terms. The presumption is that Islam is the public religion. We can see this in the women's use of religious language and arguments (Abbas-Gholizadeh and Sherkat) for what in other political contexts would be considered nonreligious topics (e.g., women's studies). In Iran, religious knowledge and rationality are appropriate to deploy for any public issue. By contrast, there is a strong presumption of pluralism in the U.S. Catholic women's rhetoric (Cahill and Isasi-Díaz). It is not that the women think that religion has no public voice, but rather they presume that Catholic arguments will be heard in a context where Catholicism is not the only option.

Values

An audience's assumed values are any object, thing, or ideal that the group agrees has influence on right action. Values therefore have an important role in assessment. The women's rhetoric demonstrates that they believe, or at least assume that their audience believes, that there are general values important to concrete actions required for women's moral lives. Shared values include survival, courage, political activism, and social responsibility—all modeled by Mary, Hagar, and Fatimah. Other values are related to the moral life in general, and apply to both men and women, such as human dignity and the sanctity of life. The women's responses share four such central general values and differ on two more.

All the women assume freedom within a religious community as an overarching value necessary for the moral life. At the same time, this is not egoism (Koulaei and Kissling). Rather we could say they assume what I called dianomy in the introduction, an account of the moral life that understands and interaction between multiple sources of freedom. At a more specific level, the Catholic women appeal to conscience (Isasi-Díaz and Kissling) and the Iranian women nod towards the Shi'i concept of *ijtihād* (Abbas-Gholizadeh, Gurji, and Ebtekar) as expressions of dianomous moral freedom.

A second shared value is actually a cluster of values: human rights. At times women use human rights as warrants (Gurji and Ebtekar) or backing (Kissling and Cahill), but all the women's rhetoric assumes the validity of the international human rights regime as an articulation of values that should have influence on right action. Human rights is a contemporary convention, consistent with, but not necessarily dependent on religious traditions. This shared source of values speaks to the success of human rights rhetoric in expressing itself in terms that conform to local assumptions.

The U.S. Catholic and Iranian Shi'i responses share the moral value of embarking on a spiritual journey to God. In the case of Fatimah, this journey increases her spiritual status, gives her access to religious knowledge, and makes her more fully human (Gurji and Ebtekar). The exemplarity of Hagar is grounded in part by the fact that God spoke directly to her in the desert (Hayes). These are not instrumental uses of religion for moral utility, but rather, as we saw with the male clerics, expressions of an understanding of the connection between mysticism and ethics.

Another group of shared values in the responses is related to women's experiences. All the rhetorical performances studied in chapters 1 through 5 assume that women's concrete experiences are sources for values about the moral life. Take motherhood, which was key in both John Paul's and Khomeini's vision of womanhood. These clerics focused on the roles of mothers in the context of a nuclear family, as bearers and rearers of children, and therefore motherhood implicated values such as service, self-sacrifice, and nurturing. Motherhood is also a central theme in the feminist ethics of the women respondents (Hitchcock and Arshad), however, the women tend to expand this vision to include a wider range of women's experiences. Women as mothers of the community are responsible for ensuring the future of the religious community (Hayes, Gurji, and Ebtekar), and as mother's of the world, women are the brokers of peace and compromise (Kissling and Sherkat).

Despite the values both groups of women share, the distinction about the value of dissent and obedience assumed in their respective rhetoric is important. In the U.S. Catholic context, Hitchcock identifies the value put on dissent, claiming that only women who are seen as resisting traditional roles are considered true feminists. This is in part because many U.S. Catholics disagree with certain aspects of papal teachings on women. But this priority of dissent also stems from an assumption that true freedom is negative freedom (freedom from a given constraint). By contrast, the Iranian Shi'i context considers such refutations to be unauthentic, driven by erroneous Western conceptions of women. Credibility comes not from dissent, but from citation and obedience. This is why the Iranian women remind their audience about their participation in the Islamic Revolution their personal connection to Khomeini, and cite the authority of men, especially male clerics, to shore up their grounds and warrants. They have successfully linked their goals to the government's development objectives.[2] Of course, the consequences for not playing by these political rules are very different in the two contexts. Being called an antifeminist, as Hitchcock argues she is because she is "too obedient," is certainly not comparable with being incarcerated in solitary confinement, as Abbas-Gholizadeh is for her beliefs, which were deemed too dissenting by the Iranian government. These consequences aside, however, the values of dissent and obedience operate in radically different rhetorical ways in the two contexts.

This is related to another distinction over value in the women's rhetoric that is cultural and linguistic. In the U.S. context, we value directness, particularly in public argumentation. For example, President George W. Bush's plain speak is credited in part with his popularity among U.S. voters in the 2004 presidential election. By contrast, Iranians put value on a form of ritualized indirect communication exemplified in the practice of *ta'āruf*. *Ta'āruf* is incredibly difficult to translate, but William Beeman provides a good working definition: "*Ta'āruf* is the active, ritualized realization of differential perceptions of superiority and inferiority in interaction. It underscores and preserves the integrity of culturally defined roles as it is carried out in the life of every Iranian, every day, in thousands of different ways."[3]

In general, the practice of *ta'āruf* involves three actions: an offer, its denial, and redirection of the offer.[4] Take a dinner party. The host offers a third helping of food, the guest refuses, protesting that she is too full. The food is offered again and again, until it is accepted in acknowledgment of the cooking skills of the host. The initial politeness (offering of food) is redirected by the guest so that a new politeness is the result: praise of the host's cooking skills. All three of these actions are stages of *ta'āruf*.

Ta'āruf can appear to an outsider as the practice of saying something one does not really mean: rhetorical insincerity. Like rhetoric, *ta'āruf* too has been defined as malice or trickery. I found while in Iran that younger Iranians in particular are critical of it. But there is no escape; its logic enters almost every social interaction. Skill in the art of *ta'āruf* is a indication of good manners, proper upbringing, and education. To read *ta'āruf* as insincerity is to miss the point.

Khomeini's practice of *ta'āruf* can be most clearly identified in the honorifics he uses to address his audience of women ("We are all indebted to your course, lion-hearted women").[5] The women also invoke *ta'āruf* in their responses through their deference to clerics and other male leaders, the timidity with which they sometimes argue, and their self-deprecating remarks. Sherkat is particularly skilled in this last practice, beginning her editorial for the hundredth issue of *Zanān* with apologies for the haste in which she writes, downplaying *Zanān*'s accomplishments, and devoting substantial time to elaborating criticisms of her magazine. By aiming at a relatively lower status using extreme praise of others or self-deprecation, an Iranian demonstrates the virtue of modesty appropriate to a higher moral status. This use of *ta'āruf* may also aim to encourage a particular action of the audience. Take the example of the dinner party. The secondary expression of politeness of the guest (your food is excellent) is anticipated and even solicited by the host's initial offer of food. Sherkat's use of *ta'āruf* creates status for *Zanān* in a similar way. Not only can *ta'āruf* encourage a higher opinion of the speaker or reinforce their assumed higher status, it can solicit concrete action, such as a comment about the skill of a cook or the praise of a magazine's courage.[6]

Hierarchies

Hierarchies work in arguments to establish greater intensity of one value over another. Although none of the women uses an explicit gender hierarchy (women are higher than men or men are higher than women), they all use gendered hierarchies in some form. Central to this analysis, some of these hierarchies are shared across religious and political contexts.

One hierarchy that many of the women's rhetoric assumes (especially that of Hitchcock, Kissling, and Arshad) is that motherhood is higher than fatherhood. In some cases this hierarchy is understood as based on a woman's special connection to her children, and therefore her unique role as moral educator (Hitchcock and Arshad). In other cases it is invoked to argue for a woman's moral right to decide whether to continue a pregnancy (Kissling).

Another shared hierarchy is that women's experiences make them a better source of moral knowledge about women's lives than male clerics are, or at least a source that can fill in gaps in the clerical logics. The idea of special ethical knowledge that arises out of women's moral praxis is central to Isasi-Díaz's *mujerista* ethics and Hayes's womanist ethics, but it also operates in Abbas-Gholizadeh's argument for the necessity of women's studies for the moral life and the work of Hitchcock's organization as a resource for moral advice for other Catholic women.

There are two assumed hierarchies between the groups of women's responses. One is related to justice and equality. If we define justice as demanding what is right, and equality as demanding sameness, then for John Paul and Khomeini these concepts do not signify the same thing in the gendered moral life, nor do they have a directly causal relationship (justice does not dictate that we treat men and women the same, but instead differently). For example, being helpmates to a spouse in a way appropriate to our gender is just, not an expression of gender equality. In contrast to the clerics, the U.S. Catholic women, with the possible exception of Hitchcock, assume that justice and equality are basically the same thing, or that equality is at least the primary way to realize justice. For example, in Cahill's argument for how to make the Catholic message on sexual ethics more successful in the U.S. context, she emphasizes the importance of equality in marriage. By contrast, the Iranian Shi'i women do not assume equality to be higher than justice; rather, they assume justice is higher than equality. Remember, this does not mean that Iranian women necessarily personally reject equality as the primary path to justice, but their rhetoric is built on the assumption that their audience will associate, per clerical teaching, equality with a neglect of men's and women's special duties and rights.

A second gendered hierarchy assumed differently in the two groups of women's rhetoric is the ontological versus cultural or material sources of gender. Some of the Catholic women assume gender is ontologically significant, a hierarchy of a woman's ontological essence versus the cultural construction of her gender. For Isasi-Díaz this is seen in her claim that not only as humans do we image God, but also in our sexed bodies. Hitchcock's rhetoric understands this hierarchy through women as representative of God's creativity (versus begetting). According to John Paul's theology of the body, the existence of Adam and Eve in the Garden of Eden means that it is ontologically significant and that we are gendered, that we are, if you like, gendered in the eyes of God. By contrast, gender is often merely material in the Iranian women's rhetoric. This tracks closely with Khomeini's teaching that men and women are equal spiritually; only material embodiment makes them different. And in this way, God is conceptualized to some extent as gender-blind.

Summary of Audience Assumptions

This Perelman-inspired rhetorical analysis is important for three reasons. It allows us to consider not only the logical structure of rhetoric that is the focus of the Toulmin-inspired analysis, but also how affective logos is deployed by references to an audience's assumptions. Without attention to these general assumptions, we neglect one important way that rhetoric persuades. For example, references to Mary or Fatimah may not necessarily make an argument more logical, but may make it more likely to motivate an action by invoking an affective response in the audience. In this way, persuasive arguments are not imposed on an audience but rather shaped through rhetorical interaction between the audience and the speaker.

Second, unlike the Toulmin analysis on its own, in combination with Perelman we gain insights into a general shared vision of feminist ethics within a community. In terms of Toulmin's specific claims, the women I study do not agree. Cahill and Kissling do not agree on the issue of abortion; Gurji and Abbas-Gholizadeh do not agree on women's ability to practice *ijtihād*. They nevertheless share assumptions about the more general beliefs of their audience—the local religious community of women—and I have been able to identify some general commonalities and distinctions of these assumptions among the U.S. Catholic and Iranian Shi'i feminist responses.

Third, the Perelman level of analysis allows us to compare the two groups of women. Such comparison is nonsensical at the level of logical form: specific evidence or rationale that is logical in the U.S. Catholic context is not necessarily logical in the Iranian Shi'i context. But at the more meta-level of assumptions, we can consider commonalities and disagreement over what is real, customary, and good.

In terms of facts, both groups of women assume in their rhetoric the reality of gender, the importance of religious history, and the cultural origins of patriarchy. The groups differ, however, on the content of religious tradition, local politics, and the role of a general "woman's nature" versus particular racial or class experiences in determining women's proper roles. The U.S. Catholic and Iranian Shi'i women's responses share presumptions about the possibility and necessity of responding to clerical rhetoric, but have different opinions about equality between men and women and the proper role of religion in public life. Both groups of rhetoric assume the values of free will, human rights, spirituality, and motherhood. However, they assume a different value of dissent versus obedience, as well as direct versus ritualized speech. In terms of hierarchies, the Catholic and Shi'i women's rhetoric assumes motherhood is higher than fatherhood and women's special access to religious knowledge about the moral life based on their experiences as women. They differ, however, on a hierarchy of equality versus justice and spirituality-ensoulment versus materiality-embodiment of personhood.

RHETORICAL (INTER)PLAY OF CLERICS AND WOMEN

Rhetoric is the object of study in this book, guided by a specific theoretical apparatus that pays many dividends. At the most basic level, it is a way to conceptually isolate women's tactics to see their impact on the moral knowledge of the community. In the process of this study, the significance of rhetoric has expanded. It turns out that rhetoric as I define it (persuasive discourse based on informal logic and affective logos) allows us to reconsider the way tradition, authority, and critique all function in the moral life of religious communities.

As others have suggested, the metaphor of a game is helpful for conceptualizing the moral life within a religious community.[7] Picture a soccer field, for example, on which the moral life of the community is "played." Our assumptions coming into this study were that male clerics set the rules for play and acted on the field as referees given the authority structure of Catholicism and Shi'i Islam. This meant that what counts as off-sides, penalty shots, out of bounds, goals, and so on, in the tradition is conveyed through clerical rhetoric. In this book's case study, all the players on the field are women. To some extent then, a woman's "play" was expected to depend on the cleric's ability to convey the rules, and her success in the moral life to depend on her ability to put the clerical rulebook into practice.

These assumptions, however, privilege the clerics as the origin of ethical knowledge or what de Certeau calls the "productive apparatus."[8] This volume, however, tells more than a simple story of men creating a game and women playing it out. John Paul and Khomeini, or by extension Roman Catholicism and Shi'i Islam, did not turn out to be something that women had to overcome in order to engage in feminist politics. Instead an effective feminism operates within the parameters of local religion through engagement with clerical rhetoric. In fact, we saw through the main chapters of this book that the women's politics depended on the clerical rhetoric. The clerics were significant not as umpires or referees, but rather as depositories of traditional moral guidance and rhetorical building blocks.

The game metaphor is also helpful in understanding the social dimension of moral authority.[9] Rather than being held and wielded by clerics, authority is created by the group dynamic in the process of playing the game. In terms of my analysis of authority in the introduction, this is another way to show how charismatic authority must be recognized by believers. But the interactive nature of authority can now can be pushed even further. We can assert that what counts as morality is a social invention, and that authority is merely the normative apparatus of the group. This is not to say that there is no ethical truth. According to Jeffrey Stout, the members of the group who care about moral knowledge (the soccer players or the religious believers), "treat inquiry into the truth-value of such claims as an objective affair, to be settled by the testimony of trustworthy eyewitnesses, the evidence of instant-replay videos, and so forth."[10] Rhetoric, then, becomes the way in which truth status of normative claims gets worked out.

Staying with the metaphor of the game, although initial assumptions may have been that male-clerics determine the game of the moral life for women in the Catholic and Shi'i traditions, in fact, both lay women and male clerics participate in deciding the parameters of the field (what counts as ethical knowledge), the rules of play (how to judge ethical action) and even the nature of the game itself (how tradition informs contemporary action). This is an important insight into the production of ethical knowledge within the community. One might initially assume that clerics are producing moral rhetoric and women merely responding, but in truth the situation is more complicated than such a simple dynamic. Both clerics and women engage in the rhetorical augmentation aimed at persuading the community about the moral life. Both interpret the tradition. Both originate discourse and respond to the discourse of others. And the clerics are not merely observing from the sidelines: they are also on the field engaged in rhetorical exchange about the moral life, muddying their shoes and staining their knees.

This interplay between clerics and women can help us gain clarity on what I refer to as dianomy. On the one hand there is the balance, or perhaps tension, between being determined by one's environment and having the freedom to work on it. In the introduction I draw on Butler to explain this as a simultaneous progress of citation and critique that is possible given the nature of discursive interaction. In terms of the moral game, this is the tension between playing by the recognizable rules and developing signature moves that push those rules to their limits. On the other hand, dianomy is also a nod to the moral life not being something we pursue in isolation using only our own reasoning. In religious communities, for example, there is a trust in the tradition, however diversely that tradition is defined. Although what counts as tradition is not wholly controlled by the clerics, clerical training and religious institutions clerics inhabit are some of the ways of allowing tradition to be maintained from one generation to the next. In this sense, women's partial obedience to clerical logics is not a substitution of clerical judgment for their own, but rather a way to access depositories of moral guidance.

If clerics act as access points to the tradition, and tradition is a necessary resource for believers in their pursuit a pious life, then the rhetorical game is how the legitimacy of religious norms are tested and ultimately affirmed or reconfigured. Discursive interactions simultaneously shift ethical knowledge and shore up traditional legitimacy. In fact, this ability to change allows the traditions to endure. Because authority is socially constructed, it can be continually and acutely relevant.

REVISITING FEMINIST POLITICS

Throughout this book I assert that Catholic and Shi'i women contribute to the truth status of gendered normative claims, or what I have called the production of ethical knowledge, through their feminist politics. This becomes clear in cross-cultural analysis.

Contribution to Ethical Knowledge

At this point we can explore the nature of this contribution that I argue takes place on three levels: the logics of ethical knowledge, judgment of ethical action, and how tradition informs contemporary action.

At the first level we observe how women recombine logical components of clerical rhetoric to make claims unanticipated by the clerical teachings. This process focuses on what I called architectonics, which has a two-fold meaning. On the one hand, it is meant to invoke the idea of building a structure: women use components of clerical rhetoric to build a logical structure about the moral life that more closely fits their lived experiences. On the other, it gestures toward tectonic plates in the earth's crust. These are always slightly shifting, much the way a religious moral tradition is always shifting. Where plates abut is where earthquakes occur and where mountains are formed. Women literally dismantle and assemble something new with the clerical rhetoric, taking advantage of the fissures and frictions that can change the literal moral landscape. In each chapter I show how the logical space of the moral life has shifted as women use some grounds, claims, warrants, backings of the clerics and morph other logical components into different sorts of components (grounds to warrants, warrants to backings, and the like).

A second way women contribute to ethical knowledge is in changing the rules for judging what is proper moral action. Despite initial assumptions that clerics were the source of these rules, the women also engage in rule making, especially when they determine the clerical codified rulebook creates obstacles in their moral life. This rule making is done at the level of tactical engagement. Again, the use of tactic instead of strategy is important here. The women's discourse examined in chapters 1 through 5 does not attempt to rebel against traditional forms of moral judgment. Instead it works within them, as perceived through the clerical rhetoric, yet at the same time slightly shifts those rules through a number of logics (logic of expansion, logic of resolution, logic of redefinition, logic of praxis, and the like). These logics aim at shifting the rules relevant to judging certain dimensions of the gendered moral life, whether motherhood, relationship to god, or citizenship; they are feminist tactics. We have seen five: the tactics of feminist symbolics, procreation, hermeneutics, embodiment, and what I call republication.

The particular ways in which these tactics change what counts as proper moral behavior is summarized at the end of each of the preceding chapters. They follow a trajectory of sorts. In chapters 1 through 4, for example, the women assume a gender dichotomy and essentialize the nature of womanhood as they work within dominant religious structures of gender. In these chapters they grapple with women's roles in the tradition, within the family, before God, and within the leadership of the religious community. By contrast, chapter 5 considers how Catholic and Shi'i women understand themselves within the more pluralistic, if not secular spaces, of U.S. and Iranian politics. In this conclusion, women's discourse has moved past an exclusive concern with the moral lives of women to address the proper role of all believers as national and global citizens. But even engagement in this more gender neutral and secular conversation is done from a theological and gendered space, and threaded through religious visions of women in the family, before God, and within a religious community. In other words, the tactics of chapters 1 through 4 make the tactic of republication possible. Any attempt to understand the secular feminist politics of religious women without first attending to their engagement in more theological matters misses the complexity of their political actions.

The first section of this conclusion, "Shared Audience Assumptions," demonstrates the ways in which the parameters for determining proper action are to some extent the same among the two groups of religious women studied, even if their specific rules emphasize different aspects of the moral life. This analysis also highlights why moral judgment is slightly different within the religious, cultural, and political contexts of the United States and Iran because audiences for the moral discourse are different. Just as the behavior of soccer fans differs—consider the fervor of European fans in contrast to low attendance at live matches in the United States—in a similar way, certain moral plays and rule-bending will meet with cheers from fans in Iran, but boos from U.S. spectators. Some arguments simply work in one context and fall flat in others.

Finally, there is the more meta-level on which feminist tactics began to change the nature of ethical knowledge. This occurs in two ways that cut across the feminist tactics studied. The first occurs on a material level. The women use the physical experience of motherhood in their political discourse as one way to gain traction within the conversation over what counts as ethical knowledge. While the clerics ground motherhood in theological understandings of procreation and child rearing, the women depend much more on biological, cultural, and emotional dimensions to derive maternal insight. Women are also able to leverage the cultural and aesthetic perceptions of their respective audiences that cast mothers as particularly powerful political symbols. Arguing for a political vision on behalf of her child, a mother's argument is harder to counter than a woman who argues merely from a position of self-interest. Women thus transform fundamental understandings of legitimate sources of ethical knowledge by emphasizing certain material experiences within the moral life.

A second meta-tactic is linguistic: women use the language of the clerics even as they work to feminize the language. In redefining what counts as ethical knowledge, women draw on the logical components of clerical rhetoric in their discourse. A process of feminization of language is also taking place, however, in which women make the genre of moral discourse their own by, for example, drawing on what they understand to be distinctly female types of authority, or invoking emotive qualities directed at persuading women. The women co-opt and redefine key terms important to determining what counts as ethical knowledge (such as freedom, conscience, and agency). In this way women's speech is different from that of the clerics, although it is all done within the language of the clerical rhetoric.

What these two meta-tactics have in common is that they both rely on the gender binary also foundational to clerical rhetoric. The women therefore acknowledge that some gendered aspects are inherent to the moral life: women will be women, men will be men, and their respective moral requirements are different. But though this signifies how some things in theory cannot be changed, at the same time it allows women to say something about ethical knowledge that men cannot say, and possibly that men cannot ultimately understand or know. Women create this discourse based on their material bodies as women, as well as their feminized forms of language, drawing on their experience and communication skills to contribute their perspective on the ethical knowledge needed to maneuver the gendered moral life.

Ironically, accepting that some things cannot be changed is a powerful way to critique from within the system itself. It allows women, who accept the essential aspects of motherhood found in the clerical rhetoric, to extend the parameters of ethical knowledge through the physical experiences of mothers. Their arguments as mothers are extremely difficult for the clerics to refute because they logically rest on the same assumptions about proper roles for women. Similarly, the meta-tactic of linguistic feminization, though building on the language of the clerics to protect itself from refutation, also uses special language to talk about the tradition. Because this feminized language works within the language of clerical instruction, women make it difficult for the same clerics to oppose their arguments. Both meta-tactics are successful because they appear to be working within the same framework as the clerics. This is how religious women are shifting the debate from one of opposition (religion versus feminism) to one of transformation (religious feminisms).

Together, these meta-tactics, one material, one linguistic, demonstrate how critique becomes possible, and potentially even more effective, despite playing by someone else's rules. Again, attention throughout this book has been on tactics from within versus strategies outside established religious logic. These meta-tactics can be understood to show how tactics can actually approach strategies, at least in terms of effect. According to de Certeau, in contemporary history we should expect to see tactical hybrids. He writes, "More and more, tactics swing out of their orbits. Loosed from those traditional communities which once circumscribed their functioning, they begin to wander throughout a space increasingly homogenized and extended."[11] It is my hunch that this "wandering" not only allows women to be active producers of ethical knowledge within the community, it also guarantees the survival of the tradition by integrating new ideas and experiences in a manner that does not appear as rebellion. This is in contrast to the rebellion of strategic action, which may "exhaust its own possibilities of transformation and come to constitute the very space (as totalitarian as the cosmos of old) of cybernetic society."[12] Even secular feminists can learn from this example, broadening not only strategies, but also tactics, in the context of their local discursive parameters.

A Craftiness That Does Not Know Itself

In the introduction I suggest that an advantage to dianomy is that it counters a tendency to romanticize resistance or even accept at face value the self-understanding of agents. This is not to suggest that individuals are incapable of self-reflection. The point is that even understanding this self-reflection does not tell us the whole story of how the arguments have productive power: there is "a craftiness that does not know itself."[13] In fact, it may be because this craftiness is unintended that it has so much impact: it will be received by the audience not as innovation, but rather as conversation from within. This is particularly true in the cases of women's responses to clerical rhetoric described in the preceding chapters, who at times have been shown to be innovative even in their attempts to affirm clerical rhetoric, and citational of clerical logics even when they intend to dissent.

Chapter 4's discussion of Hitchcock illustrates this point well. A focus on her intention alone would have obscured the fact that in the process of confirming John Paul's teaching, including his ban on women's ordination, she relies on logical components that actually critique John Paul's original rhetoric. For example, in terms of grounds supporting the ban on ordination, Hitchcock relies on theological evidence in contrast to John Paul's primarily historical evidence. This significantly shifts what is at stake in the debate, opens up an opportunity to critique the ban on different grounds, and is an implicit critique that John Paul's grounds are inadequate. Hitchcock also creates by justifying the work of WFF in facilitating women who provide moral guidance directly to other women. This sidesteps the issue of ordination entirely by setting up an alternative system of giving and receiving advice.

Pursuing "a craftiness that does not know itself" means that I have not avoided entirely the issue of offending the women I study. In fact, my project will likely elicit reactions from the women I study that rival Habibi's table slamming. This is mainly because I analyze all the women discursively within a middle ground of creativity and conformity. I consider the dissent of women who claim to be obeying as well as the obedience of those who claim to be dissenting. In other words, the analysis of this book is focused not on understanding what women think they are saying, but rather on the productive power of their arguments. Certainly some of the women I study will bristle at the thought of conforming to their religious traditions, particularly if tradition is understood in terms of the logics of male clerics. Other women will be just as offended by the suggestion that they are being innovative, because their intention is to be faithful to their tradition. However, it is by looking at their arguments within this middle space, as political actions that both obey and dissent from a given context (even if not intentionally), that the possibility of a new type of comparative study of feminist tactics emerges.

The Contribution of Comparison

Several advantages of comparison to a study of feminist ethics have been named and demonstrated such as preventing moral judgment of women's actions, decentering the norms of prominent feminist models, identifying general tactics of intellectual engagement that appear cross-culturally, and understanding diversity of assumptions at play in different communities' moral discourse. More can now be said about how this particular study of U.S. Catholic and Shi'i women helps us understand each group better than the study of either tradition alone.

The payoff on the Iranian side is seen particularly in the application of a method of rhetorical analysis that was itself developed out of a desire to analyze two distinct groups of women within their specific religious contexts. Looking at the Iranian women's rhetoric at the micro-level, and juxtaposed against the moral guidance of Khomeini, we can see moments of citation and innovation that may not otherwise be clear to us as outsiders. This approach allows us not only to describe, but also to explain women's discourse, and to begin to understand the artistry of the Iranian women's creative conformity.

Insights into the U.S. Catholic case comparison are, although perhaps less obvious, also significant, and allow us to rethink some of the limits of Western feminism. Many colleagues who have read portions of this book in progress have told me they find the creative conformity of the Iranian women more apparent. But this is not because the Iranian women are more creative, but rather that, quoting de Certeau again, "Other laws restore to us what our own culture has seen fit to exclude from its own discourse."[14] Take, for example, chapter 5. Many readers will be struck by the cleverness and courage behind Sherkat's rhetorical nets that allow her to publish without losing her license. Certainly this complicated practice of self-censorship under conditions of theocratic rule is inventive. But time should also be taken to consider Kissling's argument about the value of fetal life. Finding a middle ground that acknowledges the core values and logic of both pro-choice and pro-life factions in the United States is a rhetorical feat indeed. It is no less clever or courageous than Sherkat's self-censorship. Its significance, however, might go unnoticed unless we think about it alongside the Sherkat example.

Both women share a similar sort of intellectual engagement with their discursive context that changes the way that religious norms interact with national politics by shifting what can be said in a public space. True, Kissling does not operate under the same legal regulation of public expression as Sherkat. The abortion debate in the United States, however, has become polarized, so that each side of the debate recycles the same arguments, without any progress toward compromise in sight. Kissling breaks through this standstill, but only through a reliance on religious logics not often considered valid by the pro-choice coalition she is politically aligned with. Her argument in fact hinges on the idea that there is a legitimate role for public theology in U.S. politics and even in U.S. feminist politics. This might be unsettling to U.S. secular feminists, even if Kissling's specific claims are something we would want to support. If Kissling's argument musters force, though, it seems unclear how the religious dimension of it can be ignored. This is all to say that comparison not only helps us better understand the Iranian women's social movement, which I think it certainly does, but also encourages us to rethink feminist tactics closer to home in ways that might be at first unsettling.

NOTES

1. It is important to note that these assumptions are of the audience, and not necessarily what the author of the response herself holds to be true. Assumptions are used in responses to frame the central argument to make it more persuasive.

2. Hoodfar, "Bargaining with Fundamentalism," 31.

3. Beeman, *Language, Status, and Power in Iran*, 59.

4. Ibid.

5. Khomeini, "Address to Group of Women in Qom," 263.

6. *Ta'āruf* can also be seen as the linguistic expression of the value of mutual interdependence between speaker and audience, or cleric and common believers. *Ta'āruf* in this way might be described as a "value couplings." It is made up of two values, hierarchy and equality. Hierarchy, in terms of status differentiation, is allowed through pretence of equality, and equality, in terms of mutual duties to the moral life, is reinforced through this hierarchical exchange. Another way to think about this is as the aesthetic dimension of mutual dependence of the cleric and common believer or, on a very general level, as a dianomous cultural practice.

7. Stout, *Democracy and Tradition*, 270–86.

8. De Certeau, *The Practice of Everyday Life*, xiv.

9. "Before human beings invented [the game of soccer], there was no such things as the normative statues that soccer people refer to as 'having committed a foul.' This normative status is a creature of a social practice in which people take one another to have committed a foul or not when competing with their opponents on the playing field." Stout, *Democracy and Tradition*, 272.

10. Ibid.

11. De Certeau, "On Oppositional Practices of Everyday Life," 9.

12. Ibid.

13. Ibid., 18.

14. Ibid., 14.

EPILOGUE

Revisiting Shahla Habibi

This book begins with an anecdote of my first interaction with Habibi during which I inadvertently insulted her by labeling her feminist. Although I have addressed that faux pas, my concern is not in preventing the offense she took, but rather preventing my inability to understand the feminist politics that her offense signaled. My agenda is not merely to convey Habibi's political agenda in her own words, but rather to explain the full impact of her actions within the Iranian context. Our interaction demonstrates the analytical challenge a cross-cultural feminist project faces: a double-layered misinterpretation, or what I call academic ventroliquism, in which both scholar and subject "throw their voice" to the other. To counter this tendency, I suggested redefining what counts as feminist politics, to include tactical argumentation, and a method of analysis that can consider women's actions within a particular context—comparative rhetoric. Underlying both this redefinition and methodological invention is a theoretical construction of women's agency.

Habibi made it clear that in a study of religious women, the danger was either interpreting the religious woman's actions as opposing religious authority or as merely obeying this authority. I break from this polarized view of the moral life by proposing the neologism of dianomy to help focus inquiry on moments of creative conformity in which women manifest the tension that they experience in their moral lives between autonomy and the dictates of religious authorities. The model of agency I have assumed is therefore double: a woman is formed within a specific discursive and performative environment, but she is also able to interrogate that environment. In addition, she relies not only on her own moral judgment, but also on the moral wisdom of her religious tradition.

Returning to the interaction between myself and Habibi, I hope it has become clear why I needed a more nuanced understanding of the moral life. A scholar assuming an autonomous model of the moral life would be interested only in Habibi's arguments that resist her local conditions. Such a scholar might understand her arguments about CEDAW or her hope for a female president as authentic expressions of her moral agency. That same scholar might ignore Habibi's claims about special roles for women based on Islamic teachings of womanhood. They would never be able to get to the level of subtle citation and innovation. By contrast, an assumption of heteronomy might see her support of CEDAW as based on a Western ideological import, and understand only Habibi's statements against the validity of feminism as an authentic expression of her agency. This sort of study would never be able to conceptualize critique and thereby grasp the work her arguments do in the Iranian political context. To understand a wider range of her rhetoric, I had to develop a third alternative.

Thinking about Habibi's arguments as creative conformity requires identifying and analyzing her heteronomous discursive context. For Shi'i Iranian women I could have selected any number of traditions: socialism, Sufism, or Persian literature. I chose Ayatollah Khomeini's teaching on women, in part because of my larger comparative project and in part because of his continued importance for Iranian public discourse about women. In Habibi's case, Khomeini's rhetoric is especially apt given that she told me that she felt very close to the imam and understands his words as grounding her work in the contemporary Iranian women's movement.

Khomeini and Habibi can be read together to understand how the totality of Habibi's action both draws on components of Khomeini's logic and shifts others. For example, Habibi cites religious and cultural values found in Khomeini's arguments, such as the priority of motherhood and innate biological and emotional differences between men and women. In response to my questions about women's political duties, she insisted that "for women to have status in society they should never forget their primary role in the family, which is the source of her dignity."[1] But at the same time, Habibi's actions, such as working long hours as special advisor to women's affairs under former President Rafsanjani, demonstrate how she shifts Khomeini's argument. In practice, she has not made time with her family her priority in the precise way Khomeini might have wanted, understanding herself to have a calling to serve the Republic in a leadership capacity. In this way her political action takes on a form of creative conformity that we could call the logic of praxis: reworking theoretical arguments into practical ones based on a perceived tension among heteronomous directives.

The dianomous view of agency has a number of advantages in addressing the lessons learned from Habibi. For example, it allows one to account for the ambiguity, partiality, and imperfection in the moral life. Because agents have direct access only to autonomous moral law, their ethical actions and arguments in some way depend on a creative process of perceiving the heteronomous law. This process relies on the unpredictable actions of hearing, understanding, and interpreting discourse. Take the metaphor of an actor who is successful when she is able to play a role scripted by a playwright and staged by a director. The moral life can also be understood to be a performance, one that aims at virtue. But life does not have a fully articulated script: there are unanticipated aspects of every moral performance.

Second, agency within creative conformity moves away from an idea of empowerment that depends on an autonomous place of perfect freedom. In contrast, creative conformity is the self-representation of women who still imagine themselves within the structure of other representations, and operating inside those lines. It provides a way to consider free will as part of the model of habituation: even as local discursive contours create the possibilities and restraints on action, freedom can exist as a norm within the discursive space.

Third, creative conformity understands both enactment and resistance, dissent and obedience, as authentic moral praxis in rhetorical response. Obedience can unintentionally implicate aspects of dissent, for example, by changing the grounds for an argument or appealing to additional assumptions. Dissent always involves some level of obedience, in that one accepts the premises of the original argument, even if only insofar as the speaker is someone whose opinion on the moral law warrants a response. This is important given my specific research: U.S. Catholics as a whole tend to appear to be dissenting whereas Iranian Shi'a appear to be obeying. In fact, both groups cite and transform clerical rhetoric. In other words, novelty in religious ethics—or a shift in the discursive parameters of what is true, real, and good—can come from either resistance or enactment.

Finally, creative conformity does not imply a prior judgment on the proper role of religion in women's flourishing. In philosophical defenses of autonomy, religion can be dismissed as antithetical to women's moral lives. Obedience to heteronomous moral norms implies an equally strong judgment about religion: religion is the source of habituation for women within a religious community. The theory of agency presented in this book, however, is predicated on understanding religion as part of a network that creates the possibility of the moral life for religious women. At times women will see it as a constraining force, at other times as a liberating one. What is interesting is how women react in both these cases: their arguments are both citational (assuming adherence) and critical.

NOTE

1. Shahla Habibi, interview by the author, Tehran, August 12, 2004.

Glossary

backing: the rationale for why a warrant should be considered reliable.

chador: traditional form of Iranian hijab.

claim: both the starting and destination point of the argument and the conclusion whose merits the speaker is seeking to establish.

conscience: a threefold human capacity, process, and judgment of morality; it includes the capacity to know right from wrong, the process of moral reasoning, and the judgment about norms that guide actions.

creative conformity: a specific type of feminist politics, best defined as tactical (versus strategic) discourse.

dianomy: a neologism to account for moral agency that does not rely exclusively on either the self nor religious traditions as a source of moral authority; attempts to comprehend creative ruptures in obedience to tradition, even when these innovations are unintentional.

feminist politics: actions that engage and shape visions of women's proper roles and the resulting impact of such actions on the community.

fiqh: Islamic jurisprudence; the human endeavor to understand shari'a.

grounds: evidence explicitly appealed to support a given claim.

hijab: Islamic dress of women; in the Iranian context refers to the entirety of a woman's dress to fulfill public modesty laws (such as a *chādor* or a manteau with a head covering).

ḥiẓānat: fostering or providing necessary care; in the context of divorce refers to the physical custody of children.

Hizbullah: adherents to the political philosophy that developed in Iran in years leading up to the Revolution; considered a radicalization of Khomeini's teachings.

ijtihād: a technical term of *fiqh* that describes the process of making a legal decision by independent interpretation of the legal sources.

al-insān al-kāmil: technical *'irfān* term meaning a person who has integrated all of God's attributes.

'irfān: Shi'i discipline of mystical knowledge.

Ithnā 'Asharī: also referred to as the Twelvers, the largest branch of Shi'i Islam in Iran; name derives from their belief in twelve divinely ordained leaders, known as the Twelve imāms.

logics: intellectual coherence of how women rhetorically transform their tradition.

madrasa: school of Islamic education; also used to refer to a center of theological learning.

miqna'ah: one form of head covering worn in Iran that covers all of a woman's hair and neck.

marja'-i taqlīd: literally "source of emulation," honorific title developed in the eighteenth century to refer to a few exceptional ayatollahs.

modal qualifiers: components of arguments that convey the degree of certainty with which the warrant is being made.

mujtahad/mujtahidūn (pl.): those qualified to practice *ijtihād*.

muqallidūn (pl.): believers not authorized to use *ijtihād*.

possible responses: logics, factors, or conditions of an argument that create opportunities for counterarguments.

rhetoric: argument aimed at persuasion.

shari'a: often translated as Islamic law, a more accurate translation is the path Muslims should follow; divine law and therefore immutable but also not completely knowable to humans; historical process of interpretation and application of shari'a to the Muslim community is *fiqh*.

ta'āruf: ritualized indirectness.

tafsīr: literally "interpretation," exegesis of Qur'an.

ṭāghūt: refers to idolatry and impurity; in the Iranian context used pejoratively to refer to the prerevolutionary Pahlavi regime.

talāq: literally "repudiation," Islamic term for divorce.

taqlīd: conformity to the judgment of another; in Shi'i Islam lacks the pejorative implication in Sunni Islam, and instead used to refer to justified conformity of common believers to *mujtahidūn*.

ta'ziyah: passion plays performed to commemorate 'Ashura.'

'*ulūm*: sciences.

vilāyat: guardianship; in divorce refers to legal custody of children.

vilāyat-i faqīh: literally "guardianship of the experts in *fiqh*;" Khomeini developed a theory of Islamic government based on this idea that gave Shi'i ayatollahs powerful political offices, such as the supreme leader, in the Islamic Republic of Iran.

warrants: rule or law relied on to authorize the step from grounds to the claim.

zan girāyāneh: literally "women-oriented," a Persian phrase used instead of *fimīnīst*, which some consider a Western import.

Bibliography

Abbas-Gholizadeh, Mahboubeh. "Chirā Farzānah? *Farzānah* 1, no. 1 (1993): 3–8.

Abu-Lughod, Lila. "The Romance of Resistance: Tracing Transformations of Power through Bedouin Women." *Amercian Ethnologist* 17, no. 1 (February 1990): 41–55.

Afray, Janet. "The Human Rights of Middle Eastern & Muslim Women: A Project for the Twenty-First Century." *Human Rights Quarterly* 26, no.1 (2004): 106–25.

Ahern, Barnabas. "The Use of Scripture in the Spiritual Theology of St. John of the Cross." *The Catholic Biblical Quarterly* 14, no. 1 (Jan. 1952): 6–17.

Algar, Hamid. "Chādor." In *Encyclopedia Iranica*. Vol. IV, edited by E. Yarshater, 609–10. New York: Routledge & Regan Paul, 1990.

———. "The Fusion of the Gnostic and the Political in the Personality and Life of Imam Khomeini (R.A.)." *Al-Tawḥīd* (June 2003): 1–12.

———. "Introduction." In *Islam and Revolution I: Writings and Declarations of Imam Khomeini 1941–1980*. Berkeley, CA: Mizan, 1918.

Amir-Moezzi, Mohammad 'Ali. "Fātema: In History and Shi'ite Hagiography." In *Encyclopedia Iranica*, Vol. 9, edited by E. Yarshater, 400–2. New York: Bibliotheca Persica, 1999.

Aquinas, Thomas. *Summa Theologiae*. London: Methuen, 1991.

Aristotle. *On Rhetoric*: *A Theory of Civic Discourse*. Translated by George Kennedy. New York: Oxford University Press, 1991.

Asad, Talal. "Agency and Pain: An Exploration." *Culture and Religion* 1, no. 1 (2000): 29–60.

Beeman, William. *Language, Status, and Power in Iran*. Bloomington: Indiana University Press, 1986.

Biabangard, Esmail, and Mahmoud Hatami. "A Study on the Effects of Working Mothers on the Social Development and Educational Progression of Children." *Farzānah*, Special Edition on the Girl Child (1995): 11–20.

Billy, Dennis, and James Keating. *Conscience and Prayer: The Spirit of Catholic Moral Theology*. Collegeville, MN: Liturgical Press, 2001.

Bonavoglia, Angela. *Good Catholic Girls: How Women Are Leading the Fight to Change the Church*. New York: ReganBooks, 2005.

Bourdieu, Pierre. *Language and Symbolic Power*. Translated by Gino Raymond and Matthew Adamson. Cambridge, MA: Harvard University Press, 2001.

———. *Outline of a Theory of Practice*. Translated by Richard Nice. Edited by John B. Thompson. Cambridge: Cambridge University Press, 1977.

Brandom, Robert B. *Making It Explicit: Reasoning, Representing, and Discursive Commitment*. Cambridge, MA: Harvard University Press, 1994.

Bucar, Elizabeth. "Dianomy: Understanding Religious Women's Moral Agency as Creative Conformity." *Journal of the American Academy of Religion* 78, no. 3 (2010): 662–86.

———. "Methodological Invention as a Constructive Project: Exploring the Production of Ethical Knowledge through the Interaction of Discursive Logics." *Journal of Religious Ethics* 36, no. 3 (2008): 355–73.

———. "Speaking of Motherhood: The Epideictic Rhetoric of John Paul II and Ayatollah Khomeini." *Journal of the Society of Christian Ethics* 26, no. 2 (2006): 93–123.

———. "Women, Gender, and Non-governmental Organizations: Iran." In *Encyclopedia of Women and Islamic Cultures*, Vol. 4, edited by Suad Joseph, 99–100. Leiden, The Netherlands: Brill, 2006.

Buckley, James. "Contraception: A Challenge to Catholic Preaching." *Catholic Culture* (October 1996). www.national-coalition.org/marriage/contrace.html.

Butler, Judith. *Gender Trouble: Feminism and the Subversion of Identity*. New York: Routledge, 1990.

———. *Excitable Speech: A Politics of the Performative*. New York: Routledge, 1997.

———. *Undoing Gender.* New York: Routledge, 2004.

———. "What Is Critique? An Esssay on Foucault's Virtue." In *The Political*, edited by David Ingram, 212–26. Malden, MA: Blackwell Publishers, 2002.

Cahill, Lisa. "Abortion, Sex and Gender: The Church's Public Voice." *America* 168, no. 18 (May 22, 1993): 6–11.

———. *Sex, Gender and Christian Ethics*. Cambridge: Cambridge University Press, 1996.

Calmard, Jean. "Fatema: In Myth, Folklore, and Popular Devotion." In *Encyclopedia Iranica*, Vol. IX, edited by E. Yarshater. New York: Bibliotheca Persica Press, 1999. www.iranica.com.

Cannon, Katie. *Black Womanist Ethics*. Eugene, OR: Wipf & Stock, 1988.

Civil Code of Iran. Translated by Mahmoud Taleghany. Littleton, CO: Fred B. Rothman, 1994.

de Certeau, Michel. "On the Oppositional Practices of Everyday Life." Translated by Frederic Jameson and Carl Lovitt. *Social Text,* no. 3 (Fall 1980): 3–43.

———. *The Practice of Everyday Life*. Translated by Steven Rendall. Berkeley: University of California Press, 1984.

Constitution of the Islamic Republic. Translated by Hamid Algar. Berkeley, CA: Mizan Press, 1980.

Curran, Charles. *Contraception: Authority and Dissent*. New York: Herder and Herder, 1969.

———. "Marriage, Sexuality, Gender, and Family." In *The Moral Theology of Pope John Paul II*, 160–201. Washington, DC: Georgetown University Press, 2005.

———. *The Moral Theology of Pope John Paul II*. Washington, DC: Georgetown University Press, 2005.

Davis, Cyrian. *The History of Black Catholics in the United States*. New York: Crossroad, 1990.

Davis, Dick. *Shahnameh.* New York: Penguin Group, 2006.

Ebadi, Shirin. "Reforming Iran: A Discussion with Shirin Ebadi." *Stanford Lawyer* 73 (Fall 2005): 12–13.

Ebtekar, Masoumeh, and Fred Reed. *Takeover in Tehran: The Inside Story of the 1979 U.S. Embassy Capture.* Vancouver, B.C.: Talon, 2000.

Eftekhari, Roza. "Zanan: Trials and Successes of a Feminist Magazine in Iran." In *Middle Eastern on the Move*, 15–22. Washington, DC: Woodrow Wilson Center for Scholars, 2003.

Enayat, Halimet. *The Effects of Employed Mothers on Families in Shiraz.* Shiraz, Iran: Shiraz University, 1988.

Esfandiari, Haleh. *Reconstructed Lives: Women and Iran's Islamic Revolution.* Washington, DC: Woodrow Wilson Center, 1997.

Ferdows, Adele K. "Women and the Islamic Revolution." *International Journal of Middles East Studies* 15, no. 2 (1983): 283–98.

Firouzabadi, H. *Fatima Zahra in the Sources of the Sunni Scholars.* Tehran: Zahra, 1990.

Fischer, Michael. *Iran: From Religious Dispute to Revolution.* Cambridge, MA: Harvard University Press, 1980.

Frymer-Kensky, Tikva. "Hagar, My Other, My Self." In *Reading the Women of the Bible,* 225–37. New York: Schocken Books, 2002.

Ghazvini, Seyed. *Fatimah Zahra from Birth to Death.* Beirut: Afagh Publications, 1980.

Grant, Steven. *The Life of Pope John Paul II: The Entire Story! From His Childhood in Poland to the Assassination Attempt!* New York: Marvel Comics Group, 1992.

Griffith, R. Marie. *God's Daughters: Evangelical Women and the Power of Submission.* Berkeley: University of California Press, 1997.

Grisez, Germain. *The Way of the Lord Jesus,* Vol. 1: *Christian Moral Principles.* Chicago: Franciscan Herald Press, 1983.

Gurji, Monir, and Masoumeh Ebtekar. "The Life and Status of Fatimah Zahra: A Woman's Image of Excellence." *Farzānah* (1997): 7–19.

Haeri, Shahla. "Temporary Marriage: An Islamic Discourse on Female Sexuality in Iran." In *In the Eye of the Storm*, edited by Mahnaz Afkhami and Erika Friedl, 98–114. New York: Syracuse University Press, 1994.

Hayes, Diana. *And Still We Rise: An Introduction to Black Liberation Theology.* New York: Paulist Press, 1996.

———. "And When We Speak." In *Taking Down Our Harps: Black Catholics in the United States*, edited by Diana Hayes and Cyprian Davis. Maryknoll, NY: Orbis Books, 1998.

———. "Black Catholics in the United States: A Subversive Memory." In *Many Faces, One Church: Cultural Diversity and the American Catholic Experience*, edited by Peter Phan and Diana Hayes. Lanham, MD: Rowman & Littlefield, 2005.

———. *Hagar's Daughters: Womanist Ways of Being in the World.* New York: Paulist Press, 1995.

———. "My Hope Is in the Lord: Transformation and Salvation in the African American Community." In *Embracing the Spirit: Womanist Perspectives on Hope, Transformation and Salvation*, edited by Emilie Townes. Maryknoll, NY: Orbis Books, 1997.

———. "To Be Black, Catholic, and Female." *New Theology Review* (May 1993): 52–62.

Hirschkind, Charles. *The Ethical Soundscape: Cassette Sermons and Islamic Counterpublics*. New York: Columbia University Press, 2006.

Hirschkind, Charles, and Saba Mahmood. "Feminism, the Taliban, and Politics of Counter Insurgency." *Anthropology Quarterly* 75, no. 2 (2002): 339–54.

Hitchcock, Helen Hull. "Appendix A.I: Affirmation for Catholic Women." In *Being Right: Conservative Catholics in America*, edited by Mary Jo Weaver and Scott Appleby, 177–78. Bloomington: Indiana University Press, 1995.

———. "Ten-Thousand Names Presented to Pope John Paul II." *Women for Faith and Family Newsletter* 1, no. 1 (Aug. 1985): 4.

———. "Women for Faith and Family: Catholic Women Affirming Catholic Teaching." In *Being Right: Conservative Catholics in America*. Edited by Mary Jo Weaver and R. Scott Appleby, 163–76. Bloomington, IN: Indiana University Press, 1995.

Hollywood, Amy. "Gender, Agency and the Divine in Religious Historiography," *Journal of Religion* 84, no. 4 (2004): 514–28.

———. "Performativity, Citationality, Ritualization." *History of Religions* 42, no. 2 (2002): 93–115.

Hoodfar, Homa. "Bargaining with Fundamentalism: Women and the Politics of Population Control in Iran." *Reproductive Health Matters* 4, no. 8 (Nov. 1996): 30–40.

Hosseinkhah, Maryam. "Guftugū va shunūdhā΄ī darbārah-i ta'arużāt-i huqūq-i zan dar Islām bih huqūq-i basher." *Iranian Feminist Tribune*, October 9, 2004.

Iranian Press Law. Ratified March 19, 1986. www.parstimes.com/law/press_law.html.

Isasi-Díaz, Ada María. *En la Lucha: Elaborating a Mujerista Theology*. Minneapolis, MN: Fortress Press, 1993.

———. *Women of God, Women of the People*. St. Louis, MO: Chalice Press, 1995.

Isasi-Díaz, Ada María, and Yolanda Tarango. *Hispanic Women: Prophetic Voice in the Church*. San Francisco: Harper & Row, 1988.

Islamic Penal Code of Iran. Ratified May 22, 1996. www.unhcr.org/refworld/docid/3ae6b51b8.html.

John Paul II. "By the Communion of Persons Man Becomes the Image of God (November 14, 1979)." In *The Theology of the Body: Human Love in the Divine Plan*, 45–48. Boston, MA: Pauline Books & Media, 1997.

———. "A Discipline that Ennobles Human Love (August 28, 1984)." In *The Theology of the Body: Human Love in the Divine Plan*, 399–401. Boston, MA: Pauline Books & Media, 1997.

———. "Faithfulness to the Divine Plan in the Transmission of Life (August 8, 1984)." In *The Theology of the Body: Human Love in the Divine Plan*, 395–96. Boston, MA: Pauline Books & Media, 1997.

———. *The Gospel of Life: Evangelium vitae.* Encyclical, March 25, 1995. Boston, MA: Pauline Books & Media, 1995. www.vatican.va/holy_father/john_paul_ii/encyclicals/documents/hf_jp-ii_enc_25031995_evangelium-vitae_en.html.

———. *Lay Members of Christ's Faithful People: Christifideles laici.* Apostolic Exhortation, December 30, 1988. Boston, MA: Pauline Books & Media, 1989. www.vatican.va/holy_father/john_paul_ii/apost_exhortations/documents/hf_jp-ii_exh_30121988_christifideles-laici_en.html.

———. *On the Dignity and Vocation of Women: Mulieris dignitatem.* Apostolic Letter, August. 15, 1988. Edison, NJ: Hunter Publishing, 1988. www.vatican.va/holy_father/john_paul_ii/apost_letters/documents/hf_jp-ii_apl_15081988_mulieris-dignitatem_en.html.

———. *Ordinatio Sacerdotalis.* Apostolic Letter on Reserving Priestly Ordination to Men Alone, May 22, 1994. www.vatican.va/holy_father/john_paul_ii/apost_letters/documents/hf_jp-ii_apl_22051994_ordinatio-sacerdotalis_en.html.

———. "The Original Unity of Man and Woman (November 7, 1979)." In *The Theology of the Body: Human Love in the Divine Plan*, 42–45. Boston, MA: Pauline Books & Media, 1997.

———. "Papal Message on Women's Conference." Delivered to Gertrude Mongella, Secretary-General of the UN Fourth World Conference on Women. May 26, 1995.

———. "Responsible Parenthood Is Linked to Moral Maturity (October 3, 1984)." In *The Theology of the Body: Human Love in the Divine Plan,* 401–2. Boston, MA: Pauline Books & Media, 1997.

———. *The Theology of the Body: Human Love in the Divine Plan.* Boston, MA: Pauline Books & Media, 1997.

———. "The Unity and Indissolubility of Marriage (September 5, 1979)." In *The Theology of the Body: Human Love in the Divine Plan*, 25–27. Boston, MA: Pauline Books & Media, 1997.

———. *Veritatis splendor.* Encyclical, August 6, 1993. www.vatican.va/holy_father/john_paul_ii/encyclicals/documents/hf_jp-ii_enc_06081993_veritatis-splendor_en.html.

———. "Women: Teachers of Peace." XXVIII Papal World Day of Peace Message, January 1, 1995. www.vatican.va/holy_father/john_paul_ii/messages/peace/documents/hf_jp-ii_mes_08121994_xxviii-world-day-for-peace_en.html.

———. "Women in the Life of the Priest." Holy Thursday Letter. *Origins* 24, no. 44 (April 20, 1995): 754.

Kar, Mehranguiz. "Shari'a Law in Iran." In *Radical Islam's Rules: The Worldwide Spread of Extreme Shari'a Law*, edited by Paul Marshall, 41–64. Lanham, MD: Rowman & Littlefield, 2005.

———. "Women's Strategies in Iran from the 1979 Revolution to 1999." In *Globalization, Gender, and Religion*, edited by Jane Bayes and Nayereh Tohidi, 177–202. New York: Palgrave, 2001.

Keddi, Nikki. *Modern Iran: Roots and Results of Revolution.* New Haven, CT: Yale University Press, 2003.

Khiabany, Gholam, and Annabelle Sreberny. "The Women's Press in Contemporary Iran: Engendering the Public Sphere." In *Women and Media in the Middle East*, edited by Naomi Sakr, 15–38. London: I. B. Tauris Publishers, 2004.

Khomeini, Ruhollah. "Address to a Group of Women in Qom, March 6, 1979." In *Islam and Revolution I: Writings and Declarations of Imam Khomeini 1941–1980*, translated by Hamid Algar, 263–64. Berkeley, CA: Mizan Press, 1981.

———. "Bayānāt dar jam'-i bānuvān (Address to a Group of Ladies, March 16, 1981)." In *Jāygāh-i zan dar andīshah-i Imām Khumaynī,* 152–56. Tehran: Mu'ssisah-i tanẓīm va Nashr-i Āsār-i Imām Khumaynī, 1995.

———. "Bayānāt dar jam'-i gurūhī az bānuvān-i Dizfūl (Address to a Group of Ladies from Dezful, June 11, 1979)." In *Jāygāh-i zan dar andīshah-i Imām Khumaynī*, 150–52. Tehran: Mu'assasah-i Tanzīm va Nashr-I Āsār-i Imām Khumaynī, 1995.

———. "Bayānāt-i Imām Khumaynī bih munāsibat-i vilādat-i Ḥażrat-i Zahrā va Rūz-i Zan (Address of Imam Khomeini on the Occasion of the Anniversary of the Birth of Hazrat Zahra and Women's Day, March 2, 1985)." In *Jāygāh-i zan dar andīshah-i Imām Khumaynī*, 41–46. Tehran: Mu'ssisah-i tanẓīm va Nashr-i Āsār-i Imām Khumaynī, 1995.

———. "Bayānāt-i Imām Khumaynī dar jam'-i gurūhī az bānuvān-i Mashhad (Address of Imam Khomeini to a Group of Ladies from Mashad, May 16, 1979)." In *Jāygāh-i zan dar andīshah-i Imām Khumaynī*, 265–70. Tehran: Mu'ssisah-i tanẓīm va Nashr-i Āsār-i Imām Khumaynī, 1995.

———. "In Commemoration of the First Martyrs of the Revolution (February 19, 1978)." In *Islam and Revolution I: Writings and Declarations of Imam Khomeini 1941–1980.* Translated by Hamid Algar, 212–27. Berkeley, CA: Mizan Press, 1981.

———. "Interview with Oriana Fallaci (September 12, 1979)." In *The Position of Women from the Viewpoint of Imam Khomeini*, translated by Juliana Shaw and Behrooz Arezoo, 86. Tehran: The Institute for Compilation and Publication of Imam Khomeini's Works, 2001. www.iranchamber.com/history/rkhomeini/books/women_position_khomeini.pdf.

———. "Islamic Government." In *Islam and Revolution I: Writings and Declarations of Imam Khomeini 1941–1980.* Translated by Hamid Algar, 27–166. Berkeley, CA: Mizan Press, 1981.

———. "Payām-i Khumaynī bih munāsibat-i Rūz-i Zan (Imam's Khomeini's Message on Women's Day, May 16, 1979)." In *Jāygāh-i zan dar andīshah-i Imām Khumaynī*, 28–31. Tehran: Mu'ssisah-i tanẓīm va Nashr-i Āsār-i Imām Khumaynī, 1995.

———. *The Position of Women from the Viewpoint of Imam Khomeini.* Translated by Juliana Shaw and Behrooz Arezoo. Tehran: The Institute for Compilation and Publication of Imam Khomeini's Works, 2001. www.iranchamber.com/history/rkhomeini/books/women_position_khomeini.pdf.

———. "Tawzīh al-masā'il (Legal Rulings)." In *Islam and Revolution I: Writings and Declarations of Imam Khomeini 1941–1980.* Translated by Hamid Algar, 437–42. Berkeley, CA: Mizan Press, 1981.

Kissling, Frances. "Abortion: Articulating a Moral View." *Conscience* (Summer 2000): 21–27.

———. "Is There Life after Roe? How to Think about the Fetus." *Conscience* (Winter 2004/5): 11–18.

———. "The Paths Not Taken: Pope John Paul II Chose Not to Engage All Catholics and Leaves a Tragic Legacy of Missed Opportunities That Damaged the Church." *Conscience* (Summer 2005): 12–13.

———. "Should the Trinity Be a Quartet?" *On the Issues* (Spring 1998): 13–14.

Lazreg, Marnia. *Questioning the Veil: Open Letters to Muslim Women*. Princeton, NJ: Princeton University Press, 2009.

MacLeod, Arlene. *Accommodating Protest: Working Women, the New Veiling, and Change in Cairo.* New York: Columbia University Press, 1991.

Mahmood, Saba. "Feminist Theory, Embodiment and the Docile Agent: Some Reflections on the Egyptian Islamic Revival." *Cultural Anthropology* 16, no. 2 (2001): 202–36.

———. *Politics of Piety: The Islamic Revival and the Feminist Subject*. Princeton, NJ: Princeton University Press, 2005.

———. "Secularism, Hermeneutics, and Empire: The Politics of Islamic Reformation." *Public Culture* 18, no. 2 (2006): 323–47.

Majlesi, Muhammad Baqir. *Biḥār al-Anvār*. Vol. 43 (on Fatimah Zahra). Tehran: Islamieh Publication, 1967.

Medina, Lara. *Las Hermanas: Chicana/Latina Religious-Political Activism in the U.S. Catholic Church.* Philadelphia, PA: Temple University Press, 2004.

Mernissi, Fatima. *The Veil and the Male Elite.* Reading, PA: Perseus Books, 1991.

Messick, Brinkley. *The Calligraphic State: Textual Domination and History in a Muslim Society*. Berkeley: University of California Press, 1993.

Mir-Hosseini, Ziba. *Marriage on Trial: A Study of Islamic Family Law*. New York: I. B. Tauris Publishers, 2000.

Mohanty, Chandra. "Under Western Eyes: Feminist Scholarship and Colonial Discourses." In *Third World Women and the Politics of Feminism,* ed. Chandra Mohanty, Ann Russo, and Lourdes Torres, 51–80. Bloomington: Indiana University Press, 1991.

Mutahhari, Murtaza. *Niẓām-i huqūq-i zan dar Islam*. Tehran: Entesharat-i Sadra, 1975.

———. *The Islamic Modest Dress*. Translated by Laleh Bakhtiar. Chicago: Kazi Publications, 1988.

Najmabadi, Afsaneh. *Women with Mustaches and Men without Beards: Gender and Sexual Anxieties of Iranian Modernity*. Berkeley: University of California Press, 2005.

Namazi, M. Baquer. *Non-Governmental Organizations in the Islamic Republic of Iran: A Situation Analysis*. Tehran: United Nations Development Programme in the Islamic Republic of Iran, 2000.

O'Connell, Timothy. "Conscience." In *Principles for a Catholic Morality*, 103–18. San Francisco: HarperCollins, 1990.

Paidar, Parvin. *Women and the Political Process in Twentieth-Century Iran*. Cambridge: Cambridge University Press, 1995.

Paul VI. "Address on the Role of Women in the Plan of Salvation," January 30, 1977. *Insegnamenti* 15 (1977): 111.

———. "Declaration on the Question of the Admission of Women to the Ministerial Priesthood," October 15, 1976. *Acta Apostolicae Sedis* 69 (1977): 98–116. www.papalencyclicals.net/Paul06/p6interi.htm.

———. "Response to the Letter of His Grace the Most Reverend Dr. F. D. Coggan, Archbishop of Canterbury, Concerning the Ordination of Women to the Priesthood," November 30, 1975. *Acta Apostolicae Sedis* 68 (1976): 599.

Perelman, Chaïm. *The New Rhetoric and the Humanities: Essays on Rhetoric and Its Applications.* Boston, MA: D. Reidel, 1979.

Perelman, Chaïm, and Lucie Olbrechts-Tyteca. *The New Rhetoric: A Treatise on Argumentation*. Notre Dame, IN: University of Notre Dame, 1969.

Pinches, Charles. *Theology and Action: After Theory in Christian Ethics*. Grand Rapids, MI: William B. Eerdmans, 2002.

Pontifical Council for the Family. "Catholics for a Free Choice." *Lexicon on Ambiguous and Colloquial Terms about Family Life and Ethical Questions*. March 31, 2003.

Ruether, Rosemary. "The War on Women." In *Nothing Sacred: Women Respond to Religious Fundamentalism and Terror*. Edited by Betsy Reed, 3–10. New York: Thunder's Mouth, 2002.

Ruffle, Karen. *Gender, Sainthood, and Everyday Practice in South Asian Shi'ism* (Chapel Hill: University of North Carolina Press, in press).

_____. "The Mystical and Intercessory Powers of Fatimah al-Zahra in Indo-Persian, Shi'i Devotional Literature and Performance." *Comparative Studies of South Asia, Africa and the Middle East* 30, no. 3 (2010).

Sachedina, Abdulaziz. *The Just Ruler in Shi'ite Islam: The Comprehensive Authority of the Jurist in Imamite Jurisprudence*. New York: Oxford University Press, 1988.

Sadr, Sahdi. "Bad hijāb dar qānūn, fiqh, va ravīyah'hā-yi 'amalī." *Zanān* 107 (1382/2004): 44–49.

Schimmel, Annemarie. *My Soul Is a Woman: The Feminine in Islam*. Translated by Susan Ray, New York: Continuum, 2003.

Schmitz, Kenneth. "On Stage: New Words for Ancient Truths." In *At the Center of the Human Drama: The Philosophical Anthropology of Karol Wojtyla/Pope John Paul II*, 1–29. Washington, DC: The Catholic University of America Press, 1993.

Schüssler Fiorenza, Elisabeth. *But She Said: Feminist Practices of Biblical Interpretation*. Boston, MA: Beacon Press, 1992.

Sered, Susan. "Rachel, Mary, and Fatimah." *Cultural Anthropology* 6, no. 2 (1991): 131–46.

"The Sermon of Fatimah Zahra (AS): The Spiritual Dynamism of A Woman." *Farzānah* 4 (1994): 29.

Shahidi, Seyed. *The Life of Fatimah Zahra*. Tehran: Daftar Nashr Farhang Islami, 1988.

Shaikh, Sa'diyya. "In Search of al-Insan: Sufism, Islamic Law and Gender." *Journal of the American Academy of Religion* 77, no. 4 (2009): 781–822.

Shariati, 'Ali. *Fatimah Is Fatimah*. Translated by L. Bakhtiar. Tehran, Iran: The Shariati Foundation, n.d.

Sherkat, Shahla. "Chashmah-'i āgāhī agar bijūshad . . ." *Zanān* no.1 (1370/1991): 2–3.

———. "100 tāziyānah bih khātir-i 'ishqī mamnū'!" *Zanān* no. 100 (1382/2004): 4–6.

Sherkat, Shahla, and Elaheh Koulaei. "Iṣlāḥ'ṭalabān va sukhangūyī az jins-i dīgar: guft va gū bā Duktur Ilāhih Kūlāyī." *Zanān* no. 120 (1384/2005): 3–16.

Sherkat, Shahla, and Staff. "Bā mudīr-i mas'ūl-i gūshah-'i rīng: guft va gū bā mudīr-i mas'ūl." *Zanān* no. 100 (1382/2004): 69–78.

Spivak, Gayatri. "Can the Subaltern Speak?" In *Marxism and the Interpretation of Culture*. Edited by Cary Nelson and Lawrence Grossberg, 271–316. Urbana: University of Illinois Press, 1988.

Srinivas, Tulasi. *Winged Faith: Rethinking Globalization and Religious Pluralism through the Sathya Sai Movement*. New York: Columbia University Press, 2010.

Stan, Adele. "Frances Kissling: Making the Vatican Sweat." *Ms.* 6, no. 2 (Sept./Oct. 1995): 40–43.

Stout, Jeffrey. *Democracy and Tradition*. Princeton, NJ: Princeton University Press, 2004.

Strathern, Marilyn. "An Awkward Relationship: The Case of Feminism and Anthropology." *Signs* 12, no. 2 (1987): 276–92.

Szulc, Tad. *Pope John Paul II: The Biography*. New York: Scribner, 1995.

Torab, Azam. *Performing Islam: Gender and Ritual in Iran*. Leiden, The Netherlands: Brill, 2007.

———. "Piety as Gendered Agency: A Study of Jalaseh Ritual Discourse in an Urban Neighbourhood in Iran." *The Journal of the Royal Anthropological Institute* 2, no. 2 (1996): 235–52.

Toulmin, Stephen. *Knowing and Acting: An Invitation to Philosophy*. New York: Macmillan, 1976.

———. *The Uses of Argument*. Cambridge: Cambridge University Press, 1958.

Toulmin, Stephen, Richard Rieke, and Allan Janik. *An Introduction to Reasoning*. New York: Macmillan, 1984.

Traina, Cristina. *Feminism and Natural Law: The End of Anathemas*. Washington, D.C.: Georgetown University Press, 1999.

Trible, Phyllis. *God and the Rhetoric of Sexuality*. Philadelphia, PA: Fortress, 1978.

Weaver, Mary Jo. *New Catholic Women: A Contemporary Challenge to Traditional Religious Authority*. Bloomington: Indiana University Press, 1995.

Weber, Max. *Economy and Society: An Outline of Interpretive Sociology*. 3 Vols. Edited by Guenther Roth and Claus Wittich. Berkeley: University of California Press, 1968.

Weiss, Bernard. "Taqlīd." In *The Oxford Encyclopedia of the Modern Islamic World*, Vol. 4, edited by John L. Esposito, 187–89. New York: Oxford University Press, 1995.

Index

Definitions of commonly used Persian and Arabic terms can be found in the glossary.

Abbas-Gholizadeh, Mahboubeh
background on, 95
and creative conformity, 97–102
on Fatimah, 38
on *ijtihād*, 94, 96–98, 108n89, 166
on women's studies, 94–98
abortion, xv, 58–59, 62–65, 135, 137–42, 152, 154, 178
Abu Bakr (Caliph), 14, 34, 39–40
Affirmation for Catholic Women, 113–17
agency
and autonomy, 4–5
and heteronomy, 4–5
and intention, 4
reconceptualizing as dianomy, 4–8, 171–73, 180–83
'Ali (First Imam), 14, 34, 39–41
Amadi Qomi, Monir, 95
Aristotle, 18
Arshad, Leila
background on, xxvn21, 70
and creative conformity, 71–76
on custody reform in Iran, 70–72
on the emotionality of women, 71–72
Asad, Talal
on empowerment, xxvin4
'Ashura', 13, 28n34
authority
and charisma, 10, 14–17
social dimension of, 171–72
types of, 10

Bible
method of interpretation of, 84, 86–89
as rhetorical source, 45–49, 81–85, 86–90, 112, 138, 161
Bourdieu, Pierre, xviii
Brandom, Robert, 26n3
Butler, Judith
on citation, 6
on critique, 6, 8
on universal concepts, xvi

Cahill, Lisa
background on, 62
critique of periodic abstinence, 62
and creative conformity, 65, 72–76
on natural law, 63–65
Cannon, Katie, 48
Catholics for Choice, 139–40
de Certeau, Michel
on rhetoric, 17, 171
on strategies, 3
on tactics, 3–4, 176
on value of comparison, xxiii-xxiv, 151, 178
chador, xi, 118, 122–25, 131n45, 132n54
charisma, 7, 10, 12, 13–17
chastity, 60–61, 63
Christifideles laici, 111
Civil Code of Iran,
on custody, 69–73
on divorce, 91–94
and shari'a, 81, 91
clerics. *See* Pope John Paul II; Khomeini, Ruhollah
comparison
and case study selection, xviii–xxiv
as method, xxiii–xxiv, 17–24, 177–78

conscience, 16, 87–90, 99–101, 104n42, 140, 152, 166, 175
Convention on the Elimination of All Forms of Discrimination gainst Women (CEDAW), xii–xiii, xviii–xix, 181
creative conformity
definitions of, 1, 4
See names of individual women; feminist politics; agency
custody reform in Iran, 68–72

divorce, 69–74, 81–85, 90–94, 101, 106n68, 158n66

Ebtekar, Masoumeh
background on, 38
and creative conformity, 41–42, 49–53
on Fatimah as moral exemplar, 38–42
essentialism, 163, 169
and feminist politics, 75–76, 175
and theology of the body, 82–85
and women's emotionality, 71–72, 75–76
Evangelium vitae, 59, 138, 140

Familiaris consortio, 59
family planning, 59–63
Family Protection Law of Iran, 69, 93, 105n65
Farzānah, 95–97
Fatimah, as moral exemplar 34–42
feminism
definitions of, xvi
Islamic critiques of, xii–xiii
secular-liberal, xii–xiv, xix, 164–65
and the concept of empowerment, xiii–xiv, 182
and the concept of resistance, 26n4
feminist politics
and autonomy, xv, 3–5, 151, 180, 182
challenges to, xii–xiii
as contributions to ethical knowledge, 173–76
as co-opted by colonialism, xv–xvi
as creative conformity, 3–4
cross-cultural studies of, xiv, xv–xviii, 23
definitions of, xvii–xviii, 180
and embodiment, 127–29
vs. feminist analysis, xvii
vs. feminist description, xvii–xvii
and hermeneutics, 101–2, 103n31
and heteronomy, 5, 181
and procreation, 75–76
and "republication," 152–54
and symbolics, 51–53
as tactics, 3–4
as unintentional, 6–8, 117, 176–77, 182
Fiorenza, Elisabeth Schüssler, 102n2, 103n31, 109, 116
Fourth World Conference on Women in Beijing, xi–xii, 136–37, 139
freedom of expression in Iran, 135, 142–51
free will
and agency, 4–6, 182
and conscience, 89
and *fiat*, 43–45
and habituation, 182
and hijab, 124–25
and *taqlīd*, 17
Frymer-Kensky, Tikva, 46–47

Gabriel (Angel of God), 35–39, 41
gender complementarity, 81–83, 90–91, 98–99
gender equality, xiii–xiv, 63–64, 73–74, 90–91, 98, 109, 136, 152, 164–65, 169–70
Griffith, R. Marie, 7–8
Gurgi, Monir
background on, 38, 95
and creative conformity, 41–42, 49–53

on Fatimah as moral exemplar, 38–42

Habibi, Shahla, xi–xx, 158n62, 165, 177, 180–82
Hagar as moral exemplar, 46–49
Hasan (Second Imam), 34
Hayes, Diana
background on, 46
and creative conformity, 48–53
on Hagar as moral exemplar, 46–49
on Mary as moral exemplar, 46
on womanist theology, 46
headscarf. *See* hijab
hermeneutics
of the Bible, 84, 86–89
feminist, 80, 101–102, 103n31
of shari'a, 81, 94, 96–98, 108n89, 166
of the Qur'an, 40, 94
hijab, xi–xii, 8, 12, 109–10, 117–29, 132n54, 163
Hitchcock, Helen Hull
background on, 113–14
and creative conformity, 117, 126–29
on moral guidance, 116–17
on ordination, 114–15, 117
ḥiżānat. *See* custody reform in Iran
Humanae vitae, 59–61, 115
human rights, xv, xix, 41, 55n35, 73, 95, 126, 136–38, 152, 166, 170
Husayn (Third Imam), 13, 34

ijtihād, 17, 94, 96–98, 108n89, 166
imago dei, 60, 82–84, 86, 88
imamate, xii, 14–15, 36–38. *See also* Shi'i leadership
inheritance, 39–41, 50
Institute of Women's Studies and Research (IWSR), xi–xii, 94–95, 158n62
Iranian Press Law, 144–45
'irfān, 12–13, 27n33, 36–37, 42
Isasi-Díaz, Ada María
on authority, 86
background on, 85–86
on biblical hermeneutics, 86–88
on conscience, 87–90
and creative conformity, 88–90, 98–102
on *mujerista* theology, 85–90
Islamic dress. *See* hijab
Islamic Government, 15, 91

Jesus, 14, 42–45, 82, 85, 110–13, 128
jihad, 37, 42

Khomeini, Ruhollah
authority of, xx, 8–10, 12–17
background on, 12–13
on children's psychology, 67
on divorce, 158n66, 92–94
on employment for women, 66–68, 121
on Fatimah as moral exemplar, 34–38
on freedom, 119–22, 144–45
on hijab, 119–22
on moral anthropology, 36, 90–91
on motherhood, 66–68
and mysticism, 12–13, 28n34, 36–37
role in the 1979 Islamic Revolution of, 10, 13
on political dissent, 143–45
on *vilāyat-i faqīh*, 12
on women's rights in Islam, 90–92
Kissling, Frances,
background on, 138–39
and creative conformity, xv, 140, 142, 151–54, 178
on Pope John Paul, 139
on the value of fetal life, 141–42
on women's agency, 140
Kotlarczyk, Mieczyslaw, 11–12
Koulaei, Elaheh
background on, 122–23
and creative conformity, 125–29
on free will, 124–25
on hijab, 123–26

logics
of connectivity, 74
definition of, 18, 23–24
of distinction, 100
of expansion, 50
of perfection, 100
of praxis, 51, 74, 100–101, 127
of recombination, 73
of redaction, 152
of redefinition, 99–100, 152
of relocation, 50
of resolution, 73, 127, 152
of reversal of order, 100, 127
of specification, 73, 99, 127
of symbolic substitution, 50–51

Mahmood, Saba, xxivn11, xxvn18, xxivn3,132n52
marja'-i taqlīd, 15
marriage, 60, 62–63, 69, 72–73, 81, 84–85, 92–94. *See also* divorce
Marriage Act of 1931 of Iran, 93
Mary Magdalene, 113
Mary (mother of God)
as co-redemptrix, 42, 45–46
as evidence for ban of women's ordination, 112
as moral exemplar, 33, 42–46
as *theotókos*, 43–46
Morrison, Toni, 48
motherhood, xii, xv, 74, 168
and child rearing, 58–59, 175
and moral education of children, 66–68, 72
and pregnancy and birth, 43–45, 58–59, 61, 140–42, 168
as vocation, 66–68
Muhammad the Prophet, 14, 34–35, 39, 41, 92
Mulieris dignitatem, 42, 111, 138
Mutahhari, Murtaza, xxvn20, 91
Mu'tazila, 16–17
mysticism, xxi, 11–13, 28n34, 36–37, 147–48, 166. See also *'irfān*

natural law, 60–61, 63–65, 84–85, 163
NGO Training Center, 95

ordination of women, 109–10
Ordinatio sacredotalis, 111

Pahlavi, Muhammad Reza Shah, 13, 66–67, 118–20
Pahlavi, Reza Shah 13, 66–67, 92, 117–20
patriarchy, 98, 100–101, 161–62, 170
penal code of Iran
on freedom of expression, 114
on hijab, 118–19
on homosexual acts, 147
Perelman, Chaïm, 18, 21–22, 161, 169–70
political context in Iran, xxi–xxiii, 162–63, 165, 167
political context in the United States, 162, 165–67
Pope Benedict XVI, 28n35, 114
Pope John Paul II
authority of xx, 9–17, 111
background on, 10–12
on divorce 82–85
on family planning, 59–61
on marriage, 60
on Mary as moral exemplar, 42–45
on moral anthropology, 82–85
and mysticism, 11–13
on natural law, 60–61, 84–85
on ordination, 111–13
on secular politics, 136–38
Pope Paul VI, 59–61, 111, 115
pre-Islamic Arabia, 92

Qur'an
interpretation of, 40, 94
as a source, 28n36, 92, 106n68,

race, 46–49, 56n51, 85–90, 163–64
Redemptoris mater, 42

rhetoric
as method, 17–24
modes of, 29n42
syllogistic form of, 29n43
Ruether, Rosemary Radford, xvi

sexual ethics. *See* abortion; family planning; marriage; divorce
Shahnameh, 65
shari'a, xii–xiii, xviii, 10, 58, 72, 74, 76, 81, 90–101, 108n89, 118, 125, 162, 166
Shariati, 'Ali, 41, 55n34
Sherkat, Shahla
on Ayatollah Khomeini, 146–47
background on, 146
and creative conformity, 149–54
and mysticism, 147–48
on censorship, 147–51
Shi'i leadership, xii, 14–15, 34, 39–40. *See also* imamate.
Society for Protecting the Rights of the Child, 70
Stout, Jeffrey, 26n3, 171–72
Sufism, 91, 147–48

ta'āruf, 167–68
tactics
de Certeau on, 3–4
definition of, 3–4
feminist politics as, xix, xxii, 3–4
vs. strategies, 3
tafsīr, xix
ṭāghūt, 66–67, 92, 117–20, 144
taqlīd, 17, 124
textual interpretation. *See* hermeneutics
Time (magazine), 11
Torab, Azam, xxivn5, xxivn16, 7–8
Toulmin, Stephen, 18–20, 23, 170

Unborn Child Pain Awareness Act, 142
United Nations, xi–xiii, xv, xix, 70, 136, 138, 153. *See also* Fourth World Conference on Women in Beijing

vilāyat. *See* custody reform in Iran
vilāyat-i faqīh, 12, 15
veil. *See* hijab
Veritatis splendor, 16, 77n10, 89

Walker, Alice, 48
Weber, Max, 10, 12, 14–16
Wojtyla, Edmund, 11
Wojtyla, Karol. *See* Pope John Paul II
Women for Faith and Family, 113–17, 177
women's press in Iran, 145

Yazid, Umayyad Caliph, 13

Zanān, 122–23, 145–50, 153, 168
Zan-i rūz, 146